CONDUCTING AN INSTITUTIONAL DIVERSITY AUDIT IN HIGHER EDUCATION

CONDUCTING AN INSTITUTIONAL DIVERSITY AUDIT IN HIGHER EDUCATION

A Practitioner's Guide to Systematic Diversity Transformation

Edna Chun and Alvin Evans

Foreword by Benjamin D. Reese Jr.

STERLING, VIRGINIA

Published by Stylus Publishing, LLC.
22883 Quicksilver Drive
Sterling, Virginia 20166-2019

Library of Congress Cataloging-in-Publication Data

Names: Chun, Edna Breinig, author. | Evans, Alvin, author.
Title: Conducting an institutional diversity audit in higher education: a practitioner's guide to systematic diversity transformation/Edna Chun and Alvin Evans; foreword by Benjamin D. Reese, Jr.
Description: First edition. | Sterling, Virginia: Stylus Publishing, 2019. | Includes bibliographical references and index.
Identifiers: LCCN 2018049989 (print) |
LCCN 2019000261 (ebook) | ISBN 9781620368206
(Library networkable e-edition) | ISBN 9781620368213 (Consumer e-edition) |
ISBN 9781620368183 (cloth : acid-free paper) |
ISBN 9781620368190 (paperback :acid-free paper)
Subjects: LCSH: Universities and colleges--United States--Administration. |
Education, Higher--United States--Evaluation. | Education, Higher--Social aspects--United States. | College personnel management--United States |
Minorities--Education (Higher)--United States. | Minority college students--
United States. | Minorities in higher education--United States.|
Diversity in the workplace--United States.
Classification: LCC LB2341 (ebook) | LCC LB2341.C54548 2019 (print) |
DDC 378.00973--dc23
LC record available at https://lccn.loc.gov/2018049989

13-digit ISBN: 978-1-62036-818-3 (cloth)
13-digit ISBN: 978-1-62036-819-0 (paperback)
13-digit ISBN: 978-1-62036-820-6 (library networkable e-edition)
13-digit ISBN: 978-1-62036-821-3 (consumer e-edition)

Printed in the United States of America

All first editions printed on acid-free paper
that meets the American National Standards Institute
Z39-48 Standard.

Bulk Purchases

Quantity discounts are available for use in
workshops and for staff development.
Call 1-800-232-0223

First Edition, 2019

To Alexander David Chun
"Alex"

And I am proud to stand amongst all of you not for joining the system, but for overcoming it. For making something of the hope, promise, and potential that each of you embodies in the eyes of your families, loved ones, and professors. Let us take a moment to remember all those who believed in us along the way: may they always know, even if they can't be here to celebrate with us today, that we hold a special place for them in our hearts.

—Alex Chun, 2011

Contents

Tables and Figure

Tables

Figure

Foreword

Those of us who remember, not from reading history books but from lived experience, the "diversity strategy" of many colleges and universities in the 1960s and 1970s recall the slogans and sensitivity groups that characterized many of the approaches to institutional change. Well-meaning and committed folks, of whom I was one, reckoned that "sensitizing" leaders to behaviors that seemed to keep African Americans from staff and faculty positions in the academy was an important strategy. In hindsight, we were right . . . in a sense. Both overt and implicit individual biases related to race and gender, not to mention religion and sexual orientation, were certainly a factor in hiring, obtaining tenure, and promotions. For example, education leaders sometimes made decisions to not consider minority group members who graduated from what were considered second-rate schools, or whose research was "too racial." But what was sometimes not considered during those years were the *structural* and *institutionalized* ways in which many colleges and universities fostered racial and gender inequities. The unenlightened leaders or gatekeepers often perpetuated inequities, but the very way that traditional and well-ingrained processes and procedures operated within a school was often the most powerful factor. Certain areas of study were historically privileged over others, looking first at colleagues of current faculty was often a trusted way of locating new faculty, and the experiences and communication styles of prospective presidents and provosts were usually measured against past leaders.

This subtle but significant shift toward examining *systems* and *processes* ushered in what today seems so common, so usual. We assess diversity and inclusion in the academy not only by analyzing compositional diversity but also by showing an interest in the relationship between those individuals and how that relates to the broader campus culture. As the authors point out, there are several recognized approaches to assessing diversity and inclusion: the Equity Scorecard, the Diversity Scorecard, the diversity rubric, and diversity mapping. They all have different areas of emphasis and

analysis, as the authors describe in a well-organized chart (Table 1.1). In different ways, they go beyond a focus on simply "counting heads" and pay attention to the complex interrelated elements of a diverse and inclusive campus. But what sets the present text apart from other approaches is not only its comprehensiveness but also its organization.

After describing a rationale for their approach, the authors present nine dimensions that comprise the diversity audit:

1. Developing a common definition of *diversity* and *inclusion*
2. Defining the academic/mission-centered case for diversity and inclusion
3. Assessing compositional and relational demography
4. Evaluating strategic diversity infrastructure
5. Implementing systemic diversity strategic planning based on data analytics, collaborative input, accountability metrics, and benchmarking
6. Creating an asset inventory of diversity education and professional development programs for faculty, administrators, staff, and students
7. Evaluating the climate, culture, and readiness for diversity transformation
8. Fostering an inclusive talent proposition through search, recruitment, and hiring processes
9. Enhancing retention, total rewards programs, and talent sustainability

It's often said that it is the *questions* that one asks that stimulate reflection and deep learning. This is exemplified in this book. Each chapter is an in-depth discussion of one of the nine dimensions, and at the end of chapters 2 through 10, the authors present a comprehensive list of questions for the analysis and assessment of that dimension. The questionnaire includes "yes/no" and multiple-choice examples, as well as questions that require a written response. Chun and Evans recognize that answering this wide-ranging list of questions might raise additional questions. In that regard, each chapter includes "References for Further Study."

After one has digested the theoretical and highly practical and applied format of this text, it's only fitting that chapter 11 offers a clear, step-by-step implementation guide. The authors walk the reader through each step of the audit, reiterating the relevant rationales, providing clear guidance, and always expressing sensitivity to the uniqueness of the varied environments. You'll surely want to refer to this chapter as your audit proceeds. Chapter 12 synthesizes the nine dimensions and emphasizes their interrelationship.

If the approach of the 1960s and 1970s laid the groundwork for what the authors refer to as *the woke academy* of the twenty-first century, then the assessment approach must be different. They provide an empirically based approach to auditing campus diversity and inclusion that engages a wide range of campus constituents in comprehensively highlighting the current state of affairs and shining a light on the path to transformation. As such, it's a must-read!

Benjamin D. Reese Jr.
Vice President and Chief Diversity Officer
Office for Institutional Equity
Duke University/Duke University Health System

Acknowledgments

This book is dedicated to Alexander David Chun, whose passionate conviction, selfless courage, and insistence upon freedom and truth in his commitment to social justice and the environment are a beacon of hope. We are especially indebted to John von Knorring, president of Stylus Publishing, for his visionary work in the realization of the ideals of diversity and inclusion in higher education. We are deeply grateful to Joe R. Feagin, Ella C. McFadden professor of sociology at Texas A&M University, for his invaluable insights, unstinting encouragement, and generous guidance throughout the writing of this book. We also thank Bryan Cook, vice president of data and policy analysis for the Association of Public Land-grant Universities (APLU), for his unfailing willingness to help on the data analysis. We thank Kimberly Thompson Rosenfeld for her skilled research assistance and Maricar Cayubit for her generous help in the preparation of the manuscript.

Alvin Evans would like to thank his children, Shomari Evans, Jabari Evans, Kalil Evans, and Rashida VanLeer, for their continuous, loving support. Edna Chun thanks Jay K. Chun, David S.C. Chu, and George S.T. Chu for their loving care. She especially thanks Alex Chun's close and loving friends who have supported Jay and herself continuously throughout these difficult times.

Introduction

INSTITUTIONS OF HIGHER EDUCATION stand at the forefront of cultural change in an increasingly diverse American democracy. Yet too often diversity is seen as an add-on to the educational process—nice to have, but a luxury. The fundamental connection between diversity and student learning in the different aspects of campus life is sometimes purely accidental. Without an intentional and integrated approach to diversity and inclusion, campuses will not be able to realize the educational benefits of diversity that prepare students for collaborative work and citizenship in a global, interconnected society.

One of the most common misunderstandings about diversity is that it refers only to race/ethnicity. By contrast, building a winning diversity equation draws on all aspects of diversity: gender, sexual orientation, disability, gender identification, and other salient characteristics of difference. Just as importantly, inclusion refers to the ways in which a campus values and respects all individuals in interactions, structures, and processes. The tapestry of inclusion means that diverse members of the campus community have voice, receive access to needed resources, and can participate in decision-making. As we elaborate further in chapter 2, genuine inclusion is characterized by the principles of reciprocal empowerment and meaningful interdependence of dominant and nondominant groups. In a democratic environment, individuals can affirm their own identity without reproach or reprisal.

But how can colleges and universities operationalize diversity and inclusion across the decentralized contours of a campus? How can progress be measured and needed improvements identified?

In light of the broad and complex landscape for diversity in higher education, this book provides a concrete process for data gathering, analysis, and evaluation of institution-wide diversity efforts through a progressive, modular approach to diversity transformation. It addresses nine critical dimensions for building strategic diversity capacity. It provides campuses with the ability to audit, evaluate, and analyze diversity progress on these dimensions and prioritize areas of focus. Assessment of each of the nine dimensions will lead to a comprehensive view of an institution's diversity progress through a systematic, research-based approach that supports continuous improvement and proactively addresses accreditation criteria.

This book is designed as a collaborative tool that will enable boards of trustees, presidents, provosts, executive officers, diversity officers, deans, department heads and chairs, administrators, human resources (HR) officers, faculty senates and staff councils, diversity taskforces, multicultural centers, faculty, and researchers to

- audit the progress on each diversity dimension;
- identify gaps between research-based practices and current approaches;
- tie diversity benchmarks to accreditation frameworks and strategic plans;
- chart the organization's overall progress in the development of comprehensive diversity initiatives leading toward inclusive excellence (IE);

- prioritize institutional diversity initiatives based on a comparison of the current state and the desired state, availability of resources, and the importance of each dimension in relation to institutional diversity goals; and
- create a long-term strategy for diversity transformation that provides a concrete, research-based method for auditing progress and future planning.

The diversity audit can serve as a conduit for deeper engagement and dialogue regarding diversity and inclusion that involves stakeholders across the spectrum of academic and nonacademic areas. In an era of diminishing financial resources, investment in costly audit processes involving outside consultants or assessors can represent a significant hurdle for campuses. Our approach offers the opportunity for self-reflection and broad-based engagement in the process of inquiry and analysis and a more cost-effective method, though one that engages many stakeholders and necessarily requires considerable investment in time.

What is the value of a diversity audit as compared to other forms of diversity assessment? The diversity audit is a process-oriented and systems-based approach to evaluation. It draws on the strengths of various existing approaches, including the emphasis on action research and the engagement of organizational stakeholders in the process. In chapter 1, we provide an extensive overview of leading approaches to diversity assessment and include a comparative analysis of features of these methodologies in terms of focus, value, limitations, and cost (see Table 1.1).

Different models and instruments have been implemented over the last two decades for gauging diversity progress. As the foundation for these efforts, Daryl Smith's paradigm designating the four domains of structural representation, climate, educational and scholarly work, and institutional viability and vitality laid the groundwork for future work in this area (D.G. Smith, 1995). We discuss these models in greater depth in the first chapter, but provide here brief thumbnails of prominent examples.

- The Equity Scorecard developed by Estela Bensimon in 2000 identifies four domains that are specifically related to educational outcomes: access, retention, excellence and outcomes, and institutional receptivity. The scorecard is particularly focused on student access and success as related to race/ethnicity and equity.
- The Diversity Scorecard is another assessment model that includes the Strategic Diversity Leadership Scorecard and the Inclusive Excellence Scorecard. These models draw on Smith's four dimensions of campus diversity and measure goals, tactics, objectives, and indicators in quadrants on dimensions that include learning and diversity. The scorecard approach uses an approach similar to the balanced scorecard and as such is a snapshot of concrete performance indicators.
- The diversity rubric developed by the New England Resource Center for Higher Education (NERCHE) is a cross-sectional approach that evaluates progress through a snapshot of selected performance indicators at a given point in time. Although the rubric provides a stage-based continuum, the generality of its definitions for each level could involve approximations rather than precise measurements of progress.
- Diversity mapping is a visually based methodology that integrates both structural and thematic elements of diversity through a cross-sectional analysis. Its progressive taxonomy addresses seven levels of engagement with diversity that tend to rely on thematic references rather than content-based analysis. As a proprietary method involving extensive analysis by external consultants and evaluation using coding software, it requires a significant resource investment.

The diversity audit we describe offers a modular, research-based framework that focuses on self-study and will enable evaluation of the integration of different dimensions of diversity across the campus ecosystem. Its particular value lies in its thoroughgoing analysis of institutional diversity structures, systems, and processes. Given the budgetary constraints facing institutions of higher education, the diversity audit represents a cost-effective vehicle for evaluation that allows campuses to address specific mission-driven contextual factors and builds synergy with organizational stakeholders in the process.

Unlike more limited types of scorecard approaches with specific performance indicators, the diversity audit begins with detailed questions about the variables and data that will, in turn, lead to the determination of needed indicators and help identify gaps between the current and desired state of diversity progress. This book is designed as a resource for institutions seeking to implement structural, programmatic, and cultural change in support of diversity. As such it provides concrete strategies, best practice examples, and worksheets for reflection on each dimension.

In the audit process, we emphasize the link between diversity progress and accreditation criteria. In particular, we highlight the principles of the Academic Quality Improvement Project (AQIP) of the Higher Learning Commission that serves the North Central region. AQIP is a systems-based model that can be applied to the evaluation of diversity progress. AQIP is process oriented with an emphasis on outcomes and results. Its holistic approach involves critical self-reflection that focuses on continuous improvement. Its approach is context specific and involves self-determination in light of the many variables that differentiate college and university campuses. In each chapter, we also cite representative criteria from the regional accrediting agencies related to each dimension.

In the implementation guide in chapter 11, we map the different steps in each dimension of the audit process and indicate recommended participants for each step. As in the formulation of diversity strategic plans, gathering data for the audit needs to involve feedback and input from stakeholders and a structured process with time lines, milestones, and development of a final report of findings. To ensure successful implementation, communication about the goals of the audit and transparency in the process will facilitate greater commitment to identified goals.

Given the significant differences in institutional contexts and organizational structures, there is no single process for completing the audit. Support from senior leadership is essential for the success of the audit in order to provide the needed vision and ongoing institutional commitment.

Different approaches are possible. The audit can be led by the chief diversity officer (CDO) in concert with academic and nonacademic leaders. Depending on the reporting relationship of the CDO (i.e., to the president or provost), the president or provost can work with the cabinet to authorize the institution's next steps and approve final recommendations. Or in collaboration with the CDO, the process can involve a subset of an institutional diversity taskforce consisting of faculty, administrators, staff, and students. When an institution has a shared diversity leadership model that includes diversity officers in divisions, colleges, and schools, a collaborative coalition of these officers can lead the audit process. Alternatively a steering committee or data research team of representative stakeholders can be formed to facilitate and oversee the process. To foster greater engagement, committee leadership can include partnerships between academic and nonacademic areas.

Because colleges and universities operate in terms of a centralized administrative hierarchy working in tandem with decentralized divisions, colleges, and departments, communication is key to the process. Input needs to be received from representative academic and nonacademic groups and offices, such as the dean's council, department chairs, human resources, and student affairs/multicultural affairs. The involvement of governance bodies such as the faculty senate and student government can also enhance the process. In all cases, broad-based consultation is essential to build ownership and strengthen accountability.

The audit does not need to be completed in sequential order, although the first five modules are considered to be the foundation for further analysis. As a practical tool, the diversity audit can be implemented in stages or in a sequence desired by a given campus. One of the key advantages of this approach is its modular and progressive format. More than one component of the audit can be taken on simultaneously.

Taken as a whole, the audit can provide a holistic institutional analysis that will enable campuses to accelerate diversity progress, capitalize on existing strengths, address the appropriation of needed resources, prioritize areas for improvement, and ensure the systematic integration of programs and processes that foster equity and inclusion.

CHAPTER 1

The Evolving Context for Diversity Assessment

Higher education is littered with grand diversity plans and limited successes.

B. McMurtrie (2016c, para. 5)

THROUGHOUT HIGHER EDUCATION, SPORADIC and fragmentary approaches to diversity and inclusion have not yielded demonstrable outcomes. Even when institutions have developed ambitious and detailed diversity strategic plans, these plans often fail to materialize or do not result in discernible change. In some instances, diversity statements and programs can dissolve into mere window dressing or branding initiatives that only accentuate the disconnection between espoused and enacted diversity mission and goals. In the absence of systematic evaluation of effectiveness, diversity efforts can plateau in a litany of discrete initiatives.

Research indicates that the mere presence of diversity structures such as statements, plans, awards, and training programs can create an illusion of fairness even in the absence of evidence that these structures make a real difference (Kaiser et al., 2013). The elaboration of an institutional infrastructure for diversity in terms of talking points, websites, and statistics creates symbols of inclusion without necessarily dismantling underlying exclusionary hierarchies (Berrey, 2015). To complicate the picture, rigorous study on the impact of diversity structures is relatively rare and the conclusions reached are inconsistent (Kaiser et al., 2013). Without a data-driven, research-based approach to diversity transformation, colleges and universities may repeat past efforts in self-defeating, self-perpetuating cycles (R.R. Thomas, 1990).

At the same time, interest in gauging diversity progress is increasing as institutions recognize the importance of demonstrating a commitment to diversity (Brown, 2016). Over the last several years, the pressures arising from student demonstrations related to campus racial climate have drawn attention to the need for a comprehensive and systematic approach to diversity assessment. The tide of student protests calling for improved race relations on college campuses has been met by a countertrend in the dissemination of racist flyers and expression of White nationalist sentiments. Campuses ranging from Temple University to Boston College, Princeton University, and the University of South Carolina are among those where a flurry of hateful posters were plastered by far-right groups (Swaak, 2018). At the same time, intervention in campus governance and diversity issues by conservative state legislatures in states such as Tennessee, Missouri, and Nebraska has called into question efforts by colleges and universities to create more inclusive campuses.

The voices of students and many others on college campuses around the country are an urgent call to action for the development of concrete approaches to diversity and inclusion that lead to long-term change. Take, for example, the account of Leah, a minority student at Lehigh University, who views institutional diversity plans with a grain of salt:

Whenever our presidents or provosts . . . put out these plans and these statements and these letters, I really take them with a grain of salt. . . . I just need to see more action ongoing or even on a month-to-month basis updating students, letting students know what's going on. . . . Another huge problem with diversity is that oftentimes people only look at the president or the provost or a couple of leading people, but it is the whole organization as an institution. (quoted in Chun & Evans, 2018, p. 187)

Or consider the perspective of Achille Tenkiang, a recent African American undergraduate of Princeton University, who describes the competing interests of administrators:

There are administrators who are dedicated, but I know that at the end of the day sometimes it does sort of feel as though they are beholden to other entities and parties. . . . And to some extent as undergraduates in this institution it kind of feels like we are undercut and our concerns are not given similar weight as concerns of alumni from 30 years ago who are not experiencing the way the world is now. (quoted in Chun & Evans, 2018, pp. 132–133)

When institutions operate from a deficit-based perspective that tends to focus on student characteristics, the assumption may be made that "the burden of failure" is due to student incompetence (D.G. Smith, 1990, p. 29). Instead, colleges and universities now must address how they need to change rather than focus on the issues students bring to their doors (D.G. Smith, 1990). The benefits of diversity progress in terms of the inclusion of individuals with diverse social identities extend well beyond the campus to society at large.

The rise of colorblind and postracial perspectives reflects the view of many Americans that race, ethnicity, gender, disability, and other forms of difference are no longer defining factors limiting opportunity and leading to social inequality. The election of Barack Obama in 2008 as the first biracial president seemed to signal a sea change in race relations was under way. Yet as Ta-Nahisi Coates (2017) points out, what the nation fears collectively is black respectability or the myth of good black government, for, "at its core, those American myths have never been colorless" (p. xv). From this vantage point, colorblind perspectives that are accompanied by a denial of the origins and impact of racism have served as a method of controlling minority groups through race-neutral policies (Berrey, 2015; Picca & Feagin, 2007).

The veil of colorblindness has even permeated judicial decision-making, such as in the Supreme Court decision to strike down Section 4 of the Voting Rights Act. Consider the assertion of Chief Justice John Roberts in the 2007 *Parents Involved in Community Schools v. Seattle School District No. 1* case that "the way to stop discrimination on the basis of race is to stop discriminating on the basis of race" (Roberts, 2007).

Racial resentment played a significant role in the election of Donald Trump as the nation's 45th president in 2016. Consider the analysis of a longitudinal data set of 8,000 adults by the Voter Study Group substantiating that racial resentment was a more critical factor than economic concerns in the election of Donald Trump (McElwee & McDaniel, 2017). Even 41% of White millennials voted for Trump. The GenForward Survey of 1,816 young adults between 18 and 34 found that these individuals were more likely to believe in "white vulnerability" driven by a sense of racial resentment (Fowler, Medenica, & Cohen, 2017). In effect, the 2016 presidential election was about an open society with racial diversity viewed as a threat with "battle lines . . . drawn around issues of racial diversity and tolerance of diversity" (McElwee & McDaniel, 2017, para. 17). These battle lines were evident even abroad and exploited by America's adversaries. Prior to the election, Russian governmental interference in the electoral process attempted to exploit the racial faults in American society by creating fake Black activist accounts (O'Sullivan & Byers, 2017). These racial divisions only deepened following the 2016 presidential election.

The resurgence of a sense of vulnerability related to White racial identity is evident in a 2016 survey of 600 non-Hispanic White American adults, in which 40% of the respondents indicated that White identity was very important to them, and 54% said Whites have a lot to be proud of. White identifiers are more likely to believe that the increase in racial and ethnic groups has had a negative impact on American culture and that society should give White people greater opportunities than they currently enjoy (Jardina, 2017). About one quarter of the survey respondents rated the Ku Klux Klan at a favorability of more than 10 but under 50 on a scale of 100, indicating a shocking favorability toward a violent terrorist group (Jardina, 2017). As Ashley Jardina (2017) indicates, "White identity politics is packaged much more decorously and clearly part of mainstream opinion" (para. 11).

What has changed in America? Deep-seated racial resentment can now be openly expressed and such expression has become normalized. Leslie Picca and Joe Feagin first documented the phenomenon of frontstage and backstage or two-faced racism. Their research sample of more than 600 students demonstrated the ways in which White protagonists can present themselves as colorblind in front of diverse audiences, whereas backstage comments, actions, and emotions of White actors reveal deep-seated racist, sexist, and heterosexist assumptions. Such comments are "tolerated, if not encouraged—and sometimes even expected" (Picca & Feagin, 2007, p. 91).

The emergence of overt backstage racism and anti-Semitic sentiments on the frontstage was evident on August 12, 2017, as crowds of White nationalists marched through the University of Virginia campus bearing tiki torches and chanting "Blood and Soil" and "White Lives Matter." They were protesting the removal of a Confederate statue of Robert E. Lee from a public park and were met by a small band of 30 counterprotesters from the University of Virginia. The day was viewed by the world as one filled with "racial rage, hate, violence and death" as a counterprotester, Heather Hyer, was killed the next day by a car driven into the crowd by a rallygoer (Heim, 2017).

Given the highly charged and often perilous political environment, higher education leaders need to present a clear and convincing rationale for institutional progress in diversity and inclusion. We know from an extensive body of empirical research that experiences of diversity on college campuses impact students' civic engagement and democracy learning outcomes. Consider the findings of a meta-analytic study of 27 works with a sample of 175,950 undergraduates that found a positive relationship between college experiences of diversity and civic engagement. This relationship was found in the development of civic skills, interactions, and attitudes as well as increased cultural empathy, awareness, and knowledge (Bowman, 2011). Similarly, a longitudinal study of 4,697 students entering 10 public universities in 2000 found that positive interactions across racial lines affected students positively in terms of their pluralistic orientation and ability to understand different perspectives (Engberg & Hurtado, 2011).

> *"The core grounding that helped shape who I am and how I think were the courses that forced me to think outside of my normal focus."*
> *David, a White male graduate of a midwestern public comprehensive university (quoted in Chun & Evans, 2016, p. 95)*

Cognitive dissonance or the disequilibrium arising from encountering difference can be a trigger deepening student experiences of diversity. As Anthony, a White male doctoral student with mild autism spectrum disorder, explains, "Diversity in my mind is a matter of experiencing cognitive dissonance in such a way that it does challenge horizons of understanding" (Chun & Evans, 2016, p. 58). Cognitive dissonance requires reconciling new experiences of diversity with existing assumptions and can lead individuals to correct or modify their views and behavior.

Yet even as colleges and universities recognize the importance of creating inclusive living, learning, and working environments, the administrative hierarchy of higher education remains largely White and predominantly male. The limited number of minorities at senior-level positions in higher education suggests that historical legacies of prejudice and racism persist in predominantly White institutions (Gasman, Abiola, & Travers, 2015). A 2017 study of 1,500 college presidents by the American Council on Education found that the typical college president is a White male in his 60s; 30% are women and only 17% are members of racial and ethnic minorities (American Council on Education, 2017; Chen, 2017). Further, a survey conducted in 2013 indicates that only 11.8% of chief academic officers (CAOs) are minorities and 41% are women. The numbers of minorities declined over a 5-year period, with African American CAO representation declining from 3.7% to 2.3%, Asian American CAOs declining from 3.7% to 2.4%, and Hispanic CAOs declining from 1.5% to 0.8% (American Council on Education, 2013). As Miranda, a transracial graduate of a midwestern, White liberal arts college, noted:

> I am looking at our administration, and our president, and our provost, and all of these people. There are no people of color really at all. . . . I think

that if the representation could have been there in the faculty and the administration that would help students relate better and especially students of color. (quoted in Chun & Evans, 2016, p. 16)

A recent study by the College and University Professional Association for Human Resources (CUPA-HR) reveals that the administrative positions held by minorities increased between 2001 and 2016 from 11% to 14%. These positions include top executives, department heads, deans, and controllers. This increase, however, has not kept pace with the rise of minority groups in the United States from 30.1% in 2001 to 38.5% in 2016, as well as the increase in minority college graduates from 19.1% to 26.7% in the same 15-year period (Seltzer, 2017).

Given the importance of role models and the attainment of a representative bureaucracy, the demographic profile of institutional leadership has been shown to impact student perceptions of diversity. For example, a study of 23 public universities and 19 community colleges in Texas found a statistically significant relationship between the persistence of African American, Asian, and Hispanic students and the demographic characteristics of the executive team of the president and vice presidents that included not only race and ethnicity but also specialization, time in an executive position, and age, among other variables (Fincher, Katsinas, & Bush, 2010).

Change is not easy. The dynamics of diversity transformation are complex and layered due to the different forms that underparticipation takes, whether structural, cognitive, intentional, or interactive (Sturm, 2010). Institutions of higher education are known to be resistant to change, as demonstrated by the slow process of remedying the underrepresentation of minority and female administrators, faculty, staff, and students. As agents of stratification in terms of opportunity and advancement, colleges and universities remain far from becoming fully inclusive, democratic, and diverse (Sturm, 2010).

Damon Williams (2006) emphasizes the "brutal facts" that stall diversity efforts, including the failure to understand that diversity work involves change and shifting organizational culture. The status quo tends to be viewed as more comfortable and desirable than undertaking a disruptive change process. As Caroline Turner (2016) wisely advises, "Most people don't change, or willingly go along with change because

change is 'the right thing to do.' They do it if there is an important reason to change" (para. 1).

In light of the pressing need to assess diversity progress systematically, this book answers the fundamental question "How can we know if we are making progress?" (Turner, 2016). From this vantage point, effective change processes in higher education are rarely about imposing solutions but rather about asking the right questions (Buller, 2015). As scholars indicate, the way a question is framed impacts the methodology, shapes the research, and conditions the solutions that are explored (D.G. Smith, 1995).

Many campuses do not have sufficient data about how diversity work impacts the institution and do not have solid metrics that will enable them to determine when progress has been made toward identified goals (D.G. Smith & Parker, 2005). In asking critical questions about diversity, this book provides a concrete process for data gathering, analysis, auditing, and evaluating diversity and inclusion efforts. It offers a progressive, modular approach to gauging institutional diversity progress and will assist leaders and stakeholders in answering the following questions:

- What are the salient diversity dimensions and structures from an institution-wide perspective?
- What progress has been attained in these dimensions to date?
- How have diversity goals been operationalized within divisions, schools, colleges, and academic and administrative units?
- What is the gap between the current state and the desired state of diversity and inclusion?
- How can my institution create synergy among faculty, staff, and students to support diversity goals?
- What are the relevant best practices in higher education?
- What strategies will work best at my institution?

Designed as a practitioner's guide, this book addresses nine modular dimensions that are essential for substantive diversity progress. Because colleges and universities function through interrelated systems that work together in support of identified goals, this book offers a structured approach for systematic evaluation of the depth, breadth, and pervasiveness of diversity and inclusion at the institutional, divisional, school, and departmental levels. The audit emphasizes the need for analysis of both quantitative and qualitative data. It does not assume that the mere aggregation of diversity projects or initiatives equates necessarily to the attainment of mission-centered diversity goals. For this reason, the focus of the diversity audit is on the intentionality and integration of diversity programs and outcomes across the campus spectrum.

As a form of research-based inquiry, this guide will serve as a springboard for further engagement with campus constituencies through discussion, dialogue, and collaborative work. The benefits of the audit process are significant. It can strengthen communication, create synergy among campus units, provide interim reports to senior management, overcome prevailing myths and dispel competing narratives, and share challenges and successes along the pathway toward inclusion (D.G. Smith, 2009b). The findings that result from asking the right questions inevitably will provide valuable input to diversity strategic planning and lead to campus-specific actions. The process of inquiry in and of itself will yield benefits to stakeholders by engaging participants in the process of institutional transformation (Bensimon, Polkinghorne, Bauman, & Vallejo, 2004). Policymakers must frame the basic questions; without such framing, the quantity and quality of data will not make up for the lack of good questions (Bensimon, 2012).

Although working backward through the reductionist lens of existing practices may be fruitful, it is far more difficult to predict future advances in diversity progress. In the face of tumultuous political and social headwinds, leading diversity transformation may be viewed as a controversial undertaking and may not yield immediate results. Based on recent research, however, without sustained and courageous leadership commitment, systematic and sustainable diversity change will be unlikely to occur (Chun & Evans, 2018).

Comparative Methods of Diversity Evaluation

What is the value added of a diversity audit compared with other methods of gathering and analyzing diversity data? Over the last few decades, colleges and universities have relied on a variety of models and methods to interpret data regarding diversity progress. These models can be viewed as complementary, but they offer different approaches, lenses,

and frameworks for consideration. With the passage of time, modified and hybrid models that build on previous progress have emerged to enrich the evaluative process. Although it is sometimes difficult to categorize the different types of assessments, the primary vehicles for measuring diversity progress are as follows:

- Equity Scorecard
- Diversity Scorecard
- Diversity rubric
- Diversity mapping
- Diversity audit

In the next sections, we shall discuss these instruments in terms of the value that each methodology provides. A synopsis and comparative analysis of features of the different methods for assessing diversity progress are provided in Table 1.1 later in this chapter. In chapter 6, we discuss the creation of a diversity strategic plan and the formulation of a systemic planning system for diversity.

The Equity Scorecard

The Equity Scorecard was one of the earliest research-based instruments specifically developed to address issues related to race and ethnicity in relation to student learning in higher education. Introduced in 2000 by Estela Bensimon at the Center for Urban Education at the University of California, Los Angeles, the Equity Scorecard focuses on student access and success as well as educational outcomes. Its emphasis is on race-consciousness and the development of "funds of knowledge" (Bensimon, 2012, p. 19) that allow individuals to recognize how race is reflected in everyday practices. Funds of knowledge include background information, cognitive frameworks, cultural frames, and implicit and tacit knowledge (Bensimon, 2012). The scorecard seeks to shed light on the epistemological ways of understanding race-related issues and the "institutional malfunction" (Bensimon, 2012 p. 28) that lead to differential student outcomes. It is premised on the need to understand faculty culture and the

> *"We believe that every campus has many practitioners with the potential to become 'first-generation equity workers'" (Bensimon, Dowd, & Witham, 2016).*

role of faculty in academic decision-making in order to effect change (Bensimon & Malcom, 2012b).

The methodology of the Equity Scorecard draws on the principles of action research and practitioner engagement (Dowd & Bensimon, 2015). Kurt Lewin founded the action research tradition in the 1940s at the National Training Labs in Bethel, Maine, through collaboration with colleagues. The three principal ideas of action research are (a) change necessitates action, (b) action involves correct analysis of the situation in order to identify alternatives and determine the most appropriate course of action, and (c) the need for action must be felt and change can be achieved only when individuals reflect on the totality of the situation to obtain new insights (Burnes, 2009).

With an emphasis on practitioner inquiry, the Equity Scorecard typically deploys an evidence team of senior leaders who gather data from numerous sources over approximately 18 months to identify equity gaps and develop strategies for overcoming the gaps. The process involves 5 phases: (a) establishing the groundwork, (b) problem definition, (c) assessment of interventions, (d) development and implementation of solutions, and (e) evaluation of results (Dowd & Bensimon, 2015).

The Equity Scorecard provides an integrated, visual depiction of four domains related to educational outcomes: (a) access, (b) retention, (c) excellence and outcomes, and (d) institutional receptivity. The metric of institutional receptivity or vitality encompasses systemic and structural arrangements that support the other perspectives (Robinson-Armstrong, King, Killoran, & Fissinger, 2009). Within each area, campuses develop contextually specific baselines, improvement targets, and identified points at which equity would be attained (Bensimon, 2004). The Equity Index measures proportionality of the target group in relation to the population under analysis and provides a useful measure of needed progress in terms of educational outcomes (Bensimon, 2004; Williams, 2013).

Over the last two decades, the Equity Scorecard has undergone several redesign periods. The first-generation scorecard was named the Diversity Scorecard and, with support of the James Irvine Foundation, was pilot tested in 14 institutions in California. The second-generation scorecard, funded by the Lumina Foundation and the California Community College System, was renamed the Equity Scorecard to address the focus on racial equity (Dowd & Bensimon, 2015). The Equity Scorecard has been implemented in a number of public university systems, including the University of Wisconsin, Nevada System of Higher Education, Pennsylvania State System of Higher Education, and Colorado Higher Education System (Dowd & Bensimon, 2015).

Diversity Scorecard

Although the Equity Scorecard also began with the designation Diversity Scorecard, subsequent scorecards such as the Strategic Diversity Leadership Scorecard (SDLS) developed by Damon Williams and the Inclusive Excellence Scorecard (IE Scorecard) broadened the focus to address how multiple dimensions of diversity combine in a holistic environment for learning (Williams, 2013; Williams, Berger, & McClendon, 2005). In addition to Bensimon's groundbreaking work, these scorecards incorporate features of private sector models such as the Balanced Scorecard of R.S. Kaplan and Norton (1992) and Hubbard's (2004) Diversity Scorecard. They also draw on Smith's delineation of the four primary dimensions of campus diversity: (a) student access and success, (b) institutional climate and intergroup relations, (c) education and scholarship, and (d) institutional viability and vitality (Hubbard, 2004; R.S. Kaplan & Norton, 1992; D.G. Smith, 2009a; Williams et al., 2005).

The SDLS and IE Scorecard measure objectives, goals, tactics, and indicators (OGTIs) in four principal areas: (a) access and equity, (b) inclusive and multicultural campus climate, (c) diversity scholarship and research including the formal and informal curriculum, and (d) learning and diversity (Williams, 2013; Williams et al., 2005).

> *"Our next step is to put together the framework of the IE change model, establish what our priorities are going to be in each of those four categories of the framework, and then have an IE scorecard where we are able to actually track and monitor the success of the prioritized areas in these four categories."*
>
> *Wes Pratt, CDO, Missouri State University (quoted in Chun & Evans, 2018, p. 116)*

Like the Hubbard scorecard, the SDLS brings the importance of diversity leadership commitment to the fore, including the vision for diversity and leadership accountability (Hubbard, 2004; Williams, 2013).

Diversity Rubric

NERCHE, formerly housed at the University of Massachusetts, Boston, worked with a project team to develop the Self-Assessment Rubric for the Institutionalization of Diversity, Equity, and Inclusion in Higher Education. Designed to measure the level of institutionalization of diversity at a given point in time, the rubric comprises six dimensions: (a) philosophy and mission of diversity, equity, and inclusion; (b) faculty support; (c) curriculum, pedagogy, and research; (d) staff support; (e) student support; and (f) administrative leadership. Each dimension includes subcomponents that are evaluated in terms of three stages of institutionalization: (a) emerging, (b) developing, and (c) transforming (New England Resource Center for Higher Education, n.d.a). This methodology offers a useful cross-sectional approach to the factors and stages of diversity change. Due to the generality of the definitions, however, unless supported by specific metrics, the determinations of progress could be approximations. For example, the rubric for staff knowledge and awareness gauges the three levels of diversity transformation as ranging from very few staff to some staff to a substantial number of staff members who know what diversity and inclusion are and why diversity is essential to the educational process (New England Resource Center for Higher Education, n.d.a).

Diversity Mapping

Diversity mapping is a relatively new and much more extensive undertaking. It seeks to evaluate the ways in which diversity is addressed both structurally and thematically throughout the university or college environment by analyzing organizational dimensions that include student learning outcomes, budget allocations, policies, and curriculum (Hurtado & Halualani, 2014). It addresses curricular diversity through analysis of general education requirements, course types, and content. The overall mapping analysis is based on a taxonomy called the Diversity Engagement and Learning Taxonomy Assessment (DELTA) that identifies seven levels of campus engagement with diversity. The taxonomy will be discussed in greater detail in chapter 7. It begins with knowledge and awareness at

level 1, progresses to social agency and action at level 6, and culminates in problem-solving using multiple perspectives from all contexts and cultures at level 7 (Halualani, Haiker, Lancaster, & Morrison, 2015). As a form of inquiry, diversity mapping provides a visual portrait based on diversity analytics that identifies gaps and duplication in campus diversity efforts (Hurtado & Halualani, 2014). Due to its proprietary methodology and extensive reach, diversity mapping generally involves external consultants and a considerable investment of campus budgetary resources.

Diversity Audit

The diversity audit is a comprehensive process that can create a campus baseline across multiple dimensions of diversity, leading to the development of a diversity scorecard or more specific measures of progress. The preeminent value of a comprehensive diversity audit is its focus on self-study, a necessary aspect of accreditation review. Consistent with regional accreditation standards, the diversity audit involves self-reflection and self-assessment directed toward the goal of continuous improvement. In this regard, the audit asks questions that relate to accreditation criteria including integrity, sustainability, accountability, and quality (Evans & Chun, 2012). It will provide evidence-based data for accreditation in terms of the resources, programs, objectives, and outcomes that support the institution's journey toward inclusion.

The diversity audit examines organizational processes from a holistic, systems-oriented perspective. Unlike the Diversity Scorecard and even the diversity rubric, which are designed to be a snapshot in time or a dashboard of selected performance indicators, the audit is a process-oriented approach or deep dive into institutional systems, structures, and programs. It identifies predominant themes or drivers that will catalyze the specific parameters of transformational organizational change. The diversity audit can yield a scorecard of performance indicators in different areas as a key outcome.

Although the Diversity Scorecard is an important asset in terms of measuring progress through specific performance indicators and outcome measures, it can be limited in scope. By contrast, a diversity audit provides an empirical, systemic framework for developing discrete measures and desired outcomes. In other words, it asks detailed questions about the variables and data that will help determine the appropriate indicators of progress and allow campuses to gauge the difference between current and desired states. From this perspective, the diversity audit avoids oversimplification and the tendency to view diversity as a checklist of activities or programs.

The diversity audit also diverges from the Equity Scorecard by its focus on the different attributes of diversity and the intersectionality of these attributes. Like all the methods described in this section, an audit of diversity and inclusion can be performed by campus leaders and teams working collaboratively to define, gather, and evaluate data and create a foundation of information for further analysis and strategic planning purposes.

With the requirements of accreditation in mind, the diversity audit provides a step-by-step analysis that will enhance evidence-based self-reflection leading to goal setting and demonstrable outcomes. In this book, we focus particularly on the innovative AQIP as a model for the process of continuous diversity improvement. AQIP is 1 of the 3 pathways to accreditation of the Higher Learning Commission (HLC) that serves institutions in 19 states in the North Central region. AQIP is an alternative accreditation vehicle implemented in 1999 as part of the reform-based changes supported by the Pew Charitable Trusts. AQIP identifies 10 "Principles of High Performance Organizations" that form a template for diversity transformation. These principles are (a) focus, (b) involvement, (c) leadership, (d) learning, (e) people, (f) collaboration, (g) agility, (h) integrity, (i) information, and (j) foresight.

The AQIP principles are applicable to the processes by which institutions set diversity goals, support diverse talent, foster diversity learning outcomes, collaborate across organizational silos, operate with integrity, and gather data and information. The systems-based framework for AQIP evaluation identifies six categories for evaluation of campus work that relate to diversity and inclusion: (a) helping students learn, (b) meeting student and other stakeholder needs, (c) valuing employees, (d) planning and leading, (e) knowledge management and resource stewardship, and (f) quality overview.

The AQIP Systems Portfolio brings these categories together in a holistic approach to performance excellence with an emphasis on academic and administrative processes. The emphasis on processes and results is consistent with the focus of the diversity audit.

Processes are defined as "the series of decisive steps that an institution takes to achieve an end" (Higher Learning Commission, 2017, p. 3).

The Systems Portfolio delineates four progressive stages of systems maturity in institutional processes and results: (a) reacting, (b) systemization, (c) alignment, and (d) integration. At the highest level, institutions use data and information to optimize and implement predictable processes and achieve organizational efficiencies through analysis, sharing, transparency, and innovation (Higher Learning Commission, 2017). Convincing evidence must be provided in terms of assessment measures, how often the assessment is undertaken, and the ways in which assessment data are applied to improve effectiveness. We will return to the framework of the AQIP Systems Portfolio in chapter 12 as a vehicle for determining overall progress in diversity and inclusion.

As campuses consider accreditation requirements, the diversity audit will facilitate the systematic documentation of diversity-related processes and programs and permit evaluation of strengths, areas for improvement, and results. Table 1.1 provides a comparative analysis of the five principal methods of evaluating diversity progress in higher education discussed here.

Despite the strategic value of a diversity audit, few campuses today have the resources or unequivocal support from faculty, staff, and administrators to invest in costly audit processes. In particular, public institutions with declining legislative budgetary appropriations are under significant pressure to reduce operating expenditures. In some states, funding for diversity and inclusion initiatives has come under intense scrutiny. Most public institutions will not have the budgetary largesse to invest resources like the $1.1 million diversity audit at the University of Missouri system. Despite concerns about racial relations at the flagship University of Missouri at Columbia campus ("Mizzou") that reached the national headlines, the cost of the audit raised significant concerns in light of falling enrollment and donor numbers (Huber, 2016). Over a span of 2 years, Mizzou experienced a 35% decline in freshman enrollment, lost millions of dollars in both tuition and state funding, trimmed 185 jobs, restricted travel budgets and new technology investments, and expended $1.3 million to address its image (Bohanon, 2018; Faulk, 2018).

Given the significant financial constraints that prevail in today's higher education environment, this book represents a cost-effective resource for diversity

TABLE 1.1. Comparative Methods of Assessing Diversity Progress in Higher Education

Method	Definition and Scope	Value	Research Basis	Strengths	Limitations	Examples	Cost
Equity Scorecard	Focuses on student access and success related to race/ethnicity and equity in educational outcomes	Particularly valuable in faculty contexts in terms of culture, pedagogy, and evaluation of educational practices	Action research	Participatory process of inquiry with practitioner-as-researcher and change agent	Primary focus on race and ethnicity without consideration of other attributes of diversity	Earlier model called Diversity Scorecard; later model called Equity Scorecard (Bensimon & Malcom, 2012a)	Internal resources
Diversity Scorecard	Uses "carefully selected set of objectives and measures" that link diversity strategy with overall organizational strategy (Catalyst, 2005)	Concise dashboard	Balanced scorecard derived from the business sector	Cross-sectional view of key indicators	Snapshot of selected performance indicators; more quantitative focus	SDLS (Williams, 2013); IE Scorecard (Williams et al. 2005)	Internal resources
Diversity Rubric	Examines diversity through six dimensions: (a) philosophy and mission of diversity, equity and inclusion; (b) faculty support; (c) curriculum, pedagogy, and research; (d) staff support; (e) student support; and (f) administrative leadership (Diaz & Kirmmse, 2013)	More systemic focus than scorecard	Faculty driven in terms of rubrics	Measures institutionalization of diversity at a certain point in time through a three-stage analysis of (a) emerging, (b) developing, and (c) transforming phases	Factors may involve value judgments that result in imprecise generalizations; for example, "a satisfactory number of faculty members are supportive of diversity, . . . few faculty are advocates for infusing diversity in the overall mission and in their professional work" (New England Resource Center for Higher Education, n.d.a)	Colby College Self-Assessment Rubric (New England Resource Center for Higher Education, n.d.b)	Internal resources

(Continues)

TABLE 1.1. (Continued)

Method	Definition and Scope	Value	Research Basis	Strengths	Limitations	Examples	Cost
Diversity Audit	Process-oriented analysis of multiple dimensions of diversity and inclusion linked to mission and strategy	Focus on systems and their integration, intentionality, and coordination	Combines multiple input sources including quantitative and qualitative data to create performance indicators and identify best practices through comparative benchmarks	Process-based, data-intensive review of multiple areas; establishes baseline data and identifies gaps between current and desired states	Without research-based strategies and instrumentation the may not result in actionable strategies	University of Missouri System Diversity, Equity, and Inclusion Audit (IBIS Consulting, 2016)	Internal or external resources
Diversity Mapping	Visual methodology that evaluates both structural and thematic aspects of diversity in an integrated framework	Holistic view of campus dimensions of diversity including curriculum, cocurriculum, budget, policies, and student learning objectives	Data collection includes electronic data analysis using SPSS and qualitative coding software; data tracked in a spreadsheet that produces a visual map and addresses levels of campus engagement with diversity	Visual representation and comprehensive cross-sectional analysis	Tends to rely more on quantitative measures such as number of programs and thematic references rather than on content-based analysis of diversity programs	Penn State and California State University at Monterrey Bay reports (Halualani et al., 2015)	External consultants

evaluation. Institutions we contacted indicated that consulting fees for an audit can range from approximately $50,000 to well into the 6-figure range, depending on the size of the institution, scope of services, and time involved. Although recognizing that an in-house audit will necessarily involve a significant investment of time, it can serve as a tool for collaboration among key stakeholders by strengthening engagement in the diversity agenda. Through the assessment process, institutions can identify existing gaps as well as institutional strengths and determine areas that require further investment of time, resources, and attention.

Chapters 2 through 10 begin by establishing the pertinent research, citing representative accreditation criteria, and sharing specific best practice examples for the dimension of diversity in question. Suggested resources for further exploration are also provided. A set of audit questions for each dimension will enable institutional leaders to assess the level of current efforts and determine appropriate strategies to accelerate progress. These questions are available for download at styluspub.presswarehouse.com/landing/C-IDA-HE.

The nine dimensions addressed in the book's modular approach are

1. developing a common definition of *diversity* and *inclusion*;
2. defining the academic/mission-centered case for diversity and inclusion;
3. assessing compositional and relational demography;
4. evaluating strategic diversity infrastructure;
5. implementing systemic diversity strategic planning based on data analytics, collaborative input, accountability metrics, and benchmarking;
6. creating an asset inventory of diversity education and professional development programs for faculty, administrators, staff, and students;
7. evaluating the climate, culture, and readiness for diversity transformation;
8. fostering an inclusive talent proposition through search, recruitment, and hiring processes; and
9. enhancing retention, total rewards programs, and talent sustainability.

To assist campuses in conducting the audit, chapter 11 provides a step-by-step implementation guide, and chapter 12 synthesizes the nine dimensions in a holistic overview linked to the AQIP model.

Given the complexities of curricular change and the unique demands of each academic discipline, a review of academic programs is not within the scope of this book. With the emergence of a growing body of research on diversity in the curriculum, academic program review requires extensive consultation with faculty and needs to be undertaken in concert with the provost's office. Furthermore, faculty have primary authority over the curriculum, research, and classroom as identified in the principles of shared governance articulated in the American Association of University Professors' *Statement on Government of Colleges and Universities*, adopted in 1966 (American Association of University Professors, n.d.). Similarly, building a systematic approach to service-learning and cocurricular programs for diversity demands specialized consultation with student affairs in light of the specific needs of the campus community and the student body.

For these reasons, the audit focuses on institutional diversity and inclusion goals that involve centralized and decentralized implementation across the campus landscape. In addition, due to the complex legal requirements surrounding compliance functions such as equal employment laws, Title IX, and affirmative action, colleges and universities will benefit from a separate review of policies and practices in these areas.

In sum, this book provides a pathway to building a comprehensive diversity strategy and agenda that brings together the varied dimensions of a campus ecosystem. The book's focus is preeminently practical and designed to identify substantive areas of strength as well as opportunities for continuous improvement. It addresses the need to orchestrate institutional diversity processes across divisions, schools, colleges, and academic and administrative departments. The diversity audit can serve as a framework for catalyzing and accelerating the process of culture change and embedding diversity within the systems and structures of institutional life.

References for Further Study

Bensimon, E. M., & Malcom, E. (2012b). Introduction. In E. M. Bensimon & E. Malcom (Eds.), *Confronting equity issues on campus: Implementing the Equity Scorecard in theory and practice* (pp. 1–14). Sterling, VA: Stylus.

Feagin, J. R., Vera, H., & Imani, N. (1996). *The agony of education: Black students at white colleges and universities.* New York, NY: Routledge.

CHAPTER 2

Defining *Diversity* and *Inclusion*

The attainment of dignity at work is one of the most important challenges people face in their lives. Ensuring the dignity of employees is equally important for organizations as they attempt to make effective use of their human and social resources.

Randy Hodson (2001, p. 4)

AN ESSENTIAL FIRST STEP in the diversity audit is to reach consensus on the meanings of *diversity* and *inclusion* within the specific context of the university or college environment. Colleges and universities often wrestle with the meaning of these terms and their various nuances within the different dimensions of a campus ecosystem. Because much has been written regarding these subjects in recent years, we offer here an overview of some of the prevailing definitions that have arisen in higher education as well as possible caveats that accompany these interpretations. We then introduce prominent holistic models for integrating diversity and inclusion across the multidimensional campus landscape.

Diversity is typically defined as difference and involves the multiple dimensions that include the primary characteristics of race, ethnicity, gender, gender identity, disability, and age, as well as secondary socially acquired characteristics such as religion, marital status, geographic location, socioeconomic background, military status, and educational experience. Diversity is not a singular phenomenon—it encompasses multiple aspects of identity. The concept of intersectionality captures the ways in which different dimensions of social identity are viewed in social contexts and internalized within individuals. Intersectionality can create multiple jeopardies with the compounding of identities that are devalued and not privileged within society,

such as an individual from an underrepresented group, a female, or an individual with disabilities. Or certain aspects of identity can be privileged whereas others are not, such as when an individual is male and gay.

One of the dangers of viewing all forms of difference in an equal light is that this perspective can mask historic and long-standing power differences between dominant and nondominant groups (Myers, 1997). The concept of "diversity-in-general" (Ahonen, Tienari, Merilainen, & Pullen, 2014, p. 269) ignores the twin factors of context and power that shape the meaning of diversity within specific processes and circumstances. In other words, diversity needs to be understood through the forms of knowledge and discursive practices that are "co-constructed through relations of power" (Ahonen et al., 2014, p. 264). From this perspective, diversity is not an isolated phenomenon but is integrally linked to sociohistorical context in which dominant identities hold power and privilege in organizational settings compared with members of nondominant groups (Ragins, 2007). The social reproduction of systemic inequality refers to the ways in which institutions have transmitted and reproduced forms of social exclusion within their processes and culture (Feagin, 2006). Specifically, Feagin and Ducey (2017) describe how sexist, classist, and racist subsystems in society are co-reproduced and interconnected through what these scholars describe as an overarching elite-White-male-dominance system.

Rather than simply viewing diversity as difference, a more nuanced understanding of diversity in higher education refers to the "difference that differences make" (Owen, 2009, p. 187). The *discourse of difference* takes into account the ways in which diversity is described, represented, and actualized in institutional contexts (Prasad, 2001). This definition recognizes that some differences can impact life opportunities, whereas others have few material consequences. Although an institution of higher education can appear to implement neutral practices that simply reflect ways of doing business, invisible norms and assumptions often derived from society can lead to interpretations of excellence that reward certain groups and not others (D.G. Smith, 2014). By contrast, diversity for equity means that organizational change seeks to eliminate or mitigate structures and processes that create barriers for certain social identities and advantages for other privileged identities (D.G. Smith, 2014). This process of leveling the institutional playing field can be understood in terms of the goal of social justice in higher education. In addition to understanding and appreciating difference, social justice challenges systems of privilege and oppression and seeks to dismantle these systems (Pope, Mueller, & Reynolds, 2009).

The concept of diversity brings into play different philosophical lenses. These lenses can help clarify the relation of diversity and inclusion to academia and the disciplinary canon. Unlike private corporations, the purpose of higher learning is not to obtain profits but to expand critical understanding based on knowledge drawn from the humanities, natural sciences, and the arts. With this purpose in mind, through an epistemological lens, diversity can be understood as referring to the diversity of viewpoints as well as differences in power and privilege and how power is exercised (Chun, 2017a). From an ontological perspective, diversity is viewed as fundamental to the very nature of being. From an ecological perspective, diversity is reflected in biodiversity. Although these different vantage points may seem esoteric, each sheds light on the role of diversity in relation to the creation and extension of knowledge.

Danowitz (2015) invokes the notion of *diversity management* derived from the corporate sector as a concept relevant to higher education with four primary elements: (a) valuing difference, (b) strategic planning to promote inclusion and equity, (c) structure and initiatives to enhance representation of nondominant groups, and (d) added value in terms of student learning outcomes. Nonetheless, a cautionary approach needs to be taken toward the frame of "managing diversity" within the context of higher education. A counterargument can be made that this language is more applicable to the corporate sector and that the complexity and nuances of diversity on college campuses are not captured within the nomenclature of diversity management. The notion of managing diversity could even be susceptible to the guise of "magical thinking" in terms of how institutions realistically can create environments that support the attainment of the educational benefits of diversity (Chang & Ledesma, 2011).

Moving beyond the presence of demographic or compositional diversity, the concept of inclusion is a dynamic one that addresses the extent to which diverse individuals are empowered to participate and have voice in organizational contexts, receive access to material resources, are treated equitably within institutional processes, and are valued and respected in terms of behavioral interactions within the normative culture of the college or university. Inclusion has been described as a practice or a mutually reinforcing system of organizational structures, values, micro and macro climates, and individual and collective behaviors (Ferdman, 2013).

Yet how can we discern the presence of genuine inclusion? Reciprocal empowerment is a paradigm that offers an in-depth approach to determining the extent to which institutional culture, structures, policies, processes, and practices are inclusive. Reciprocal empowerment invokes interdependence and interrelationship among dominant and nondominant groups. In essence, it implies the sharing of power held by privileged groups with groups that have been historically oppressed and excluded. It is a revolutionary phenomenon in light of the pervasive forms of inequality that persist within the fabric of institutional norms, culture, processes, and behavioral interactions.

Prilleltensky and Gonick (1994) offer three value-based pillars that gauge the attainment of reciprocal empowerment: (a) self-determination, (b) distributive justice, and (c) collaboration and democratic participation. As yardsticks of inclusion, these three values are polar opposites to forms of oppression. They denote the power of individuals to affirm their own identity, obtain sufficient resources on an equitable basis, and participate in decision-making. To determine if reciprocal empowerment has been actualized, in-depth review of decision-making processes and resource allocation is necessary. Such review will help ascertain the degree to which diverse individuals participate in organizational life or are excluded from consequential involvement.

With this background in mind, let us consider representative themes and elements in the definitions of *diversity* and *inclusion* at several private and public institutions. These themes are typically articulated through the institution's core values, mission statement, and strategic diversity plans. A common fallacy of how institutions approach *diversity* and *inclusion* is the lack of a clear definition of these two terms on institutional web pages and even within strategic planning documents. Although one might assume that the definitions of *diversity* and *inclusion* are widely understood, the ways in which diversity and inclusion are described can actually impact the focus of programs, the prioritization of initiatives, and resource allocation. Several representative definitions of *diversity* and *inclusion* are displayed in Table 2.1.

TABLE 2.1. Representative Definitions of *Diversity* and *Inclusion*

Institution	*Definitions of* Diversity	*Definitions of* Inclusion	*Themes*	*Reference*
Yale University	Includes range of experiences and characteristics (e.g., race, gender, sexual orientation, physical/mental ability, age, national origin, etc.) "that makes us uniquely who we are"	"Creating a *work environment* where each person has the opportunity to participate fully to achieve the mission of the University and is valued for their distinctive skills and capabilities"	Breadth of difference connected with institutional identity; inclusiveness in valuing individuals and work environment	*Diversity & Inclusion* (It's Your Yale, 2017)
Brown University	References "historical legacies of oppression and discrimination" in the United States	Refers to learning environments, physical access, behavioral issues, financial support	Links to sociohistorical experiences; inclusion in all aspects of university life	*Pathways to Diversity and Inclusion: An Action Plan for Brown University* (Brown University, 2016, p. 3)
University of California System	"Diversity . . . refers to the variety of personal experiences, values, and worldviews" resulting from "differences of culture and circumstance" and is "integral to the University's achievement of excellence" as it broadens and deepens the educational process and scholarly environment, "as students and faculty learn to interact effectively with each other, preparing them to participate in an increasingly complex and pluralistic society"		Links to excellence and educational outcomes	*Regents Policy 4400: Policy on University of California Diversity Statement* (University of California Board of Regents, 2010)

Prominent Integrative Frameworks

Developing a common understanding of diversity and inclusion requires consideration of how multiple dimensions of the campus environment work in concert to create an intentional ecosystem for diversity and inclusion. In this regard, several leading conceptual models provide a comprehensive view of how diversity and inclusion are operationalized on a college or university campus. These frameworks differ in emphasis but offer a holistic, environmental perspective in terms of the integration of multiple dimensions of the campus environment. As these frameworks have evolved over the last decade, increasing emphasis has been placed on the centrality of social identity and the impact of social identity on student learning outcomes.

The most widely adopted, holistic frameworks are IE, Daryl Smith's integrative model, the multi-contextual model of diversity learning environments (MMDLE), and the culturally engaging campus environments (CECE) model. All four frameworks offer a systems perspective and seek to evaluate the integration of diversity processes and programs in support of educational outcomes.

IE

IE is the principal organizing model used by many colleges and universities to translate diversity and inclusion strategy into concrete educational goals and outcomes. Introduced by the Association of American Colleges & Universities (AAC&U), IE is a change model that emphasizes how diversity and quality bond together and create a stronger and more lasting alloy. This view of the interrelationship of diversity and quality serves as a counterweight to frequent assertions that diversity dilutes excellence or even that it prioritizes the concerns of minorities over majority interests.

Prevailing descriptions of the IE model often fail to emphasize its focus on student concerns. The IE framework is built on four key elements that directly relate to student learning outcomes: (a) creating a welcoming campus community, (b) focusing on the intellectual and social development of students, (c) purposefully distributing resources that support student learning, and (d) valuing the cultural differences students bring to the educational experience (Clayton-Pedersen & Musil, 2005). As such, IE foregrounds the integration of campus diversity experiences that include climate, resource distribution, curricular and cocurricular offerings, and valuing difference. In chapter 6 we discuss how IE has been adopted as an integrative framework for diversity strategic planning.

Smith's Progressive Diversity Framework

The diversity framework developed by Daryl Smith is one of the earliest and most widely adapted paradigms for understanding the interrelationships among key diversity dimensions of campus life. Smith (1995) sees diversity as an evolving concept with multiple strands operating simultaneously on a college campus. Her foundational framework began with the identification of four principal aspects of diversity: (a) structural representation, (b) climate and responses to intolerance with a focus on institutional behavior and practices and how these affect the psychosocial environment, (c) educational and scholarly mission including efforts to broaden the curriculum and acknowledge groups that have been excluded, and (d) transformation as institutions address multiple perspectives and educate a diverse student body for citizenship and future careers (D.G. Smith, 1995). Later iterations of this model identify the following four dimensions: (a) student access and success, (b) institutional climate and intergroup relations, (c) education and scholarship, and (d) institutional viability and vitality (D.G. Smith, 2009a; D.G. Smith & Parker, 2005). The framework offers a progressive pathway toward institutional success with diversity as a capability linked with institutional vitality and sustainability that can move a campus from a local to a global platform.

In an era of high competition and uncertainty as budgets constrict and higher education comes under increasing fire from conservative forces, the link between diversity capability and institutional viability has particular relevance. As efforts to eliminate and consolidate diversity programming have arisen, such as in the North Carolina, California, and Tennessee university systems, Smith's framework offers a compelling argument for ensuring that diversity and inclusion remain a core rather than a peripheral consideration in ensuring the continued vitality, success, and transformation of institutions of higher education.

The MMDLE and the CECE

Two recent frameworks offer an environmental focus that places student experiences with diversity in an ecological framework with the learner at the center. The MMDLE, developed by Sylvia Hurtado and others, creates a multilayered, contextual perspective that moves from the direct experiences of students to include the ways in which campus climate and institutional policies and systems mirror, replicate, and transmit sociohistorical context within institutional settings (Hurtado & Guillermo-Wann, 2013). The breadth of these interlocking spheres of experience addresses three primary levels: (a) student interactions in the classroom and with the curriculum at the meso level; (b) involvement with the community in the exosystem; and (c) engagement with the political, social, and policy context of the overarching macrosystem. At the core of the MMDLE is social identity as the defining element that differentiates and individuates student experience.

Samuel Museus's (2014) CECE framework builds on the concept of social identity to focus on the experiences of diverse students on predominantly White campuses and delineate the factors contributing to student success. The model presupposes the value of cultural multiplicity and the contributions of diverse identities. Its nine-factor analysis includes five factors that pertain to culturally engaging and validating environments and four indicators that address how campuses respond to the needs and cultural norms of diverse students (Museus, 2014). In 2017 the CECE project was subsumed under the newly established National Institute for Transformation and Equity at Indiana University, Bloomington, with goals that include documenting how campuses bring about change to advance equity. The institute is also expanding the scope and reach of equity and inclusion

surveys to shift to strategies for cultivating more inclusive campuses (National Institute for Transformation and Equity, 2017).

Hurtado's and Museus's theoretical approaches both underscore the disconnection between the identity of diverse students that can create a sense of marginalization and a lack of belonging on college campuses. These frameworks point to the need for a systems-based, ecological approach to diversity and inclusion.

We now proceed to the first step in the data-gathering process that considers the development of campus-specific definitions of *diversity* and *inclusion*: the Audit Questionnaire.

References for Further Study

Harper, S. R., & Hurtado, S. (2007). Nine themes in campus racial climates and implications for institutional transformation. *New Directions for Student Services, 120,* 7–24.

Knox, M. W., & Teraguchi, D. H. (2005). Institutional models that cultivate comprehensive change. *Diversity Digest, 9*(2), 10–11.

Office of Diversity, Equity, and Community Engagement, University of Colorado, Boulder. (n.d.). *Defining and enacting diversity, equity, & inclusion.* Available from https://www.colorado.edu/odece/diversity-plan/resources/defining-enacting-diversity-equity-inclusion

Owen, D. S. (2009). Privileged social identities and diversity leadership in higher education. *The Review of Higher Education, 32*(2), 185–207.

Williams, D. A. (2013). *Strategic diversity leadership: Activating change and transformation in higher education.* Sterling, VA: Stylus.

Audit Questionnaire Step 1: Developing Common Definitions of *Diversity* and *Inclusion*

1. My institution has developed common understandings and definitions of *diversity* and *inclusion*.

   ____Yes ____No

   a. If yes, how is *diversity* defined by my institution?

   _____

   _____

   _____

   _____

   b. If yes, how is *inclusion* defined?

   _____

   _____

   _____

   _____

2. Are diversity and inclusion listed as separate headings on the institution's home page?

   ____Yes ____No

3. Is the definition of *diversity* included in the mission, vision, and values statements and the strategic plan(s), including the diversity strategic plan?

   ____Yes ____No

   a. If no, which university or college documents do not address the definition?

   _____

   _____

   _____

   _____

b. If no, list the primary definitional variations:

_____

_____

_____

_____

4. Are the definitions of *diversity* and *inclusion* consistently applied throughout the colleges and schools of the institution?

____Yes   ____No

   a. If no, list some of the primary variations:

_____

_____

_____

_____

5. Which domains do the definitions of *diversity* and *inclusion* specifically reference? Check all that apply.

   ☐ Campus climate and culture

   ☐ Civility and community

   ☐ Cocurriculum

   ☐ Curriculum

   ☐ Demographics and compositional diversity

   ☐ Educational outcomes and student intellectual/social development

   ☐ External community relations

   ☐ Institutional viability and vitality

   ☐ International programs

   ☐ Interpersonal interactions and intergroup relations

   ☐ Leadership

   ☐ Policies

   ☐ Research and scholarship

   ☐ Student access and success

   ☐ Other:

   _____

6. What specific aspects of the definitions of *diversity* and *inclusion* can be strengthened, modified, consolidated, or solidified to develop a common institutional perspective?

_____

_____

_____

_____

7. What elements or dimensions of the definitions remain contested or require further discussion to reach consensus?

_____

_____

_____

_____

Summative Evaluation: Please provide a summative evaluation of the results of this questionnaire and concrete steps for enhancement:

_____

_____

_____

_____

Goals for enhancement:

1. _____

2. _____

3. _____

The Academic/Mission-Centered Case for Diversity and Inclusion

As humans spread over the Earth, we fractured ourselves by ethnicity, culture, history, religion, wealth, nationality, and ideology. As a result we often failed to see our various journeys as parts of a single evolving enterprise.

David Orr (2016, p. 5)

MOVING FORWARD, THE NEXT step in a diversity audit is to consider how the institution's mission, vision, and values statements and strategic plan reference diversity and inclusion. Why is this important? The mission of an institution represents the locus or central point of gravity where its purpose is defined and its values and priorities are identified. The mission and vision statements drive strategic planning and prioritization processes. Key decisions relating to academic and cocurricular programs, administrative structure, and budget derive from institutional mission. Over time and as administrations change, colleges and universities frequently revisit mission and vision statements and strategic planning goals, with corresponding impact on the ways *diversity* and *inclusion* are defined and framed.

A marker of the importance of diversity and inclusion is the prominence of the diversity function on the institution's home page. If diversity is a priority, it will occupy a visible space on the home page. In this way, current and prospective students, faculty, and staff, as well as external constituencies, will understand the degree to which the institution values diversity and inclusion. When linking from the university home page to the diversity home page, it is equally important to provide contact information for members of the diversity and inclusion team rather than a single generic office phone contact. The availability of university or college diversity spokespersons who can be contacted readily reflects the centrality of diversity to campus mission, climate, and the day-to-day experiences of students, administrators, faculty, and staff.

Context-Specific Factors

In developing a persuasive case for diversity and inclusion, consideration of context-specific factors will help identify the specific elements pertinent to the institutional diversity mission. Given the breadth of institutional types in American higher education, Harris (2013) delineates five overarching factors that differentiate the missions of colleges and universities:

1. Systemic—institutional type, size, and oversight (public, private, for profit)
2. Programmatic—degree level, range of disciplines, emphases, and comprehensiveness
3. Procedural—curricular programs, modes of study, student policies
4. Constitutional—difference in student goals, demographics, educational preparation
5. Positioning—appeal to segment of the educational map/student population

Research over the last two decades suggests that this taxonomy is incomplete when describing the academic mission as it relates to diversity. Critical factors include the institution's legacy of exclusion or inclusion;

geographic location; the structural diversity of leadership, faculty, and staff; normative culture; intergroup relations; and organizational structures including policies and programs that pertain to diversity (Hurtado, Clayton-Pedersen, Allen, & Milem, 1998; Hurtado, Griffin, Arellano, & Cuellar, 2008; Hurtado & Guillermo-Wann, 2013; Hurtado, Milem, Clayton-Pedersen, & Allen, 1999). When considering these factors, the academic case for diversity needs to address how institutions seek to maximize the educational benefits of diversity such as through the framework of IE. As a result, building a compelling academic case for diversity requires careful analysis and evaluation to bring together the disparate strands of these components to develop an institution-specific rationale.

Articulation of the academic/mission-centered case for diversity can also help mitigate legal risk in the pursuit of diversity goals. The challenges to race-sensitive or race-conscious policies in recent Supreme Court cases make it imperative for colleges and universities to articulate why diversity is a compelling interest in terms of preparing graduates for careers and citizenship in a diverse global society (Chun & Evans, 2015a).

Representative Themes

To begin the process, consider the predominant rationales for diversity and inclusion articulated by CDOs in a study of 107 campuses identified in 2009 as members of the National Association of Diversity Officers in Higher Education (NADOHE): remedial ($n = 19$), educational ($n = 11$), and mixed ($n = 72$) (Antonio & Clarke, 2011). The most common arguments for diversity and inclusion identified in the higher education research literature fall into the following 10 general categories:

1. Moral:
   Social justice and overcoming historical legacies of inequality
2. Legal:
   Nondiscrimination and equal opportunity
   Civil rights laws
   Affirmative action
3. Social progress:
   Social mobility and opportunity for underrepresented groups
   The public good
   Civic mission

   Democratic outcomes
4. Demographic:
   Changing demographics of the nation and of the student population
   Global society
   Representative bureaucracy
5. Talent and knowledge/innovation:
   Innovation, creativity, and problem-solving
   Advancement of knowledge
6. Institutional success:
   Academic excellence, institutional performance, and vitality
7. Educational benefits of diversity:
   Student intellectual and social development (e.g., critical thinking and cognitive skills, intellectual self-confidence, pluralistic orientation, perspective-taking)
   Exploring difference through cognitive dissonance
   Future leadership and citizenship of students, contributions to a diverse workforce
8. Community and intergroup relations:
   Climate of belonging and inclusion
   Cross-racial relations and campus racial climate
   Mutual respect
   Intrinsic worth of all individuals
9. Student success:
   Access, retention, and graduation
   Engagement
   Sense of belonging
10. Economic:
    Global competitiveness

These 10 primary themes or guiding rationales for diversity emanate from the growing literature on the educational benefits of diversity. The evolution of university and college mission statements in relation to diversity and inclusion is ongoing. Leadership by the president and board of trustees is essential in ensuring that the academic case for diversity is front and center in the institutional mission statement. Many institutions share their aspirations and goals for diversity and inclusion through the medium of diversity plans (see chapter 6) or strategic planning documents.

At times, mention of diversity in college and university mission statements can be indirect and elliptical, such as noting the need for a diverse student body and diverse perspectives without reference to equity or inclusion. In some cases, references to diversity and inclusion simply are missing. For example, a 2009 study of the websites of 80 institutions from different Carnegie Classifications found that 59 institutions, or 75%, mentioned diversity in their mission statements and 52, or 65%, had a separate diversity statement. Only 18 of those with a separate diversity statement identified this statement as official. In addition, only 16% of the mission statements mentioned inclusion (J.H. Wilson, Meyer, & McNeal, 2012).

Framing the academic case for diversity in a formal diversity statement is another avenue that can crystallize the institution's distinct and differentiated goals for diversity and inclusion. Examples include Pennsylvania State University's *Statement on Diversity, Equity, and Inclusion* (Penn State, 2018) that calls for

faculty, staff, and students to be social justice advocates and the *Statement on Diversity* issued by the Faculty Council at Indiana University, Bloomington (2016), which seeks to remedy historic imbalances in resource allocation to teaching, research, and campus culture in the effort to build greater understanding of community, citizenship, and national and global relationships.

> *"We affirm the inherent dignity in all of us, and we maintain an inclusive and equitable community."*
> The Principles of Our Equitable Community, *Lehigh University (n.d.)*

TABLE 3.1. Representative Themes in the Academic/Mission-Centered Case for Diversity

Institution	Representative Statements	Themes
Amherst College	"Diversity is a natural condition of the modern world. . . . We believe that a great intellectual community should look like the world" (Amherst College, n.d.a, para 1). Residential liberal arts education as "socially necessary and valuable" in a changing world (Amherst College, 2015). "To help students balance the need for familiarity and comfort with the fundamental educational need to explore, risk discomfort, and allow change" (Amherst College, n.d.b).	Demographic diversity in a global society; social responsibility; talent and intellectual diversity; community; risking discomfort in the educational process
University of Michigan	"Excellence is not possible without diversity in the broadest sense of the word" (University of Michigan, 2016, p. 3). "Diversity is key to individual flourishing, educational excellence, and the advancement of knowledge" (University of Michigan, 2017). "[A] campus . . . where every individual feels a sense of belonging and inclusion" (University of Michigan, n.d., p. 1). "Our commitment . . . to contribute to a just society and to affirm the humanity of all persons" (University of Michigan, n.d., p. 2).	Student success, academic excellence, advancement of knowledge; community of inclusion and belonging; moral and social
Pennsylvania State University	"We value inclusive excellence as a core strength and an essential element of our public service mission . . . [to] educate our faculty staff and students to be social justice advocates [to] foster and maintain a safe environment of respect and inclusion [to] address intergroup disparities in areas such as representation, retention, learning outcomes, and graduation rates" (Penn State, 2016, p. 1).	IE; public good; social justice; student success

"Diversity at all levels of the University—from the board of trustees to the student body—enriches our learning environment and expands our institutional ability, intelligence, and creativity."

   Eric Spina (2017), president, University of Dayton

Listed in Table 3.1 are examples of multifaceted arguments that delineate the academic case for diversity based on institutional mission and goals. Each example reflects the specific educational milieu that the institutions serve and the environment they seek to cultivate.

Accreditation and Diversity Mission

With these examples in mind, consider the critical importance that the six regional accrediting agencies give to institutional mission and, by extension, the relation of mission to diversity and inclusion. The academic case for diversity ideally resides within the institution's overarching mission statement but can be articulated in greater specificity within the mission of divisions, schools, colleges, and departments, as well as through curricular goals such as general education requirements and cocurricular objectives. Table 3.2 summarizes accreditation criteria that pertain to the institutional diversity mission.

Given the centrality of diversity to institutional mission, Audit Questionnaire Step 2 raises specific

TABLE 3.2. Accreditation Criteria Related to Diversity Mission and Goals

Accrediting Agency	*Criteria*	*Definition*
Higher Learning Commission (HLC)	Criterion 1: Mission	Mission clear, publicly articulated, guides operations 1c. Mission understood in relation to diversity of society: 1. Addresses role in multicultural society. 2. Processes and activities give attention to diversity in terms of mission and constituencies (Higher Learning Commission, 2014).
Southern Association of Colleges and Schools (SACS)	Section 2: Mission	Mission defines uniqueness, qualities, values that identify distinctiveness in diverse higher education environment (Southern Association of Colleges and Schools Commission on Colleges, 2017).
Western Association of Schools and Colleges (WASC)	Standard 1: "Defining institutional purposes and ensuring educational objectives"	Integrity and Transparency: 1.4 "Consistent with its purposes and character, the institution demonstrates an appropriate response to the increasing diversity in society" through policies, curriculum and cocurriculum, hiring, admissions, organizational practices. *Diversity policy:* demonstrated commitment to the WSCUC Diversity Policy (WASC Senior College and University Commission, 2015).
New England Association of Schools and Colleges (NEASC)	Standard 1: Mission and purpose	1.1 Mission identifies institution's unique character, addresses social needs, and provides basis for priorities and future plans. 1.3 Mission defines educational and other dimensions (New England Commission of Higher Education, 2016).
Middle States Commission on Higher Education	Standard 1: Mission and goals	Mission indicates purpose within higher education, students the institution serves, what it seeks to accomplish, how it will fulfill mission. Goals focus on student learning and institutional improvement (Middle States Commission on Higher Education, 2014).

questions that will help determine the degree to which the academic case for diversity is articulated in the university's, or college's mission, vision, and values statements and strategic planning documents.

References for Further Study

Coleman, A. L., Palmer, S. R., Lipper, K., & Milem, J. F. (2010). *A diversity action blueprint: Policy parameters and model practices for higher education institutions.* Available from https://secure-media.collegeboard.org/ digitalServices/pdf/diversity/diversity-action-blueprint .pdf

College Board, American Council on Education, & Education Council. (2015). *A policy and legal "syllabus" for diversity programs at colleges and universities.* Available from https://professionals.collegeboard.org/pdf/adc-diversity-syllabus-institutions.pdf

Taylor, T., Milem, J., & Coleman, A. (2016). *Bridging the research to practice gap: Achieving mission-driven diversity and inclusion goals.* Available from http://www.aacu .org/sites/default/files/BridgingResearchPracticeGap .pdf

Audit Questionnaire Step 2: Defining the Academic/Mission-Centered Case for Diversity and Inclusion

1. Is diversity mentioned in the mission statement?

   ____Yes ____No ____Indirectly (e.g., diverse community)

   Please include the specific reference here:

   _____

   _____

2. Is inclusion mentioned in the mission statement?

   ____Yes ____No ____Indirectly

   Please include the specific reference here:

   _____

   _____

3. Is diversity mentioned in the vision statement?

   ____Yes ____No ____Indirectly

   Please include the specific reference here:

   _____

   _____

4. Is inclusion mentioned in the vision statement?

   ____Yes ____No ____Indirectly

   Please include the specific reference here:

   _____

   _____

5. Are diversity and inclusion included in a values statement?

   ____Yes ____No ____Indirectly

   Please include the specific reference here:

   _____

   _____

6. Does the institution have a separate diversity statement?

   ____Yes ____No

7. Is the diversity statement an official statement of the institution?

   ____Yes ____No

8. Is the academic case for diversity and inclusion clearly identified in the institution's mission statement?

   ____Yes ____No

9. Is the academic case for diversity and inclusion clearly identified in the strategic plan?

   ____Yes ____No

10. Is the academic case for diversity and inclusion aligned with accreditation standards?

    ____Yes ____No

11. Is the academic/mission-centered case for diversity and inclusion articulated in university or college policies?

    ____Yes ____No

    a. If yes, which policies? List all—use additional sheets of paper as needed.

    _____

    _____

    _____

    _____

    b. Which policies will need to be revised to include this reference? List all.

    _____

    _____

    _____

    _____

12. Do the institution's mission statement and/or mission-related policy statements link the academic case for diversity to educational outcomes and the students served? (Questions 12–14 are derived from criteria identified in Coleman et al., 2010.)

    ____Yes ____No

13. Do the institution's mission statement and/or mission-related policy statements reflect the value and priority given to diversity?

    ____Yes ____No

14. Do the institution's mission statement and/or mission-related policy statements describe multiple dimensions of diversity in relation to strategic goals?

    ____Yes   ____No

15. Are institution-specific historical barriers to diversity referenced in the mission statement and/or mission-related policies?

    ____Yes   ____No

16. Is the academic/mission-centered case for diversity and inclusion published on the university or college website?

    ____Yes   ____No

    If yes, please provide the location(s):

    _____

    _____

17. Is specific attention given to the academic/mission-centered case for diversity and inclusion in college or university processes?

    ____Yes   ____No

    a. If yes, which processes? Check all that apply.
       ☐ Academic decisions
       ☐ Advertising
       ☐ Approval for new positions
       ☐ Branding/marketing
       ☐ Budgetary decisions
       ☐ Cocurricular and service-learning
       ☐ Compensation programs
       ☐ Curricular offerings
       ☐ Faculty evaluation/promotion/tenure
       ☐ Hiring
       ☐ Performance evaluation for administrators
       ☐ Performance evaluation for staff
       ☐ Position descriptions
       ☐ Recruitment (job postings)
       ☐ Staff advancement
       ☐ Student evaluations
       ☐ Other (please specify):

       _____

b. If no, what processes should take priority in making the academic case for diversity?

_____

18. Has the academic/mission-centered case for diversity and inclusion been communicated publicly to the university or college community other than through the website or strategic planning documents?

_____Yes _____No

19. If the answer to the preceding question is yes, what communication vehicles have been used?

_____

_____

20. How familiar are most faculty, administrators, and staff with the academic/mission-centered case for diversity and inclusion? Use the rating of Familiar, Somewhat Familiar, Not Familiar.

Faculty: _____

Administrators: _____

Staff: _____

21. How often is the academic/mission-centered case for diversity and inclusion reviewed and discussed?

_____Never

_____Annually

_____Reviewed in conjunction with strategic planning cycle

_____Other (please explain):

_____

22. Does each college or school have a diversity plan?

_____Yes _____No

a. If no, what number and percentage of the colleges and schools have a diversity plan?

_____(number) _____(%)

b. Do college and school diversity plans state the academic/mission-centered case for diversity and inclusion?

_____Yes _____No _____Some do

Please explain:

_____

_____

c. Are college and school statements aligned with the larger institutional diversity and inclusion statements?

_____Yes _____No _____Some are

Please explain:

_____

_____

Summative Evaluation: Please provide a summative evaluation of the results of this questionnaire and concrete steps for enhancement:

_____

_____

_____

_____

_____

Goals for enhancement:

1. _____

2. _____

3. _____

CHAPTER 4

The Building Blocks of Compositional and Relational Demography

So after being exposed to diversity in college, and meeting with different people with different religious beliefs, different family and cultural backgrounds, I feel that I am prepared to recognize difference and I need to also have respect for difference as well.
    Mai, an Asian American administrator and graduate of a private Midwestern liberal arts college (quoted in Chun & Evans, 2016, p. 73)

THIS CHAPTER IS DESIGNED to assist campuses in gauging the level of structural or compositional diversity of faculty, staff, and students. Structural diversity is a threshold requirement for inclusion, but does not guarantee its attainment (Clarke & Antonio, 2012). What it can help identify, however, are the mountain peaks—the discernible contours of an organization that affect the prevailing climate and culture and the norms that govern day-to-day processes and activities.

An expansive body of empirical research identifies the impact of structural diversity on factors that include student success, educational outcomes, cross-racial interactions, enhanced intergroup relations, campus climate, and institutional vitality (e.g., Bowman, 2012; Chang, 2011; Chun & Evans, 2015a; Milem, Chang, & Antonio, 2005; Pike & Kuh, 2006). The mere presence of structural diversity is a necessary although not sufficient condition for realizing the educational benefits of diversity. The creation of a campus culture that provides opportunities for a racially diverse student body to interact freely and responsibly in both formal and informal settings will require interventions and intentional programs

supported by high-level administrators that address historical legacies of discrimination (Chang, Chang, & Ledesma, 2005). Conscious commitment to disrupting legacies of exclusion will help students garner the benefits of educational diversity and gain the knowledge, competence, and skills necessary for success in a global society.

"I learned many lessons from being a minority on a college campus. Lessons lost to my white peers who don't have to be placed in a group where they are a minority. Lessons necessary to survive in a diverse world."
    Kiara, an African American research technician (quoted in Chun & Evans, 2016, p. 129)

Viewing the campus as a unitary environment does not offer insight into how institutions can maximize the benefits of diversity, because significant variations exist within a given campus for different groups and different contexts (Clarke & Antonio, 2012). Race, ethnicity, gender, sexual orientation, and disability are salient and often intersecting attributes of structural diversity. Although considerable research has focused on gender, relatively little research has focused solely on the impact of race/ethnicity on barriers to advancement in higher education (Jackson & O'Callaghan, 2009). This lack of focused attention may fail to acknowledge the unique challenges associated with racial diversity that are different from other types of diversity (Chang et al., 2005).

Methodological Approaches

From a 30,000-foot perspective, boundary-spanning metrics will generate data about the process of transformation and build capacity for multilevel systems change (Sturm, 2010). A critical approach to demography is essential to interpret the results of institution-level metrics. These metrics will provide an evaluation of the institution's effectiveness and the ways in which its mission and highest level purposes are attained through multiple dimensions (Ruben, 2016). Because higher education functions as an agent of social stratification, the use of critical demographic information will help identify the complex dynamics of structural inequality that can result in differential opportunity, participation, and advancement for faculty, administrators, and students (Sturm, 2010).

Whereas conventional demography is descriptive and focuses on trends, statistical variables, and estimates, critical demography is theory driven and poses reflective questions that challenge the existing order. As such, compositional diversity is part of the contextual paradigm within which critical demography is situated (Horton, 1999). Similarly, the lens of quantitative demography will help decipher patterns of inequity in the institutional landscape. Over the last decade, the concept of quantitative criticalist has been used to describe researchers who use quantitative methods to identify inequities in educational processes and outcomes and the systematic reproduction of these inequities (Stage & Wells, 2014). This vantage point offers insight into the oppression and underrepresentation of minoritized groups, leading to critical examination of policies and practices and reframing traditional questions about nontraditional groups (Stage & Wells, 2014).

Two major conceptual approaches provide analytical perspectives on structural diversity in higher education: *compositional demography* and *relational demography*. The first conceptual approach, compositional demography, addresses structural attributes of the group and the impact on outcomes at multiple levels, including the department, division, and institution as a whole (Tsui, Porter, & Egan, 2002). It is the fundamental yardstick that measures whether or not institutions have addressed the representation of nondominant groups among governing boards, executive officers, faculty, administrators, staff, and students. It represents an empirical barometer of where an institution is on the journey to diversity and where it needs to go. For administrators and faculty, an important measure of compositional diversity is the degree to which a bureaucracy is representative in terms of the comparative presence of institutional leaders who reflect the demographic composition of its constituents or students (Jackson, 2004).

A second major conceptual approach to demographic analysis is relational demography. This aspect of demographic study is rare in higher education today and requires a much more finely tuned analysis. Relational demography takes into account social relationships between the individual and the group or with another individual in dyadic relationships (Tsui et al., 2002). Although straightforward statistical measures of composition diversity provide the ability to gauge the demographic profile of the group, such measures do not consider how individual attributes relate to the organizational unit or institution as a whole (Tsui & Gutek, 1999). For example, although research indicates the demography of the supervisor-subordinate relationship plays an important role in workplace outcomes, little institutional attention is typically paid to the impact of the demography of this relationship (Chun & Evans, 2012).

In gauging the impact of demographic diversity on student learning, the concept of critical mass has gained considerable legal attention. Critical mass refers to the sufficient representation of minoritized individuals (those with a nonmajority identity) that will promote inclusion, dispel stereotypes, and overcome social isolation. In the 2003 Supreme Court case *Grutter v. Bollinger* that challenged the denial of admission to Barbara Grutter, a White female, to the University of Michigan Law School, the university described "critical mass" as "meaningful representation" that would prevent minority students from being spokespersons or "tokens" for their race and encourage classroom participation (*Grutter v. Bollinger*, 2017). Yet only nine years later in the 2012 *Fisher v. University of Texas at Austin* case, Chief Justice Roberts pushed the university's lawyer, Gregory Garre, for a quantification of critical mass, indicating that there has to be "a logical endpoint to the use of race" (*Abigail Noel Fisher v. University of Texas at Austin; David B. Pryor*, 2014).

Although critical mass has come under fire in terms of how institutions will know when it has been attained and how it is measured, it is a highly relevant concept for consideration in relation to structural diversity

(Chun & Evans, 2015a). Clearly, it cannot be quantified precisely and needs to be understood within a specific campus context (Garces & Jayakumar, 2014). Critical mass is an antidote to tokenism that transpires in the hiring of a single minoritized individual or a few isolated individuals to satisfy the need for diversity. Research indicates that tokenism can lead to marginalization and stress for diverse individuals who are often subjected to pressure to conform while enduring both hypervisibility and invisibility (Evans & Chun, 2007; Maramba, 2011).

An alternative way of thinking about critical mass is what Lilian Garces and Uma Jayakumar (2014) term *dynamic diversity* or how contextual factors in the university or college environment promote productive intergroup relations. Dynamic diversity is characterized by interdependence, cross-racial interactions, and participatory engagement of group members under conditions that facilitate equal status relations (Garces & Jayakumar, 2014). From this perspective, the tapestry of structural diversity creates the potential for enhanced intergroup relations and the creation of dynamic diversity.

Determining the Variables for Analysis

The field of research on institutional demography is rapidly evolving through the impact of technology. Analytical reporting ranges from fact books published by institutional research on university or college websites to interactive applications that allow users to drill down through institutional data and view longitudinal comparisons.

Traditional fact books are necessarily limited not only by the data available but also by the degree to which institutional research provides in-depth analysis of processes and results in connection with demographic variables. Usually such resources portray an institutional perspective and may not include data that reflect areas of concern in the demographic portrait. Although a helpful starting point, such reports tend to be static because they focus on a discrete set of statistical measures of diversity. Published reports generally focus more heavily on student outcomes and typically do not address process-based outcomes for faculty, administrators, and staff in areas such as promotion and tenure, compensation, hiring, and turn-over. In addition, institutionally created resources may not meet social science research criteria in terms of quality and may require cross-checking through both quantitative and qualitative data sources.

Ascriptive characteristics such as sexual orientation and gender identity/expression are typically not available for analysis through institutional sources. Supplementary data may be available for study through climate studies or other in-house resources, although questions of confidentiality may apply. The relative invisibility of sexual orientation and the decisions involved in disclosure make studying the impact on workplace and educational outcomes difficult (Ragins & Wiethoff, 2005). Similarly, gender identity may or may not be expressed outwardly (di Bartolo, 2015).

Other characteristics for consideration in evaluating structural representation in the student body include first-generation student status and measures of socioeconomic disadvantage, such as the number of Pell-eligible students. The variable of religious affiliation adds another dimension to the analysis that is usually not available for study although it can be a significant component of intersectionality. With increased discrimination arising relative to Muslim students, campus attention needs to be directed to acts of religious intolerance.

In some instances, faculty have taken the lead in calling for more intensive scrutiny of institutional data. Take the *Report of the Senate of the Faculty of Arts and Sciences* (FAS) at Yale University in May, 2016. The FAS report specifically calls for extensive data analysis including publication of data on faculty diversity overall and by division. It requests graphs showing trends that include data on promotion, tenure, and retention by department and requests a faculty survey that will provide qualitative information on the faculty experience. It asks for evaluation of the equitable distribution of faculty resources such as through research funds, hiring and retention packages, and awards. In addition, the FAS report requests that the administration maintain a dashboard of performance indicators on faculty diversity available online with a data profile of faculty that analyzes relevant diversity indicators (*Report on Faculty Diversity,* 2016).

Best practice examples of institutional fact books include the analysis published by Iowa State University that offers a breakdown of different employee groups and students by gender and race/ethnicity (Iowa State University Institutional Research, 2018). The University of Wisconsin System has taken data analysis to the next level through publication of an extensive fact book and implementation of the University of Wisconsin's UW System Accountability Dashboard. Accountability areas include financial and administrative management, educational performance, and research and economic development. Topics explored through the dashboard that pertain to diversity include access, progress and completion, and faculty and staff. Each of these dashboard topics contains questions that explicitly relate to race and ethnicity. The section on faculty and staff addresses the rate of faculty turnover and faculty compensation but does not provide data specific to race/ethnicity and gender in relation to these variables (University of Wisconsin System, 2018).

At an advanced technological level, the University of California, Los Angeles' BruinX Dashboards are interactive visualizations that allow users to drill down through each population of students, faculty, staff, and executive leadership on the website. The dashboards provide comparative longitudinal data for each grouping. For faculty, 5 years of data are provided and can be filtered by school/division, department, academic series, and title. For executive leadership, the dashboard provides 11 years of data on department chairs, deans, and senior administrators by position. The extensive research team of BruinX is located within UCLA's Office of Equity, Diversity and Inclusion (2018b) and this focused resource configuration allows for rapid evolution and application of technological innovation directed toward enhancing demographic diversity. Under the vice chancellor for equity, diversity, and inclusion, an inaugural position has been created for associate vice chancellor, BruinX, as team lead (UCLA Equity, Diversity and Inclusion, 2018a). The resources and infrastructure for data analysis related to diversity, equity, and inclusion provide the capacity for rapid adaptation.

From this portrait of the components of structural diversity, it is clear that compositional diversity is a multifaceted construct, although institutions may be limited in terms of data on certain important demographic characteristics. Within the confines of the data available, disaggregated data will allow institutions to determine specific issues related to different identity groups in order to develop context-specific strategies.

Relational Demography and Process-Based Outcomes

Given the predominance of majority group members within the academic and administrative hierarchy, the impact of demographic relationships on workplace outcomes will yield insight into disparate outcomes and patterns of exclusion that are not readily evident from cursory examination of structural diversity statistics. As demonstrated by research findings, the reproduction of inequality takes place through organizational processes in which in-group preferences by majority decision-makers can limit access to power and block opportunities for non-White, nonmale individuals (Elliott & Smith, 2001; Ragins, 1997; Ragins & Sundstrom, 1989; R. A. Smith & Elliott, 2002). Inequality occurs through a dynamic interactive process when dominant group members preserve privilege through actions (termed *closure*) that reify prevailing patterns of stratification (Roscigno, 2007; Roscigno, Garcia, & Bobbitt-Zeher, 2007).

Asymmetrical power relations among dominant and nondominant group members, particularly in supervisory-subordinate relationships, rarely undergo scrutiny by boards of trustees in terms of the dynamics of decision-making processes (e.g., Chun, 2017b). The demography between White supervisors and minority employees can result in different expectations, as demonstrated in the narrative of Lisa, an African American administrator in an elite research university:

> I have gone out of my way to control everything around me, because I believe that it is viewed differently if I let a ball drop. Everyone pays attention if I let a ball drop. Whereas the mainstream white male or white female drops a ball, no one even looks in that direction. (quoted in Chun & Evans, 2012, p. 43)

Studies also indicate that diverse individuals in leadership positions may have difficulty attaining the respect and organizational authority associated with their positions from both their supervisors and their predominantly majority staff members (Chun & Evans, 2012).

> *"And again my experience is that institutions have a certain set of people that they consider for particular decision-making. And even though in my case my official position warrants my presence, I wasn't part of that group, so it is very much an ingroup-outgroup situation."*
>   *Mark, an Asian American administrator in a private research university (quoted in Chun & Evans, 2012, p. 75)*

A pivotal concept applicable to the study of institutional equity and relational demography is the glass ceiling. The *glass ceiling* does not just pertain to gender discrimination. It has been defined in terms of the barriers or multiplicity of effects that women and minorities face in terms of career advancement that increase with movement to higher organizational levels after controlling for other relevant factors (Jackson & O'Callaghan, 2009; Jackson, O'Callaghan, & Leon, 2014).

Accompanying the metaphor of the glass ceiling is the parallel metaphor of the sticky floor in which chances of authority gain for nondominant groups concentrated at lower levels of the organization are limited (R.A. Smith & Elliott, 2002). Research also indicates that the negative effects of race/ethnicity and gender on career progression are additive over the course of a career and may even worsen as individuals attempt to break through the glass ceiling. Due to such cumulative barriers, longitudinal data sets are needed to track career progression (Jackson & O'Callaghan, 2009; Jackson et al., 2014).

For administrators, faculty, and staff, process-based outcomes need to be reviewed regularly for equity in relation to demographic characteristics. Relevant processes for consideration include recruitment, outreach, and hiring; representation within job groups, retention, and promotion; faculty rank and tenure; compensation; and disciplinary representation, conflict resolution, evaluations, grievances, disciplinary actions, layoffs, and terminations. For students, admission, retention, time to degree, representation in fields of study, graduation rates, disciplinary actions, and degree attainment are focal processes for study.

Patterns of stratification are not limited to race and ethnicity. A study of 335 supervisor-subordinate dyads in 10 companies found that when the supervisor is younger than the subordinate, subordinates were consistently rated the lowest on four performance measures. The study also provided support for the similarity-attraction concept that could lead to positive bias and differential treatment of subordinates by supervisors (Tsui et al., 2002). And as shown by the so-called queen bee syndrome, women in power can also thwart opportunities for other women due to their efforts to distance themselves from gender stereotypes and their feeling that they have worked hard to reach their current position and feel other women should do the same (Cooper, 2016; Snipes, Oswald, & Caudill, 1998).

Caveats in the Data Analysis

One of the dangers of looking narrowly at structural diversity is the assumption that the reporting of data regarding diversity necessarily leads to intentional actions on the part of a campus in terms of strategic planning, budgetary support, and prioritization of diversity and inclusion as critical aspects of the institutional agenda. From a national perspective, little information exists as to whether campuses have taken action in relation to annual reports and any resulting accountability for diversity goals (Hurtado & Halualani, 2014). At times, the lists of discrete diversity indicators articulated in campus diversity planning documents can be overwhelming, without necessarily providing an overall explanatory portrait or yielding a cohesive narrative. Providing numerical indicators without an accompanying narrative will likely fail to capture the underlying thematic trends that lead to specific equity outcomes. As a result, the diversity audit will benefit from the following principles identified by Ewell and Cumming (2017):

- Avoid measuring everything that moves; allocate resources to the most focused questions.
- Because outcomes are end results, try to determine the processes that led to these results and to identify causal inferences.

TABLE 4.1. Accreditation Criteria and Structural Diversity

Accrediting Agency	Criteria	Definition
Southern Association of Colleges and Schools (SACS)	N/A	*The Principles of Accreditation: Foundations for Quality Enhancement* (Southern Association of Colleges and Schools Commission on Colleges, 2017)
Western Association of Schools and Colleges (WASC)	Standard 3: Developing and Applying Resources and Organizational Structures to Ensure Quality and Sustainability	Faculty and Staff, 3.1 "The faculty and staff are sufficient in number, professional qualification, and diversity . . . to achieve the institution's educational objectives" (WASC Senior College and University Commission, 2015, p. 18).
New England Association of Schools and Colleges (NEASC)	Standard Five: Students	Standard Five "The institution addresses its own goals for the achievement of diversity among its students and provides a safe environment that fosters the intellectual and personal development of its students." 5.12 "In providing services, in accordance with its mission and purposes, the institution adheres to both the spirit and intent of equal opportunity and its own goals for diversity."
	Standard Six: Teaching, Learning, and Scholarship	Faculty and Academic Staff: 6.5 "The institution ensures equal employment opportunity consistent with legal requirements and any other dimensions of its choosing; compatible with its mission and purposes, it addresses its own goals for the achievement of diversity among its faculty and academic staff."
	Standard Nine: Integrity, Transparency, and Public Disclosure	9.5 "The institution adheres to non-discriminatory policies and practices in recruitment, admissions, employment, evaluation, disciplinary action, and advancement. It fosters an inclusive atmosphere within the institutional community that respects and supports people of diverse characteristics and backgrounds" (New England Commission of Higher Education, 2016).
	Equity and Inclusion Policy	Good practices for valuing diversity indicate that "institutions seek and nurture diversity within their student bodies, faculty, administrative staff, and governing boards." Institutions can compare their demographic diversity to regional, state, or national populations, depending on the constituency served and its unique mission (WASC Senior College and University Commission, 2017, p. 3).

- Do not expect final answers; provisional conclusions can raise questions for the next level of inquiry.
- Do not expect to be finished; the inquiry process is ongoing.

For these reasons, the questions in the diversity audit offered at the close of this chapter focus on gathering and analyzing boundary-spanning measurements. Comparison to national and peer data will help benchmark institutional progress. Although comparative data may not take into account factors such as sociohistorical legacy, geographic context, and organizational climate, the benchmarking process will raise questions, identify organizational silos and where attention needs to be directed, and lead to a deeper inquiry as to why differences may exist.

Following comparison with institutions in a specific Carnegie Classification as well as a subset of peer institutions, an in-depth view of the demographic data needs to be organized by divisional areas and then by departments and disciplines. Affirmative action data will yield additional comparative information on job groups and underrepresentation based on the reasonable recruitment area for the types of positions in question.

Moving deeper in the data analysis, institutions need to probe process-based outcomes based on race/ethnicity and gender. Although organizational data may be aggregate in nature, they can be further analyzed by divisions and departments to locate areas of concern that may require further review. Institutions typically review data related to the demographics of recruitment and hiring, but the regular review of other process-related outcomes in relation to compositional and relational demography is far less frequent. For example, awarding of merit pay and adjustments need to be analyzed in terms of impact on minoritized individuals. Although the concept of merit itself invokes the concept of an equal playing field, in reality the similarity-attraction paradigm or homophily can come into play and result in different application of standards.

Sample tables for both demographic analysis and outcomes-based review are provided later in this chapter. These tables can be supplemented with a number of other relevant analyses as part of an institutional audit process. Before proceeding further, however, we examine how accreditation criteria provide an important vehicle for measuring progress in compositional diversity.

Accreditation and Structural Diversity

Accreditation criteria provide a significant institutional rationale for measuring and analyzing the impact of structural diversity. Because accreditation focuses on processes of continuous improvement, longitudinal metrics will help identify how institutions are responding to the need for greater demographic diversity. As shown in Table 4.1, these criteria vary in terms of the components addressed in the review process. WASC and NEASC are the most explicit.

Audit Questionnaire Step 3 provides the opportunity to assess current levels of compositional and organizational diversity in order to create a baseline for comparative review.

References for Further Study

College and University Professional Association for Human Resources. (2017). *Data on demand*. Available from http://www.cupahr.org/surveys/dataondemand/hr-benchmarking/

Ruben, B. D. (2016). *Excellence in higher education guide: A framework for the design, assessment, and continuing improvement of institutions, departments, and programs* (8th ed.). Sterling, VA: Stylus.

Audit Questionnaire Step 3: Building a Compositional and Outcomes-Based Diversity Baseline

Step 3 of the audit questionnaire consists of three main sections: (a) compositional (or structural) diversity metrics, (b) analysis of process-based outcomes, and (c) overall analysis of results and a planning matrix. Sample data tables are provided for the first and second sections that can be adapted or elaborated based on institutional needs and context.

A. Compositional Diversity Metrics

In alignment with the concept of a representative bureaucracy, this segment of the audit establishes baseline metrics for diversity. Sample data tables are drawn from the Integrated Postsecondary Education System (IPEDS) database. These tables can be further refined by institutional type and compared to peer institutions. Additional tables can be developed for executives (vice chancellors, vice presidents, administrative officers), academic leadership (deans, department heads and chairs), staff (full- and part-time), and part-time faculty. Longitudinal comparisons are critical in order to gauge progress over an appropriate time period and to answer questions about increases or decreases in the representation of minoritized groups. In addition, for federal contractors, affirmative action data by job group can be used to compare incumbency versus availability in the appropriate recruitment area and establish goals for women and minorities as aggregate groups rather than by specific minority groups. For institutions that recruit students primarily within a given state, the demographics of the state population can be used as another comparative indicator in the baseline analysis.

In the first example, Table 4.2 addresses the race/ethnicity and gender of full-time instructional faculty at doctorate-granting institutions. An institution-specific table can be developed for statistical comparison to public or private institutions of the same Carnegie classification and type.

Table 4.3 assesses the diversity of the undergraduate student population in terms of race/ethnicity and gender. The results of this analysis will be used in Table 4.6.

Table 4.4 analyzes the race/ethnicity and gender of the graduate student population.

Table 4.5 addresses administrative diversity in terms of education-related administrative positions (student and academic affairs) as reported through the IPEDS database. It provides a point of comparison for certain types of administrative positions.

Table 4.6 compares the demographics of the student population with the demographics of full-time instructional faculty, a key ratio for analysis. Comparisons can be drawn for undergraduates and graduates or a combination of both groups.

B. Outcomes-Based Metrics

This aspect of the audit considers key outcomes such as turnover, merit pay awards, and performance evaluations by employee group. Turnover statistics are a key indicator measured by institutions of higher education that can provide insight into comparative levels of job satisfaction. Table 4.7 can be adapted for use in gauging a range of process-based outcomes. Additional columns may be needed, depending on the institutional process under review and the level of detail desired. Table 4.8 is a sample provided to illustrate the comparison between the turnover of White tenure-track faculty compared to minority faculty.

TABLE 4.2. Full-Time Instructional Faculty Diversity at Doctorate-Granting Institutions: Instruction, Research, and Public Service

Carnegie Classification	GENDER		RACE/ETHNICITY																	
	Total Male %	Total Female %	American Indian or Alaskan Native (Male) %	American Indian or Alaskan Native (Female) %	Asian (Male) %	Asian (Female) %	Black or African American (Male) %	Black or African American (Female) %	Hispanic or Latino (Male) %	Hispanic or Latino (Female) %	Native Hawaiian or Other Pacific Islander (Male) %	Native Hawaiian or Other Pacific Islander (Female) %	Non-resident Alien (Male) %	Non-resident Alien (Female) %	Race and Ethnicity Unknown (Male) %	Race and Ethnicity Unknown (Female) %	Two or More Races (Male) %	Two or More Races (Female) %	White (Male) %	White (Female) %
Public Doctoral Universities (highest research activity)	56.0%	44.0%	0.2%	0.3%	6.5%	3.3%	2.2%	2.5%	2.6%	2.6%	0.0%	0.0%	3.1%	1.7%	1.9%	1.6%	0.4%	0.4%	39.1%	31.6%
All Public Doctoral Universities (highest, higher, moderate research activity)	58.5%	41.5%	0.2%	0.2%	7.4%	4.1%	1.8%	2.1%	2.4%	2.1%	0.0%	0.0%	5.3%	2.7%	1.8%	1.4%	0.4%	0.4%	39.2%	28.4%
Private Doctoral Universities (highest research activity)	61.2%	38.8%	0.1%	0.1%	8.2%	5.6%	1.5%	1.8%	2.1%	1.6%	0.0%	0.0%	7.3%	3.8%	1.7%	1.2%	0.3%	0.3%	39.9%	24.3%
All Private Doctoral Universities (highest, higher, moderate research activity)	59.8%	40.2%	0.1%	0.1%	7.3%	4.9%	1.9%	2.3%	2.3%	2.0%	0.0%	0.0%	5.8%	3.1%	1.8%	1.3%	0.4%	0.3%	40.3%	26.2%

Source: National Center for Education Statistics (2015, 2016), Fall Enrollment Survey, and Institutional Characteristic Survey. Analysis by authors.

TABLE 4.3. Undergraduate Student Diversity at Doctorate-Granting Universities

Carnegie Classification	GENDER		RACE/ETHNICITY																	
	Total Male %	Total Female %	American Indian or Alaskan Native (Male) %	American Indian or Alaskan Native (Female) %	Asian (Male) %	Asian (Female) %	Black or African American (Male) %	Black or African American (Female) %	Hispanic or Latino (Male) %	Hispanic or Latino (Female) %	Native Hawaiian or Other Pacific Islander (Male) %	Native Hawaiian or Other Pacific Islander (Female) %	Non-resident Alien (Male) %	Non-resident Alien (Female) %	Race and Ethnicity Unknown (Male) %	Race and Ethnicity Unknown (Female) %	Two or More Races (Male) %	Two or More Races (Female) %	White (Male) %	White (Female) %
Public Doctoral Universities (highest research activity)	46.8%	53.2%	0.3%	0.4%	2.1%	2.1%	4.6%	7.0%	5.9%	7.6%	0.1%	0.1%	2.3%	1.4%	1.4%	1.5%	1.5%	2.0%	28.6%	31.2%
All Public Doctoral Universities (highest, higher, moderate research activity)	47.8%	52.2%	0.2%	0.3%	4.0%	4.0%	3.8%	5.6%	6.3%	8.0%	0.1%	0.1%	3.2%	2.2%	1.2%	1.2%	1.7%	2.0%	27.4%	28.7%
Private Doctoral Universities (highest research activity)	47.8%	52.2%	0.1%	0.1%	7.2%	8.1%	2.5%	3.5%	5.0%	5.6%	0.0%	0.0%	6.3%	6.5%	2.2%	2.5%	1.8%	2.4%	22.7%	23.5%
All Private Doctoral Universities (highest, higher, moderate research activity)	42.9%	57.1%	0.1%	0.2%	3.5%	4.3%	3.3%	6.8%	5.2%	7.4%	0.1%	0.1%	3.7%	3.4%	4.2%	6.5%	1.5%	2.4%	21.2%	26.1%

Source. National Center for Education Statistics (2015, 2016), Fall Enrollment Survey, and Institutional Characteristics Survey. Analysis by authors.

TABLE 4.4. Graduate Student Diversity at Doctorate-Granting Institutions

Carnegie Classification	GENDER		RACE/ETHNICITY																	
	Total Male %	Total Female %	American Indian or Alaskan Native (Male) %	American Indian or Alaskan Native (Female) %	Asian (Male) %	Asian (Female) %	Black or African American (Male) %	Black or African American (Female) %	Hispanic or Latino (Male) %	Hispanic or Latino (Female) %	Native Hawaiian or Other Pacific Islander (Male) %	Native Hawaiian or Other Pacific Islander (Female) %	Non-resident Alien (Male) %	Non-resident Alien (Female) %	Race and Ethnicity Unknown (Male) %	Race and Ethnicity Unknown (Female) %	Two or More Races (Male) %	Two or More Races (Female) %	White (Male) %	White (Female) %
Public Doctoral Universities (highest research activity)	46.8%	53.2%	0.3%	0.4%	2.1%	2.1%	4.6%	7.0%	5.9%	7.6%	0.1%	0.1%	2.3%	1.4%	1.4%	1.5%	1.5%	2.0%	28.6%	31.2%
All Public Doctoral Universities (highest, higher, moderate research activity)	47.8%	52.2%	0.2%	0.3%	4.0%	4.0%	3.8%	5.6%	6.3%	8.0%	0.1%	0.1%	3.2%	2.2%	1.2%	1.2%	1.7%	2.0%	27.4%	28.7%
Private Doctoral Universities (highest research activity)	47.8%	52.2%	0.1%	0.1%	7.2%	8.1%	2.5%	3.5%	5.0%	5.6%	0.0%	0.0%	6.3%	6.5%	2.2%	2.5%	1.8%	2.4%	22.7%	23.5%
All Private Doctoral Universities (highest, higher, moderate research activity)	42.9%	57.1%	0.1%	0.2%	3.5%	4.3%	3.3%	6.8%	5.2%	7.4%	0.1%	0.1%	3.7%	3.4%	4.2%	6.5%	1.5%	2.4%	21.2%	26.1%

Source. National Center for Education Statistics (2015, 2016), Fall Enrollment Survey, and Institutional Characteristics Survey. Analysis by authors.

TABLE 4.5. **Full-Time Administrators in Student and Academic Affairs and Other Education Administrative Services in Doctorate-Granting Institutions**

Carnegie Classification	GENDER		RACE/ETHNICITY																	
	Total Male %	Total Female %	American Indian or Alaskan Native (Male) %	American Indian or Alaskan Native (Female) %	Asian (Male) %	Asian (Female) %	Black or African American (Male) %	Black or African American (Female) %	Hispanic or Latino (Male) %	Hispanic or Latino (Female) %	Native Hawaiian or Other Pacific Islander (Male) %	Native Hawaiian or Other Pacific Islander (Female) %	Non-resident Alien (Male) %	Non-resident Alien (Female) %	Race and Ethnicity Unknown (Male) %	Race and Ethnicity Unknown (Female) %	Two or More Races (Male) %	Two or More Races (Female) %	White (Male) %	White (Female) %
Public Doctoral Universities (highest research activity)	28.7%	71.3%	0.2%	0.3%	1.0%	1.7%	3.0%	10.0%	2.1%	4.3%	0.0%	0.1%	0.4%	0.6%	1.0%	1.8%	0.3%	0.9%	20.6%	51.5%
All Public Doctoral Universities (highest, higher, moderate research activity)	29.7%	70.3%	0.2%	0.4%	1.2%	2.7%	3.0%	8.2%	2.0%	5.0%	0.1%	0.2%	0.6%	0.8%	1.0%	2.2%	0.4%	1.1%	21.2%	49.7%
Private Doctoral Universities (highest research activity)	28.3%	71.7%	0.1%	0.1%	1.0%	4.5%	3.2%	11.3%	1.8%	5.6%	0.0%	0.0%	0.6%	1.3%	1.0%	1.8%	0.4%	1.0%	20.1%	46.1%
All Private Doctoral Universities (highest, higher, moderate research activity)	30.2%	69.8%	0.1%	0.3%	1.0%	3.3%	3.0%	9.0%	2.3%	6.0%	0.0%	0.1%	0.6%	1.0%	1.2%	2.3%	0.4%	1.0%	21.6%	46.8%

Source. National Center for Education Statistics (2015, 2016), Fall Enrollment Survey, and Institutional Characteristics Survey. Analysis by authors.

TABLE 4.6. Comparison of Full-Time Faculty Demographics With Undergraduate Student Population

Race/Ethnicity	Male	Female	Total	Percentage	Comparison With Student Population (%)
American Indian or Alaska Native					
Asian					
Black or African American					
Hispanic or Latino					
Native Hawaiian or Other Pacific Islander					
Nonresident Alien					
Race and Ethnicity Unknown					
Two or More Races					
White					
Total					

TABLE 4.7. Determining Process-Based Outcomes

Academic Year _____   Job Group _____   Process _____

Race/Ethnicity	Total in Job Category	Male	Female	Total	Racial/Ethnic Group in Job Category (%)
American Indian or Alaska Native					
Asian					
Black or African American					
Hispanic or Latino					
Native Hawaiian or Other Pacific Islander					
Nonresident Alien					
Race and Ethnicity Unknown					
Two or More Races					
White					
Total					

TABLE 4.8. Sample Turnover Statistics for Tenure-Track Faculty

Academic Year _____   Job Group <u>Tenure-Track Faculty (Pretenure)</u>   Process <u>Turnover</u>

Race/Ethnicity	Total in Job Category	Male	Female	Total	Turnover by Race/Ethnicity (%)
American Indian or Alaska Native	1	0	1	1	100
Asian	12	2	1	3	25
Black or African American	8	1	2	3	37.5
Hispanic or Latino	7	1	0	1	14.2
Native Hawaiian or Other Pacific Islander	0	0	0	0	0
Nonresident Alien	9	0	1	3	33
Race and Ethnicity Unknown	5	0	1	1	20
Two or More Races	8	1	0	1	12.5
White	57	3	1	4	7
Total (includes overall turnover percentage)	107	8	7	17	15.9

Note. Assumption: 107 Tenure-Track Faculty (Pretenure).

C. Overall Analysis of Results and a Planning Matrix

This section of the audit examines the results of the analysis to use as a basis for future planning.

1. What boundary-spanning thematic inferences about the institution can be drawn from the data analysis?

    a. _____

    b. _____

    c. _____

    d. _____

2. What are the areas of strength/IE in the analysis?

    a. _____

    b. _____

    c. _____

    d. _____

3. What areas require further study?

    a. _____

    b. _____

    c. _____

    d. _____

4. What opportunities exist for improvement?

    a. _____

    b. _____

    c. _____

    d. _____

5. What additional qualitative data need to be considered to cross-check results?

    a. _____

    b. _____

    c. _____

    d. _____

6. What resources (both financial and nonfinancial) will catalyze progress in areas that require improvement?

    a. _____

    b. _____

    c. _____

    d. _____

7. In what areas has progress been made over a discrete time period?

    a. _____

    b. _____

    c. _____

    d. _____

What factors may have produced these results?

_____

_____

_____

_____

8. In what areas has there been little or no progress or even backward movement?

   a. _____

   b. _____

   c. _____

   d. _____

   What factors may have produced these results?

   _____

   _____

   _____

   _____

9. Going forward, what specific strategies will address needed areas of improvement?

   a. _____

   b. _____

   c. _____

   d. _____

   e. _____

Summative Evaluation: Please provide a summative evaluation of the results of this questionnaire and concrete steps for enhancement:

_____

_____

_____

_____

_____

Goals for enhancement:

   1. _____

   2. _____

   3. _____

CHAPTER 5

Strategic Diversity Infrastructure

Predominantly white institutions often align in similar fashion, operating under a set of like administrative practices and assumptions. . . . [The CDO] might come to be viewed as an unfortunate add-on to the administrative lineup, such that some campus personnel may develop the attitude of tolerating the presence of the CDO rather than valuing the skills that the CDO brings to serving campus constituents.

Charles Robinson (2015, p. 217)

THIS CHAPTER ADDRESSES COORDINATION of the strategic organizational infrastructure for diversity. Three measures will help in the evaluation of the infrastructure: (a) centrality, (b) pervasiveness, and (c) integration. Measures of centrality look at the macro aspects of the diversity infrastructure in terms of overall campus diversity leadership. Measures of pervasiveness evaluate micro aspects in terms of the extent to which the infrastructure is operationalized across a campus, and measures of integration evaluate the overall coordination of the infrastructure (Knox & Teraguchi, 2005).

In terms of centrality, a recent review study of 448 texts from 5 scholarly research databases found only 10 manuscripts that addressed diversity leadership and leadership style in higher education. All the texts identified the importance of transformational change and focused on campus diversity and organizational culture as the target of change efforts (Adserias, Charleston, & Jackson, 2017). This finding indicates that greater emphasis needs to be placed on the leadership of diversity and on the specific strategies that will foster transformational change.

If transformational change is to become a reality, then courageous and sustained diversity leadership is essential. Yet the ability to effect transformational change is affected by the positionality of leadership or the ways in which social hierarchies and power relationships are linked to leadership identities. For example, a study of 27 presidents found that more than half of the minority presidents expressed difficulty in exerting transformational diversity leadership because their advocacy could be viewed by White constituents as advancing a personal agenda rather than establishing an institutional priority. As one minority president explained:

If a president of color supports diversity, people expect that and they don't think that it is part of a campus agenda, instead they think that it is part of a personal agenda. Instead, I focus on creating a shared vision and getting other individuals to support the diversity agenda publicly. If I do it, it can be a liability for the agenda. White presidents often do not face this same issue. (quoted in Kezar & Eckel, 2008, p. 397)

As indicated earlier, a 2017 survey of 1,500 colleges and universities found that the presidency still remains largely White and male. Seven out of 10 presidents were male and only 17% were minorities. More than half of those surveyed indicated that racial climate on campus had increased in importance compared to 3 years previously and a majority of the respondents felt that presidents need to address campus climate issues. At the same time, 92% believed that it is very important for presidents to make clear, public statements about the inclusion of racial minorities on campus (Gagliardi, Espinosa, Turk, & Taylor, 2017).

Although diversity leadership emanates from the president and board of trustees, it also flows from executive officers, deans, department heads, and governance bodies such as the faculty senate. The pervasiveness of diversity leadership across a college or university will benefit from grassroots activism by empowered groups, notably the faculty. For example, Hart (2009) cites the example of coalitions of full-time faculty working as "insiders without" (p. 126), employed by the university but instigating change on their own without formal reward or recognition. Feminist faculty collectives have lobbied for change on issues such as salary inequities, hostile climates, and the need for family-friendly campuses (Hart, 2009). Grassroots leadership can create greater equity for different communities on campus and undertake changes that are less likely to happen due to constraints on administrators (Kezar & Lester, 2011).

> *"I think we use every strategy we can think of. We are not always coordinated as well as we should be. We are not always able to push with the right legislative people or the right people in town. Part of it is because we all have full-time lives and full-time professions."*
> *Beth Newman, Faculty Women's Caucus, University of Nebraska, Lincoln (quoted in Hart, 2009, p. 135)*

The third factor—integration of diversity leadership—looks at the coordination of diversity efforts across divisions and departments.

Models of Diversity Leadership

Over the past two decades, the architecture for diversity leadership has continued to evolve in higher education. Despite growth in the infrastructure for diversity, reliance on a small, disempowered cohort of individuals to lead diversity efforts can fail to create traction in the context of larger, more stable academic structures (Brimhall-Vargas, 2012).

The creation of the CDO role reflects the recognition that diversity involves multiple dimensions of the campus ecosystem and requires more than compliance with federal and state antidiscrimination laws. In the first decade of the twenty-first century alone, 60 leading institutions undertook reframing of the senior administrative diversity role (Williams & Wade-Golden, 2013).

Ironically, the CDO role remains the single executive leadership role in which the majority of the incumbents are diverse. The employment conditions for CDOs tend to be tenuous, because often these leaders serve "at will" without the protection of tenure status and may lack the power that is needed to challenge the status quo (Chun & Evans, 2018). As a result, CDOs must primarily rely on the power of persuasion and collaboration. As one CDO explains:

> And a [CDO] is always in a very delicate situation where their primary task is to create change. They are supposed to be change agents; that's in most of the job descriptions. But institutions are very traditional and don't like change; and if you change too fast or too slow you're seen as a troublemaker. (quoted in Woodard, 2014, p. 80)

Due to the potential for political crosswinds and diversity backlash, employment protections or contracts for diversity officers will enable these positions to exercise greater leverage.

> *"This role in itself is a risk. I think that anybody that takes on this role must go into this role with the understanding that they are at risk all the time. . . . [T]he reality is that this work challenges power."*
> *Yekim, an Afro-Latino CDO (Chun & Evans, 2018, p. 62)*

Williams (2013) delineates four prominent archetypes of leadership by the CDO: (a) the collaborative officer model or single person leader, with limited staff and relatively little independence in implementing programmatic initiatives; (b) the unit-based model with enhanced vertical capacity including larger budgets and increased staffing; (c) the portfolio divisional model that includes line leadership of a number of direct reporting units and typically holds executive rank; and (d) the multi-institutional model that operates across multiple campuses in a statewide system (Williams & Wade-Golden, 2013). All four models rely heavily on collaboration with other divisions and units. In many cases, the CDO position has a direct or dotted line reporting relationship to the president and has a seat in the president's cabinet.

A fifth model or matrix of shared diversity leadership is rapidly emerging. Williams's (2013) analysis touches on this model in terms of matrix reporting relationships rather than as what he terms a *structural organizational archetype*. Nonetheless, we are seeing the rapid evolution of the matrix model as a full-fledged typology or archetype that relies principally upon horizontal rather than vertical integration. It consists of diversity leadership positions in key divisions or schools.

A matrix model may offer advantages by building breadth and pervasiveness while enhancing disciplinary specialization. As Williams (2013) notes, this complexity can be problematic without clear delineation of responsibility, setting of goals, and creative ways to negotiate issues of overlapping responsibility. As diversity positions have become increasingly specialized, consideration still needs to be given to overall coordination, clear lines of reporting, and accountability. Shared leadership requires processes that are genuinely consensual, shared interests, and delegation of authority at different levels within the institution (Kezar & Lester, 2011).

This synergistic model or shared leadership model may include diversity positions in student affairs as well as school-focused positions that reside in the larger schools such as arts and sciences and schools of medicine or health sciences. For example, a dean for diversity and inclusion in the office of the vice president for student life at Princeton University was established upon the recommendation of the Special Task Force on Diversity, Equity, and Inclusion. College campuses have also recognized the contributions of student affairs to the student experience of diversity and campus climate and their relation to student persistence and success. The dean for diversity and inclusion works collaboratively with the vice provost for equity and diversity housed in the provost's office (Chun & Evans, 2018). In other examples, Stanford University does not have a CDO but houses diversity officers in each of its seven schools. Yale University recently appointed a deputy dean for diversity and faculty development in the College of Arts and Sciences.

With the continued evolution of diversity officer positions, placing the lead diversity officer in academic affairs may create greater authority due to the close proximity to academic mission and location of significant budgetary resources. The solidification of authority through an academic title such as vice provost may permit greater leverage in faculty-related areas such as diversity curriculum, teaching and learning, and tenure-related issues. Surprisingly, however, these positions may or may not have tenure. Other specialized positions in academic affairs have emerged that focus explicitly on faculty diversity and faculty development.

Important considerations in building a successful diversity leadership model include creation of a research team dedicated to institutional demographic issues and establishment of dedicated, full-time positions for diversity education and organizational learning. As a result, a fully staffed diversity structure will encompass sufficient staffing and budgetary resources to deploy diversity development programs, conduct research, and coordinate diversity initiatives across the variegated campus terrain.

Challenges in Organizational Integration

Regardless of organizational design, distinct challenges arise in terms of the efforts to integrate diversity programs. As Robinson (2015) points out, in academic affairs, although diversity is viewed as an important educational outcome, it often is not seen as a critical aspect of the teaching and learning experience. For this reason, it may not be used as a learning tool in the classroom. Robinson notes that even when vested with an academic title, "the CDO has the constant struggle of demonstrating that he/she possesses an academic mind-set and approach to dealing with diversity issues" (p. 218).

On the financial side of the house, few universities bring business affairs and issues of minority contracting within the scope of the CDO role (Robinson, 2015). The increased influence of chief finance officers in strategic decision-making has arisen in an area of budgetary constraints and resulted in the consolidation of a broad set of nonacademic functions (Chun & Evans, 2012). The absence of CDO involvement in financial and budgetary administration perpetuates the divide between academic and nonacademic functions. As one president warned:

The most important advice I would give presidents is to maintain control over the budget and strategic planning process. The president should use the budget to support diversity initiatives, which will likely not receive support early on. No matter how limited your budget is, it can be used to support change. (quoted in Kezar, 2007, p. 427)

A more focused budgetary model, such as those adopted at Princeton University and the University of Michigan, consolidates budgetary functions under the provost, who then is responsible for coordinating administrative and support functions and diversity commitments with university mission (Chun & Evans, 2018). At the University of Michigan, oversight of the budget by the provost allows the review of departmental and unit diversity goals in alignment with institutional mission as a key aspect of the allocation process (Chun & Evans, 2018).

Another area typically within the business or financial affairs purview is campus safety and security. With the rise of hate crimes on campus coupled with the shootings of unarmed Black men both on and off university campuses, diversity, antibias, and cultural competency training for police officers has become an important priority. As of 2011–2012, campuses had more than 14,000 sworn police, 75% of whom were armed. Incidents such as the shooting death of an unarmed African American driver by a University of Cincinnati police officer during an off-campus traffic stop in 2015 have called attention to the urgency of systematic diversity training ("U. of Cincinnati Shooting," 2015). At Indiana University, Bloomington, for example, the police department appointed its first CDO, who will increase outreach efforts; develop a training curriculum on social justice and prejudice; and build relationships with faculty, staff, and students ("Indiana University Police," 2017).

Regardless of organizational design and the availability of permanent funding resources for diversity, the collaboration inherent in the strategic diversity officer model requires partnerships and collaboration with divisions, schools, and departments. A common practice at many institutions is to pool funds across units to allow for a wider range of programmatic offerings. Although not always recognized as a major diversity partner, HR leadership is essential due to its expertise in change management principles and its ability to work collaboratively on a wide range of professional development programs that promote diversity learning.

Many institutions have created diversity and inclusion taskforces or commissions composed of faculty, administrators, staff, and students. These taskforces typically provide advice to the CDO and the president or chancellor. Although diversity reports prepared by such taskforces often present the problem in clear terms and offer helpful recommendations, these reports usually don't provide an inventory of existing capabilities, articulate the steps in the implementation process, or identify a detailed budget (Williams, 2013). As a result, such reports can gather dust on the shelf, be recycled in subsequent years, and fail to activate meaningful change.

We now proceed to evaluation of the diversity infrastructure in Audit Questionnaire Step 4 in order to assess the centrality, pervasiveness, and integration of diversity-related staffing and structures. In chapter 7, we delve further into the breadth, range, and depth of diversity education programs.

References for Further Study

Stanley, C. A. (2014). The chief diversity officer: An examination of CDO models and strategies. *Journal of Diversity in Higher Education, 7*(2), 101–108.

Williams, D. A., & Wade-Golden, K. C. (2013). *The chief diversity officer: Strategy, structure, and change management.* Sterling, VA: Stylus.

Audit Questionnaire Step 4: Evaluation of the Strategic Diversity Infrastructure

Measures of Centrality

1. Does the institution have a CDO?

   ____Yes ____No

2. What is the reporting relationship of the CDO or lead diversity officer?

   ☐ To the president or chancellor

   ☐ To the provost

   ☐ To the vice chancellor for student affairs

   ☐ To the CEO of the medical center

   ☐ Other (please explain);

   _____

3. If the CDO or lead diversity officer does not report to the president or chancellor, is there a dotted line reporting relationship to that position?

   ____Yes ____No

4. Does the CDO or lead diversity officer sit in the president's or chancellor's cabinet?

   ____Yes ____No

5. Does the CDO or lead diversity officer have tenure?

   ____Yes ____No

6. Which diversity officer model best describes the organizational design at your campus?

   ☐ Collaborative officer model (single CDO)

   ☐ Unit-based model (CDO with staffing including research and other diversity officers)

   ☐ Portfolio divisional model (vertically integrated portfolio with units reporting to CDO)

   ☐ Multi-institutional model

   ☐ Matrix or shared leadership model (horizontally integrated)

   ☐ Other variant (please explain):

   _____

7. If the model selected is the portfolio divisional model, please indicate the units within the CDO portfolio.

   _____

_____

_____

_____

_____

_____

8. Does the CDO oversee compliance-related functions?

____Yes ____No

   a. If yes, which functions does the CDO oversee?

      ☐ Affirmative action

      ☐ Code of conduct

      ☐ Disability services

      ☐ Sexual harassment

      ☐ Title IX

      ☐ Other (please explain):

      _____

   b. If not, how are these functions handled?

      _____

9. Does the CDO oversee complaints or grievances related to discrimination?

____Yes ____No

   a. If not, how is this function handled?

      _____

   b. Is the CDO involved in dispute resolution including mediation?

   ____Yes ____No

10. Does the central diversity office have staffing for research and data analysis?

____Yes ____No

If yes, please indicate staffing levels and full-time equivalent (FTE):

Title _____ FTE _____

Title _____ FTE _____

Title _____ FTE _____

11. Is the annual operating budget for the central diversity office exclusive of salaries consistent with the goals of the diversity strategic plan?

____Yes ____No

   a. If no, please explain:

      _____

b. Is the annual operating budget exclusive of salaries comparable to peer institutions, of similar size? (See, e.g., Williams, 2013, p. 117.)

____Yes   ____No

Please explain:

_____

12. Please attach an organizational chart for the diversity and inclusion function(s) at your institution.

Measures of Pervasiveness

13. What other diversity officer positions exist on campus?

Title	Location	FTE	Reporting Relationship	Tenure (Y/N)
_____	_____	_____	_____	_____
_____	_____	_____	_____	_____
_____	_____	_____	_____	_____

14. How is the work of these positions coordinated?

_____

_____

15. Does the campus have a presidential taskforce or commission on equity, diversity, and inclusion?

____Yes   ____No

a. If yes, how many years has the taskforce or commission been operating?

_____

b. If yes, is an annual report with recommended action steps provided to the president?

_____Yes   _____No

c. Taking last year's report as an example, what action steps recommended are in progress or are implemented?

_____

_____

_____

_____

16. What governance bodies have subcommittees, councils, or taskforces related to diversity?

Governance Body	Subcommittee/Taskforce
_____	_____
_____	_____
_____	_____

17. What independent commissions or grassroots groups have been formed related to diversity and inclusion?

_____

_____

18. Does the institution have diversity affinity groups?

____Yes   ____No

a. If yes, please name the groups:

_____

_____

_____

b. Does each group have an executive sponsor?

____Yes   ____No

c. How is the work of the groups coordinated?

_____

_____

19. Does the institution have specific centers for different identity groups?

____Yes   ____No

If yes, please list here.

Name   Reporting Relationship

_____   _____

_____   _____

_____   _____

_____   _____

_____   _____

Measures of Integration

20. What formal mechanisms or practices facilitate the integration of diversity efforts across the campus?

_____

_____

_____

21. How would you rate the integration of diversity efforts (see Knox & Teraguchi, 2005)?

☐ Nominal

☐ Limited to certain sectors

☐ Balanced

☐ Institutionalized

22. What specific aspects of the diversity infrastructure would benefit from further review or study?

_____

_____

_____

Summative Evaluation: Please provide a summative evaluation of the results of this questionnaire and identify specific steps for enhancement:

_____

_____

_____

_____

_____

Goals for Enhancement

1. _____

2. _____

3. _____

CHAPTER 6

The Strengths and Pitfalls of Diversity Strategic Planning

Now here, you see, it takes all the running you can do, to keep in the same place. If you want to get somewhere else, you must run at least twice as fast.
The Red Queen in Through the Looking-Glass, and What Alice Found There
(Carroll, 1897, p. 50)

ALTHOUGH THE METAPHOR OF the Red Queen running twice as fast to stay in place has been widely applied across many disciplines, it is especially relevant to diversity initiatives, which often appear to cover the same ground without advancing forward. As an antidote for running in place, diversity strategic plans are an important vehicle for overcoming organizational inertia and catalyzing progress.

But what do diversity strategic plans measure and how are they operationalized? These two critical questions lie at the heart of diversity strategic planning. This chapter begins with the premise that institutions may not always be able to define the results they expect to obtain from diversity strategic planning. The start of the planning process requires articulating desired outcomes and working backward from these outcomes in terms of plan design. We do not focus on the sheer instrumentation of diversity strategic plans, due to the fact that over the past two decades the instrumentation has been well established and even standardized. Rather, we address aspects of diversity strategic planning that are frequently overlooked or underemphasized but that represent essential aspects of diversity transformation.

As noted throughout this book, diversity strategic planning is about change. Without systemic, process-based change, campuses will cycle through repetitive efforts and become entangled in circuitous pathways that do not lead to results. A common lament of

campus stakeholders in diversity-related initiatives is that they expect to be in the same place in a few years' time, without having made tangible advances on the diversity agenda. Diversity councils similarly may find themselves repeating past efforts in submitting recommendations over a period of years without noticeable improvements.

Recall the alignment described in chapter 3 between diversity strategic plans and the college's or university's mission, vision, values, and goals. Diversity strategic planning is not a separate or discrete aspect of planning but forms an integral part of overall institutional planning. In the early twentieth century, a wide swath of colleges and universities initiated diversity strategic plans as instruments for identifying diversity goals. Yet in interviews with CDOs regarding their college's or university's diversity plans a decade ago, the response we often received was that the public diversity plans had not been operationalized. In other words, the plans were largely aspirational (Evans & Chun, 2007). Some institutions may have adopted them as obligatory evidence of a commitment to diversity. In this sense, the creation of diversity plans can serve a rhetorical purpose as branding and marketing tools. When this occurs, diversity plans may be abstract documents when not operationalized and linked to day-to-day experiences and process-based outcomes.

One of the earliest initiatives in diversity strategic planning was the Michigan Mandate, established by President James Duderstadt in 1988 at the University of Michigan. This evolutionary strategic planning effort was data driven with a financial resource pool underpinning its forward-looking objectives. It featured an explicit focus on organizational learning, called for the establishment of a senior administrative diversity role, and linked academic goals and diversity progress (Williams, 2013). Just as importantly, the Michigan Mandate recognized the importance of faculty in driving diversity change. Interestingly, one of the recommendations was the formation of a faculty committee (without deans or chairpersons) to monitor the recruitment and retention of minoritized faculty (Lomax, Moore, & Smith, 1995).

Only a small percentage of early plans reached beyond structural diversity to address issues of reciprocal empowerment, participation in decision-making, equitable resource distribution, and inclusion (Evans & Chun, 2007). Exclusionary decision-making practices, differential treatment, and asymmetrical power relations remained outside the realm of such plans. Consider, for example, the observations of Mark, an Asian American administrator in a private, religiously oriented midwestern institution:

> Not being invited to meetings or, to serve, be on committees that my job should be considered for (not me personally), oh yeah, this happens quite often. And again my experience is that institutions have a certain set of people that they consider for particular decision-making. And even though in my case my official position warrants my presence, I wasn't part of that group so it is very much an ingroup-outgroup situation. The outgroup may be that I am a person of color or it may be something else. (quoted in Chun & Evans, 2012, p. 75)

Or note the observations of Therese, an African American administrator in a prestigious university:

> We tend to have a group of people who go to lunch on a regular basis. Instead of holding a meeting for all of the stakeholders, a group of three or four people will go to lunch and make the decisions. . . . I have a responsibility to pull together some projects and programs and there was a time where I had the authority to make decisions about my programs. And as of lately, after being excluded from these luncheons, I have been directed by my superior to check in with my colleagues to get essentially their permission to move forward with my program, when I didn't have to in the past. But it's not the reverse. Some things in my areas might be impacted greatly. (quoted in Chun & Evans, 2012, p. 99)

These narratives reveal that the relationship between rank and power differ for minority and majority groups with minority group members. Minority group members are more likely to be vulnerable to attack and lack of stability in their positions due to biased attributions (Ragins, 1997). Exclusion from decision-making for members of nondominant groups and differential levels of authority in terms of rank and power are symptomatic of an exclusionary and even discriminatory culture. Yet if diversity plans do not touch on the quality of organizational culture and practices of reciprocal empowerment, they may fail to address prevailing cultural norms and assumptions and how these norms are operationalized within day-to-day interactions. They may omit references to behavioral interactions, attitudinal shifts, and inclusive practices of participation and decision-making.

> *"I don't think the university was diverse or the culture embraced diversity. It certainly didn't live up to its mission, but I did see a lot of people working toward that. It [the mission] certainly wasn't operationalized through some behavior that people demonstrated."*
> Seth, a gay, White student affairs administrator (quoted in Chun & Evans, 2016, p. 50)

Principal Components of Diversity Strategic Plans

The ready availability of strategic planning templates offers an outline of major components. The tendency in recent years to approach diversity planning in a standardized fashion has yielded instrumentation that includes the following:

- *A values, vision, or mission statement* that links diversity to institutional strategic planning and a broader national and global context
- *Definitions of* diversity *and* inclusion in order to create a common vocabulary
- *A conceptual framework* that often identifies multiple dimensions for study within a campus environment
- *Input* from campus constituencies in the process of plan development
- *Goals and strategies*

- *Accountability* for goal attainment including divisions, offices, and leadership
- *Incentives* such as for hiring initiatives
- *Assessment and measures* such as campus climate surveys, diversity mapping, and other evaluative mechanisms
- *Time frames* for attainment of goals
- *Campus resources* including centers, offices, and programs that contribute to diversity
- *Tools* to assist organizational units in diversity planning
- *A communication plan* to disseminate goals and objectives (Evans & Chun, 2007)

The initial formulation of early diversity strategic plans led to the evolution of second-generation diversity planning. Second-generation plans build on the foundation established in earlier planning documents and provide a comparative reference point through longitudinal assessment and benchmarking. Ideally, the planning framework for diversity is process based rather than simply serving as a check-box report card. Progress is measured through both quantitative and qualitative measures as well as through benchmarking with peer institutions.

Nevertheless, because most diversity plans are multi-year and time limited, turnover in presidential leadership means that plans are often reshaped to address new priorities and perspectives. In Table 6.1 (found later in this chapter), we compare earlier plans with the most recent developments at a number of public doctoral research universities. Interestingly, some institutions like Indiana University, Bloomington; Ohio State University in Columbus; and Pennsylvania State University, College Park, have moved away from the creation of a separate diversity strategic plan to incorporation of diversity objectives in the context of overall strategic planning. The use of diversity mapping at Indiana University, Bloomington and Pennsylvania State University has helped identify specific diversity objectives.

Second-Generation Diversity Strategic Planning

Whereas early diversity plans may have focused on organizational characteristics such as structural diversity, accountability mechanisms, goals, and time lines, more advanced planning includes a focus on behavioral practices, the quality of interactions across difference, cultural change, and organizational learning. Specific areas of importance in second-generation diversity planning include the following:

- Recognition of socially embedded forms of inequality and asymmetrical institutional power structures and systems
- Review of process-based outcomes for equity and inclusion
- Measures of behavioral and attitudinal change
- Expected diversity leadership competencies
- Research-based approaches to systemic culture change and organizational learning

If the goal is diversity organizational transformation, diversity plans cannot be merely diagnostic in nature but need to address the root causes of organizational and behavioral barriers to diversity. These barriers include the prevailing power dynamic, lack of structural diversity, and relative absence of equitable resource distribution and participation in decision-making processes.

In recent years, the framework of IE has been widely used as a foundation for diversity strategic planning. The IE framework typically addresses the integration of diversity efforts across different dimensions of the campus environment. Due to the emphasis of IE on student learning outcomes and a welcoming campus environment, second-generation plans often include results of campus climate surveys as an important reference point. Yet surveys sometimes focus extensively on quantitative data, with only secondary consideration of qualitative feedback and the day-to-day experiences of faculty, staff, and students regarding diversity and inclusion.

Even with IE as an explicit framework in diversity strategic plans, overt articulation of goals that speak to social justice, reciprocal empowerment, critical intercultural perspectives, and inclusive leadership is rare. Even less prevalent is an emphasis on cultural change that recognizes the ways that power and privilege can perpetuate the status quo, legitimize inequality, and reinforce racial stratification (McDonald & Coleman, 1999; R.A. Smith & Elliott, 2002). As Yekim, an Afro-Latino CDO in a private western university emphasizes, simply articulating the principles of IE is not sufficient. IE requires actual structural change and the resources needed to accomplish the change:

"I believe the (IE) work is [often] done in a way that doesn't address power . . . not necessarily centralizing of the work that needs to happen structurally" (quoted in Chun & Evans, 2018, p. 98). Amplifying this point, Frank Tuitt (2016), senior adviser to the chancellor and provost on diversity and inclusion at the University of Denver, explains:

> These [IE] programs, though important, are usually not linked to institutional structures and systems, which severely diminishes their ability to transform campus culture. Such practices are the equivalent of putting Band-Aids on cuts, while leaving the sharp instrument that created the cuts in place.

Two promising exceptions built on the IE framework offer models for consideration. The plan for "Diversity, Inclusion, and Institutional Excellence" now under way at the University of Colorado, Boulder is built on a model of cultural change that emphasizes strategic actions and strategic innovations (University of Colorado, Boulder, Office of Diversity, Equity, and Community Engagement, n.d.).

American University's (AU); (2018) *Plan for Inclusive Excellence* begins by offering a candid assessment of the experiences of minority students:

> We found that more students of color experience bias, and feel alienated and unsafe, compared to their white peers. The institutional policies and practices that could respond to these experiences are considered inconsistent and opaque, even biased. (p. 2)

AU is investing $60 million in fiscal year 2018 for diversity, equity, and inclusion initiatives, $53 million of which will be in scholarships. The university's IE plan focuses on five priority goals: (a) training, learning, and development; (b) campus climate and culture; (c) systems, policies, and procedures; (d) access and equity; and (e) curriculum and instruction. As a whole, the plan addresses the need for organizational change and learning. Rather than reinventing the wheel, it seeks to build on promising practices and highlights a model practice with each priority goal.

According to Jesus Trevino, vice provost for IE and senior diversity officer at the University of Arizona, Tucson, the process of change can be compared to the metaphor of a ballroom. If the ballroom itself never changes, it is unlikely that a shift in power will occur. Rather than repackaging existing systems, a systemic approach to change requires learning new steps, recruiting new dance instructors, and ensuring that everyone is invited to the dance. In this sense, change can be compared to a campaign, like running for office, rather than an automatic process (J. Trevino, personal communication, February 9, 2018).

With this expanded focus in mind, diversity strategic plans can serve as a powerful conduit for cultural change and progressive organizational learning. They can catalyze the development of organizational capabilities that move an institution forward in both talent development and diversity learning outcomes. In addition, diversity plans can serve as a persuasive communication tool that reinforces the values, attitudes, and identity of the campus. When viewed as a driver in the change process, diversity strategic plans look beyond statistical measures to gauge the level of inclusion on a campus and within campus units. They are not formulaic but approach inclusion in terms of context, geographic location, historical legacy of exclusion, and existing culture. And they identify the resources necessary for systemic change.

Diversity strategic plans also provide a mechanism to ensure accountability for equitable outcomes. In this regard, boards of trustees can play an important balancing role in monitoring process-based outcomes at an institutional level in order to reinforce the need for equality. More often, however, board review tends to defer to limited review of demographic statistical reports without in-depth consideration of decision-making processes as they evolve and their differential impact on organizational outcomes (Chun, 2017b).

Systemic Diversity Planning

Diversity strategic planning is sometimes viewed as a centralized activity initiated by campus or system leadership. Although the development of centralized diversity plans offers the opportunity for engagement with all constituencies, the implementation process does not always reach the different layers and organizational strata of the campus ecosystem. As we have noted earlier, plans often remain disconnected from day-to-day experiences within an institutional setting.

> *"The mission of our great university is to discover, disseminate, preserve and apply knowledge. To this end we must confront many uncomfortable societal issues, that once confronted will make us stronger."*
>   *Michael Middleton, former interim president, University of Missouri System (CNN, 2015)*

By contrast, a systems perspective on diversity planning encompasses both centralized and decentralized school or college diversity plans. The formulation of a centralized plan provides overall institutional goals that create a framework for decentralized planning. At the institutional level, planning processes take place in consultation with all campus constituencies, including campus governance bodies. Systemic diversity planning is a multilevel undertaking that requires leadership commitment at all levels, including divisions, schools, colleges, and departmental units (Williams, 2013). In essence, it is a networked planning process that involves multiple branches. By creating responsibility at different organizational levels, it allows for expression of the individual identity and goals of different organizational units and academic disciplines while ensuring accountability for outcomes. At the division, school, and departmental levels, individualized plans respond to specific diversity goals that pertain to outcomes in the academic or administrative area.

A survey of 772 CDOs conducted in 2013 found that 59% had a centralized diversity plan, 86% included diversity in the general academic plan, and only 34% had decentralized plans. In addition, public institutions were more likely than private institutions to have a centralized diversity plan (66% compared to 47%) and also more likely to include diversity in their mission statements (85% compared to 80%) and academic plans (88% compared to 82%). Similarly, whereas 68% of public institutions reported the attainment of an institutional definition of *diversity*, only 47% of private institutions had formulated a campus definition (Williams, 2013).

Best Practices in Diversity Strategic Planning

To create a comprehensive framework for diversity strategic planning, university systems and boards of regents have established guidelines that charge each campus with the development of its own diversity plan. For example, the University of Wisconsin Board of Regents, set forth a mandate in 1998 for each campus in the system to establish a diversity plan (Williams, 2013). In 2016 the State University of New York (SUNY) with its 64 institutions issued guidelines for campuses in the development of their plans. SUNY's *Campus Guide for Strategic Diversity & Inclusion Plan Development* mandated the creation of a CDO at each campus by August 1, 2017. The CDO is responsible for implementing best practices in regard to recruitment and retention based on the overarching SUNY Diversity, Equity, and Inclusion Policy. The guidelines provide examples of goals related to the policy, implementation strategies, and approaches to outcomes-based assessment (SUNY, 2016). SUNY has articulated its aspirational goal to be the most inclusive state university system in the country.

A leading-edge best practice is the University of California, Berkeley's (UC Berkeley) carefully mapped administrative and academic toolkits and resources for departmental diversity planning. The toolkits refer specifically to the need to transform daily work in support of the values of diversity, equity, and inclusion articulated in the *UC Berkeley Strategic Plan for Equity, Inclusion, and Diversity: Pathway to Excellence* (2009).

The strategies outlined in the UC Berkeley toolkits articulate the need to address the deepest levels of change by living and breathing the university's priorities in every department. Areas of prioritization are to (a) grow leadership in both teaching and scholarship related to diversity, (b) expand the access and success of underrepresented groups, and (c) create a welcoming and inclusive climate where diversity is valued. Departmental planning is mapped in successive stages and uses campus climate survey results as a metric for comparative analysis. Emphasis is placed on self-assessment and engagement in the planning process by departmental stakeholders, with the centralized Equity and Inclusion Office as a resource. Questions for reflection are positively focused by asking departments to consider areas of strength, areas in which the department can be viewed as a leader, and areas in which the department would be excited about expanding its work. A self-assessment worksheet provides a standardized instrument for gauging diversity and inclusion in different dimensions of the department's work (UC Berkeley Division of Equity & Inclusion, 2018).

TABLE 6.1. Comparative Analysis of Representative Diversity Strategic Plans for Selected Public Doctoral Research Universities

Institution	Type	Enrollment	Title/Date	Key Features	Update	Title/Date	Key Features
Auburn University (Auburn, Alabama)	Higher Research Activity	25,912	Strategic Diversity Plan, 2005	Five goals with multiple strategies, includes tactics, partners, and measures; career development and succession planning program; communication plan for diversity	Change in diversity administration, planning in progress (Auburn University, 2006)		
Indiana University (Bloomington, Indiana)	Highest Research Activity	46,416	20/20: A Vision for Achieving Equity and Excellence at IU-Bloomington, 2003	Addressed progress in diversity goal attainment over past five years with emphasis on minority student enrollment, diversity hires, travel funds and retention initiatives for minority faculty	20/20 plan superseded by Bicentennial Strategic Plan for university campuses	*The Bicentennial Strategic Plan for Indiana University* (Indiana State University, 2014)	Schools and colleges address core values of diversity of community and ideas and respect for the dignity of others (Indiana University, 2014)
Kent State University (Kent, Ohio)	Higher Research Activity	29,477	Diversity Implementation Plan, 2001–2005; A Framework to Foster Diversity in Kent State's Eight-Campus System	The framework focused on recruitment, retention, and enrollment management with accompanying goals and strategies		*Equity Action Plan* (Kent State University, 2018)	Transformational change based on fairness, justice, and integrity and informed by equity in terms of historical and cultural circumstances; (a) plan framework of four dimensions; (b) institutional climate, culture, and community relationships; (c) student access, recruitment, retention, and success; (d) education and scholarship; and (e) institutional accountability (Kent State University, 2018; also see Case Study 9 in Chun & Evans, 2014b)

University	Carnegie Classification	Enrollment	Plan and Years	Actions	Notes	Core Values
Ohio State University (Columbus, Ohio)	Highest Research Activity	58,322	Diversity Action Plan, 2000; Diversity Plans: An Analysis 2004–2005	Identified six major objectives and report card with progress reports from divisions, colleges, and schools	Separate diversity plan superseded by *Ohio State's Strategic Plan—Time and Change: Enable, Empower and Inspire* (Ohio State, n.d.)	Among core values are diversity in people and ideas, inclusion, access, collaboration; plan states that diversity and inclusion are "essential components of our excellence" (Ohio State, n.d., p. 3)
Pennsylvania State University (University Park, Pennsylvania)	Highest Research Activity	47,040	A Framework to Foster Diversity, 2004–2009; this framework concluded its third and last five-year cycle in 2015 (Penn State, 2018); diversity mapping project completed in 2013	Used Smith's four-dimensional framework to address seven diversity challenges with midpoint review and targeted areas for improvement	Goals set forth under the university's strategic plan: *Our Commitment to Impact: The Pennsylvania State University's Strategic Plan for 2016 to 2020*, and specifically within a plan component: "Foundations: Fostering and Embracing a Diverse World—Strategic Plan 2016–2020" (Penn State, n.d.)	Strategic plan guided by six foundations that include "fostering and embracing a diverse world," "enhancing global engagement," and "enabling access to education" (State University of New York, 2016)

(Continues)

TABLE 6.1. (Continued)

Institution	Type	Enrollment	Title/Date	Key Features	Update	Title/Date	Key Features
University of Arizona (Tucson, Arizona)	Highest Research Activity	42,236	Diversity Action Plan, 2002	Addressed retention, mentoring, and campus climate assessment; specific action steps and responsibilities identified	IE framework and infrastructure under way with more than 24 committees to embed in institutional processes; Diversity Coordinating Council working with CDO on practices of IE; committee structures in schools following guidebook for diversity planning; diversity and inclusion to be further embedded in overall university strategic plan (University of Arizona, 2002)		
University of California, Los Angeles (Los Angeles, California)	Highest Research Activity	41,845	Diversity@ UCLA	Extensive website, including assessment of climate for faculty	CrossCheck Live, an online platform designed to change thinking about diversity, equity, and inclusion (UCLA Equity, Diversity and Inclusion, 2018a)		

University of California, San Diego (San Diego, California)	Highest Research Activity	30,709	Diversity Matters (website)	Included short-, intermediate-, and long-term plans with incentives for changes in work models and organizational structures	New Strategic Plan for Inclusive Excellence under way with focus groups, online data gathering, and workshops	*Strategic Plan for Inclusive Excellence* (in progress) (UC San Diego Office for Equity, Diversity, and Inclusion, 2018)	Framework: student-centered, research-focused service-oriented public university (UC San Diego Office for Equity, Diversity, and Inclusion, 2018)
University of Colorado, Boulder (Boulder, Colorado)	Highest Research Activity	32,432	Campus Diversity Plan: A Blueprint for Action, 1999	Diversity goals identified in climate for living, learning, and working; student access and opportunity; and diversity of faculty and staff	Diversity planning model for cultural change under way based on IE and incorporating strategic actions and innovations	*Diversity Plan: An Update on Making Excellence Inclusive* (to be completed in 2018) (University of Colorado, Boulder, Office of Diversity, Equity, and Community Engagement, n.d.)	Foregrounds cultural change and common understanding of university's mission, vision, and strategic goals regarding diversity and inclusion (University of Colorado, Boulder, Office of Diversity, Equity, and Community Engagement, n.d.)

(Continues)

TABLE 6.1. (Continued)

Institution	Type	Enrollment	Title/Date	Key Features	Update	Title/Date	Key Features
University of Louisville (Louisville, Kentucky)	Highest Research Activity	21,561	Achieving Our Highest Potential: Diversity Plan for the University of Louisville, 2003	Required each unit to submit diversity plan linked to strategic plan; evaluated deans and vice presidents on success in implementing unit plans	Plan reformulated as a result of the state of Kentucky's *Policy for Diversity, Equity, and Inclusion* (University of Louisville, 2016); this policy requires state institutions to set annual goals for underrepresented minorities defined as Hispanic/Latino, American Indian or Alaska native, Black or African American, Native Hawaiian or Other Pacific Islander, or two or more races	*Diversity Plan: 2017–2021* (University of Louisville, 2017)	The plan focuses on three groups: (a) African American, including those included in two or more races; (b) Hispanic/Latino; and (c) low income as well as services for other groups. Plan components are success, opportunity, and impact with strategies and tactics designed to enhance student access and success (University of Louisville, 2017)
University of Maryland (College Park, Maryland)	Highest Research Activity	37,610	Diversity database	Database of diversity-related syllabi, institutional diversity initiatives, and other resources	Ten-year plan developed in 2010 after 18 months of data gathering; creation of CDO position and Office of University Diversity	*Transforming Maryland: Expectations for Excellence in Diversity and Inclusion* (2010)	Foundation is IE and focuses on impact, leadership, and excellence; concrete goals in six areas: leadership, climate, recruitment and retention, education, research and scholarship, and community engagement (*Transforming Maryland*, 2010)

Institution	Classification	Enrollment	Plan	Description	Plan	Description	Thematic areas
University of Massachusetts, Amherst (Amherst, Massachusetts)	Highest Research Activity	28,635	Diversity and Inclusion at UMass Amherst: A Blueprint for Change, 2005	Emphasized inclusion and empowerment and systemic, planning-centered diversity efforts; recommended establishment of incentives and rewards for implementing diversity goals	*Diversity Strategic Plan* (University of Massachusetts, Amherst, 2015)	Steering committee appointed in 2014, identified five thematic areas	Thematic areas: campus as destination of choice for underrepresented groups, improve climate of inclusion, enhance curricular diversity, improve recruitment and retention of diversity faculty and staff, and increase outreach with external communities (University of Massachusetts, Amherst, 2015)
University of New Hampshire (Durham, New Hampshire)	Higher Research Activity	15,117	Diversity Strategic Plan, 2004–2009	Seven comprehensive strategies to be assessed in 2009; strategies in five categories: recruitment and retention, curriculum, climate, organizational structure, and outreach and engagement	*2010–2020 Inclusive Excellence Strategic Plan* (University of New Hampshire, 2012)	Extension of earlier plan and based on IE paradigm; establishes structure of the University Council on Inclusive Excellence and Equity	Thematic areas: organizational structure; curriculum; campus climate; recruitment and retention; and campus engagement with themes, strategies, and actions (University of New Hampshire, 2012)
University of South Florida (Tampa, Florida)			Strategic Diversity Plan, 2004, or CLEAR (Climate, Leadership, Excellence, Access, and Representation)	Draws on results of 2002 Campus Climate Survey and highlights faculty enrichment program for increasing diversity (College of Business Administration, 2004)			

(Continues)

TABLE 6.1. (Continued)

Institution	Type	Enrollment	Title/Date	Key Features	Update	Title/Date	Key Features
University of Washington (Seattle, Washington)	Highest Research Activity	44,784	Diversity Appraisal	Synthesizes appraisal results from three campuses and addresses curricular and research diversity; student access and opportunities; student development and retention; and structural diversity of faculty, staff, and administrators	Builds on 2010–2014 Diversity Blueprint, which focused mainly on student experience	*UW Diversity Blueprint: 2017–2021* (University of Washington, 2017)	Emanating from the University of Washington's Diversity Council, blueprint organized around goals focused on building an inclusive campus climate; recruiting and retaining diversity faculty, staff, and students; addressing tri-campus diversity needs; and enhancing accountability and transparency (University of Washington, 2017)
University of Wisconsin, Madison (Madison, Wisconsin)	Highest Research Activity	42,977	Plan, 2008 (2003–2008)	Followed University of Wisconsin System Design for Diversity and built on 1988 and 1993 campus plans; identified specific representation and academic success goals for American Indian, African American, Latino and Latina, and Southeast Asian American groups (University of Wisconsin System, n.d.)	A series of initiatives undertaken including a Strategic Diversity Update completed in 2011 and a Strategic Diversity Framework compiled by the Ad Hoc Diversity Planning Committee titled *Forward together: A framework for diversity and Inclusive Excellence, 2014* (Forward Together, 2014).	*Affecting R.E.E.L. Change: Retain, equip, engage, lead for diversity & inclusion* (University of Wisconsin, Madison, 2015)	The Diversity Implementation Plan for affecting R.E.E.L. change sets forth 3 stages for implementing the 5 goals of the framework established in Forward Together (2015) to be accomplished in a 10-year period.

Institution	Carnegie Classification[a]						
Virginia Polytechnic Institute and State University (Blacksburg, Virginia)	Highest Research Activity	31,224	University Diversity Plan, 2000–2005	Aligned with the university's six strategic directions and "Implementation Plan of the Academic Agenda"; goals addressing structural diversity, education and training, responsibility, climate, accountability and recognition, and internal and external partnerships and collaboration (Virginia Polytechnic Institute and State University, 2000)	Focus groups revisited goals of previous plan and made revisions based on current achievements in Inclusive Excellent and drew on an external benchmark study of 31 peer institutions.	*Toward an Inclusive Community: Diversity and Inclusion at Virginia Tech; Diversity Strategic Plan 2013–2018* (Virginia Polytechnic Institute and State University, n.d.).	Builds on the work of the first diversity strategic plan in 2000 and aligns with the university's strategic "Plan for a New Horizon." Goals and objectives are framed in terms of the four dimensions of the Inclusive Excellence framework: access and success; campus climate and intergroup relations; education and scholarship; and institutional infrastructure.
Washington State University (Pullman, Washington)	Highest Research Activity	28,686	Framework for the University Strategic Plan for Equity and Diversity, 2005	Established strategic goals and benchmarks	An associate vice president for community, equity, and IE hired effective June 1, 2018		

[a]Carnegie Classification of Institutions of Higher Education (2017).

The University of Michigan's (2016) *Diversity, Equity, & Inclusion: Strategic Plan* also offers a comprehensive, systemic framework for centralized and decentralized planning. The campus-wide plan articulates three overarching strategies: (a) creating an equitable and inclusive campus climate; (b) recruiting, retaining, and developing a diverse community; and (c) supporting inclusive and innovative scholarship (University of Michigan, 2016). These commitments are reflected in the planning updates submitted by 49 units and documented in a summary report of nearly 2,000 action items in the first year of implementation (University of Michigan, 2018). The first-year progress report acknowledges that the work outlined in the plan will be challenged "by a national climate that portends an extremely volatile space" for diversity (University of Michigan, 2017, p. 51).

An example of a strategic diversity plan built on a framework of social justice is the University of Massachusetts, Amherst's (2015) *Diversity Strategic Plan*. The plan identifies the following core values that foster a culture of excellence:

- Social progress and social justice—instilling in students a commitment to a more just society
- Diversity, equity, and inclusiveness—fostering a sense of belonging and creating an environment of dignity and respect
- Opportunity—"a corollary to inclusiveness" (p. 1) in welcoming those who share institutional aspirations and standards of performance

Specific goals include establishing the institution as a university of choice for students from underrepresented groups and improving the campus climate of inclusion. Articulation of the value of opportunity in relation to inclusion links directly to underscore process-based outcomes such as advancement and promotion. Further, as we will share in chapter 7, diversity strategic planning efforts led to the implementation of a campus climate survey. This development is a testament to the efficacy of the plan in driving institutional actions.

Table 6.1 shows diversity plans at public doctoral research universities that updates an earlier table published over a decade ago (Evans & Chun, 2007). The comparative data give perspective on these institutions' diversity journeys and the ways in which their diversity and inclusion efforts have been operationalized. Please refer to the accreditation standards cited in Table 3.2 that refer to the relationship between diversity and institutional mission.

We now proceed to Audit Questionnaire Step 5 in order to assess the progress of diversity strategic planning efforts.

References for Further Study

Reyes, K. A. (n.d.). *Developing a strategic inclusion & diversity action plan: Lessons learned from research & practice.* Available from https://www.sreb.org/sites/main/files/file -attachments/diversity_and_inclusion_webinar.pdf

State University of New York. (2016). *Campus guide for strategic diversity & inclusion plan development.* Available from https://www.newpaltz.edu/media/diversity/1%20 -%20SUNY%20Guide%20-Strategic%20Diversity %20Plan%20Development%203-16.pdf

Audit Questionnaire Step 5: Gauging the Progress of Diversity Strategic Planning

1. Does the institution have a current diversity strategic plan?

    ____Yes ____No

2. Are diversity values and goals incorporated within the university's or college's overall strategic plan?

    ____Yes ____No

    Please note where and how diversity values and goals are reflected in the university or college strategic plan:

    Section: _____

    Reference: _____

    Section: _____

    Reference: _____

    Section: _____

    Reference: _____

    Section: _____

    Reference: _____

    Add additional pages as needed.

3. What is the time frame identified for diversity planning and goal achievement?

    _____

4. Are interim reports required?

    ____Yes ____No

    The following questions pertain to diversity strategic plans that are separate from institutional strategic plans.

5. If a separate diversity plan has been developed, what frameworks or models are used? Check all that apply.

    ☐ Diversity or Equity Scorecard

    ☐ IE

    ☐ Multicontextual model for diverse learning environments

    ☐ Smith's progressive model

    ☐ Social justice

    ☐ Other (please identify):

    _____

6. When was the last diversity plan or update to a plan completed?

   _____

7. Were the results (outcomes) from the last plan incorporated into the current plan?

   ____Yes ____No

8. What specific dimensions or themes relating to diversity and inclusion are identified for study/assessment?

   _____

   _____

   _____

   _____

9. Which constituencies provided input for the plan?

   ☐ Administrators

   ☐ Board of trustees

   ☐ Diversity council

   ☐ Diversity officer(s)

   ☐ Executive leadership

   ☐ Focus groups

   ☐ Faculty senate

   ☐ Tenured and tenure-track faculty

   ☐ Non-tenure-track full- and part-time faculty

   ☐ Staff

   ☐ Student body council

   ☐ Students

   ☐ Other (please specify):

   _____

   _____

10. Does the plan define key terms such as *diversity, inclusion, underrepresented,* and so on?

    ____Yes ____No

11. Is the plan concise and easy to read?

    ____Yes ____No

12. Does the plan include specific time frames, evaluative measures, and accountability for the accomplishment of objectives?

    ____Yes ____No

If no, what elements are lacking?

_____

13. What measures of cultural change are addressed in diversity planning?

_____

_____

14. Does the plan provide specific mechanisms for the evaluation of process-based outcomes for equity?

For nonacademic administrators ____Yes ____No

Specific processes: _____

For academic administrators ____Yes ____No

Specific processes: _____

For full-time faculty ____Yes ____No

Specific processes: _____

For part-time faculty ____Yes ____No

Specific processes: _____

For staff ____Yes ____No

Specific processes: _____

For students ____Yes ____No

Specific processes: _____

15. What is the role of the board of trustees identified in terms of process review? Please explain with specific examples:

_____

16. In what ways does the plan address how behavioral practices and intergroup relations will be enhanced and improved?

_____

_____

17. In what specific dimensions of the plan is diversity organizational learning addressed?

_____

_____

18. Does the plan address diversity leadership competencies and how these are evaluated?

____Yes ____No

19. Does the plan include resources for goals that have been identified?

____Yes ____No

20. Does the plan provide guidelines for colleges and schools for decentralized diversity planning?

_____Yes _____No

21. Does the plan require annual updates from decentralized units on goal attainment?

_____Yes _____No

22. Does the plan address recognition for goal attainment?

_____Yes _____No

Systemic Diversity Planning

23. Please explain how divisional/departmental/and unit plans contribute to the institution's overall diversity strategic planning process.

_____

_____

_____

_____

Summative Evaluation: Please provide a summative evaluation of the results of this questionnaire and concrete steps for enhancement:

_____

_____

_____

_____

_____

Goals for enhancement:

1. _____

2. _____

3. _____

CHAPTER 7

Creating a Comprehensive Inventory of Diversity Education Programs

Higher education is the usher of progress and change.
And change is the defining force of our time.
Joseph E. Aoun (2017, p. xvii)

IN THESE CHANGING TIMES, Joseph Aoun (2017) foresees an educational shift and indicates that college should shape students into not only professionals but also creators who can thrive in a global economy. How then can higher education prepare students as creators in a rapidly changing and diverse global world? An answer to this question lies in the central role of diversity organizational learning in reshaping the educational context. With this vision in mind, this chapter draws on the research literature on organizational learning and identifies the steps in building a comprehensive inventory of diversity education programs.

Organizational learning addresses both the conditions and processes by which an organization changes and learns. It is cross-institutional and reflective in nature, transcending internal boundaries and engaging stakeholders in the process (Chun & Evans, 2018). For these reasons, organizational learning is one of the most effective levers of cultural change in institutions of higher education. Yet transformational change is extremely difficult and rare because it alters the underlying culture and norms of an institution and requires intentionality in order to sustain deep and pervasive change (Kezar & Eckel, 2002). Single events are not a "quick fix" to long-standing barriers to inclusion. Instead, culture change requires long-term, comprehensive, strategic efforts. As a result, the commitment and persistence of top institutional leadership is essential to the success of diversity organizational learning.

In the process of cultural change, organizational learning can serve as a catalyst in raising awareness of hidden norms and prevailing assumptions about diversity and inclusion. It can help shift and recalibrate mind-sets and modes of behavior and promote meaningful interaction across difference. Consequently, organizational learning needs to consider the existing culture, because diversity programs can trigger resistance when they do not build on existing strengths or create blame or guilt (Chun & Evans, 2018).

Without a nuanced approach, the volatility of campus politics can undermine the success of diversity initiatives and even destabilize employment relationships for administrators and untenured individuals when sponsoring events that deal with controversial subjects. Political crosswinds, whether arising from state legislatures, alumni, or divisive national trends, can limit, foreclose, and stall diversity learning efforts.

Connecting the plethora of diversity education programs is a challenging proposition. Building partnerships across internal organizational divides will require leadership support to convey the needed vision, focus, and urgency of integrated and effective diversity education. This chapter is designed to help overcome the tendency toward creation of siloed and piecemeal programs in different areas of the university and provide a vehicle for assessment of programmatic infrastructure and resources.

From an institutional perspective, the focus of diversity education programs is twofold: (a) to build the overall diversity capability of the college or university and (b) to enhance individual diversity competencies.

As we shall discuss further in chapter 10, diversity capability is a core intangible asset that differentiates an institution in terms of excellence and quality and is an integral aspect of the institution's identity (Evans & Chun, 2012). Built over the past two decades, a significant body of empirical research demonstrates that although intangible assets cannot be measured in strict accounting terms, they nonetheless affect organizational effectiveness and performance and have a significant impact on the institutional bottom line (e.g., Chun & Evans, 2014b; Ulrich, Allen, Brockbank, Younger, & Nyman, 2009; Ulrich, Brockbank, Johnson, Sandholtz, & Younger, 2008). In other words, diversity is not something "nice to have" but a necessary driver of organizational performance and success. On an individual level, building diversity competencies involves enhancing the awareness, knowledge, and skills to collaborate, communicate, and engage across difference with reciprocity, respect, and understanding (Pope, Reynolds, & Mueller, 2004).

In assessing a systematic approach to diversity organizational learning, the content and focus of diversity education programs should be at the forefront, rather than the sheer number of programs. Absent a clear alignment with institutional strategy, diversity programming can dissolve into numerous redundant activities and one-shot training events. Such programming too often suffers from "projectitis" or the failure to probe deeply into the underlying institutional logic that impedes the attainment of strategic diversity goals (Williams, 2013). Furthermore, diversity programs cannot be "one size fits all," but need to be tailored to the roles, contextual settings, and types of interactions that pertain to faculty, academic and nonacademic administrators, staff, graduate assistants, and students. For example, faculty development programs need to

> "I think I personally was pretty hapless in that regard, especially with African American students. I received no formal training about how to do that. . . . I grew up in a pretty lily white community and certainly felt those social values . . . but I personally didn't have any skills, and I am sure that I had negative skills, of not really knowing how to do it."
>
> A White female, lesbian psychology department chair in a midwestern liberal arts university (Chun & Evans, 2015a, p. 63)

be led by faculty and address issues through learning modules that are pertinent to concrete issues faced by faculty in the classroom and academic department.

With these concerns in mind, we identify three principal reasons for the failure of diversity education programs (Chun & Evans, 2018):

1. Programs tend to be atheoretical and not based on substantive research findings (Bezrukova, Jehn, & Spell, 2012). The research literature on diversity often lacks theoretical rigor and relies on nonexperimental approaches (Paluck & Green, 2009).
2. Diversity programs are frequently viewed as outside the mainstream university agenda and may be siloed in various areas of responsibility. As a result, programming can be redundant, piecemeal, and not well coordinated.
3. Diversity education programs often focus on the celebratory aspects of difference and do not address difficult sociohistorical realities or controversial topics. Programs that focus on antiracist training or social justice issues can cause considerable backlash.

The breadth of diversity education programs needs to address organizational culture, strategies, policies, and practices and not simply focus on one aspect of organizational learning such as implicit bias. As the *Report on Faculty Diversity and Inclusivity in FAS* (2016) at Yale University points out, "While implicit/unconscious bias are key aspects of any diversity strategy, the university should broaden current strategies for talking about the challenges of diversity and inclusivity" (p. 7).

Structurally, one of the most frequent pitfalls of diversity education programs is the lack of follow-up and evaluation of the transferability of learning to workplace or classroom settings. As a result, an iterative planning process for diversity education necessarily includes the following key phases:

- Preassessment and needs analysis
- Identification of gaps
- Gathering of feedback
- Programmatic development
- Evaluation (Chun & Evans, 2018)

Recognizing that diversity is often a contested topic in higher education, we now consider how institutions can clarify the guiding logic that underpins diversity organizational learning and develop a progressive taxonomy for evaluation. This taxonomy needs to take into account both qualitative and quantitative data regarding diversity and inclusion and cross-check institutional data sources with in-depth analysis of process-based outcomes.

Developing an Organizational Learning Taxonomy for Diversity

At the heart of an organizational learning taxonomy for diversity are the guiding principles that move the institution toward greater inclusion. The framework of learning principles will benefit from the groundbreaking research of Christopher Argyris and others. Argyris identifies single-loop or first-order learning as incremental and instrumental in that it involves relatively minor adjustments to routinized activities and behaviors (Argyris, 1993, 1997; Argyris & Schon, 1996). Such learning is primarily tactical and does not address underlying reasons for misalignment or the governing theory-in-use. In contrast, second-order or double-loop learning addresses underlying values and logic and

seeks to understand why outcomes have been produced and then develop strategies in response to these findings (Argyris, 1993, 1997; Argyris & Schon, 1996). A third-level or triple-loop learning not explicitly posited by Argyris and others has been conceptualized since the 1990s in the organizational learning literature as a meta- or superordinate level of learning (Tosey, Visser, & Saunders, 2011). Williams (2013) posits that triple-loop learning in higher education takes into account the institution's strategic context and challenges. Williams's triple-loop strategic diversity learning model moves in linear fashion from environmental context to the institution's governing diversity logic to the development of specific tactics and finally to implementation of strategic diversity goals (Williams, 2013).

With the framework of triple-loop learning in mind, the model of reciprocal empowerment shared in chapter 2 provides a dynamic model for embedding governing diversity principles into the evaluation of educational impact and effectiveness. In the context of hierarchical modes of power and interaction, institutional intervention is needed when those in power refuse to share resources and power with those from marginalized groups (Prilleltensky & Gonick, 1994). Empowerment is the guiding principle that

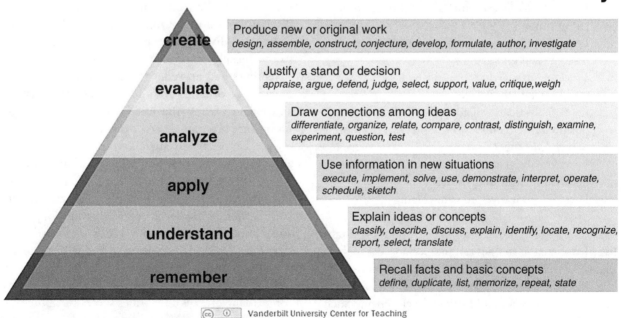

FIGURE 7.1. Bloom's taxonomy.

Source. Armstrong (2018). Reprinted with permission.

can bring together the necessary organizational factors that lead to successful diversity change initiatives (Kezar, Glenn, Lester, & Nakamoto, 2008). Guided by empowerment, a revolutionary reconceptualization of leadership is inclusive, collaborative, collective, and context oriented rather than based on hierarchical control (Kezar & Carducci, 2009).

In building a taxonomy for diversity education, institutional thought needs to be given to a progressive approach to diversity learning. Such approaches move from initial stages of awareness and understanding to analysis, evaluation, and creative problem-solving and innovative action based on synthetic understanding. As a starting point, Benjamin Bloom's foundational framework developed in 1956 (Figure 7.1) presents an important conceptualization of the stages of learning and inclusion applicable to diversity.

The DELTA shared in chapter 1 is a progressive path for gauging organizational learning focused on diversity and inclusion. This taxonomy begins with awareness of difference but ultimately results in institutional change through a critique of power differences as reflected in organizational practices and creative problem-solving across multiple contexts. A brief summary of the seven levels is as follows (Halualani et al., 2015; Halualani, Haiker, & Lancaster, 2010):

> Level 1: Knowledge awareness
> Level 2: Skill sets including intercultural competence
> Level 3: Interaction, particularly in terms of intercultural interactions
> Level 4: Advanced analysis through perspective-taking
> Level 5: Evaluation and critique in terms of positionality, compassion, and critique of power differences
> Level 6: Social agency and action including decision-making and advocacy
> Level 7: Innovative problem-solving

Once the organizational learning taxonomy is established, a thematic analysis can provide a visual tool for identifying programmatic focus, gaps, and redundancies. It will highlight areas in which offerings are concentrated or may require further development. Such an analysis will not only address topical areas but also focus specifically on the following (Halualani et al., 2015):

- Is there an intentional learning plan for faculty, staff, and administrators?
- How are individuals encouraged to transfer learning to roles in the university or college?

One of the primary challenges in an institution of higher education is obtaining faculty buy-in for diversity education. The literature on the effectiveness of faculty development has begun to erode the myth that faculty do not need ongoing training (Kezar, 2005). Nonetheless, methods of delivery of diversity education need to be tailored to the specific audience in higher education in order to address relevant issues and role-based needs.

Modes of Diversity Organizational Learning

A problem facing offices that offer diversity development is the lack of research on the effectiveness of diversity education programs (Chun & Evans, 2018). Given the difficulty of shifting mind-sets and norms, determining the most effective mode of delivery of diversity education remains a prominent consideration. Approaches to faculty audiences, for example, benefit from relating to the specific field or discipline in question.

Purely cognitive approaches can fail to address the deep-seated affective and psychological aspects of diversity education. Organizational and behavioral barriers to diversity are particularly intractable due to the socially embedded nature of prevailing social stereotypes and attitudes (Chun, 2009). As a result, didactically oriented training can increase resistance and fail to address the underlying assumptions and norms that preclude diversity progress.

An important avenue for consideration is to approach diversity organizational learning through strengths-based rather than deficit-based models. One such approach to positive change is appreciative inquiry (AI), a framework developed by David Cooperrider and Suresh Srivastva in the 1980s (Cooperrider & Srivastva, 1987). AI begins by surfacing what already works well and then builds on existing practices to identify desired goals. Its value lies in the fact that it is contextually oriented, identifies successful approaches already in use that are yielding positive results, and through collaborative input determines a pathway to an envisioned future state.

Diversity education is more likely to promote changes in mind-sets when it is experiential, because change is not only a cognitive process but also an affective one. Experiential learning promotes participation and involvement and can also provide a level of safety and depersonalization. Experiential methods include use of professional actors or diversity troupes such as Temple University's InterACTion Theater in the learning and development area of HR, journaling, group exercises, video excerpts, and visits to local landmarks and community groups. The use of case studies is effective, because it enables participants to view problems and issues outside of the immediate institutional context.

Because diversity topics are difficult and even controversial, casting blame and creating a sense of guilt may create backlash. For example, Marcy, a Latina CDO at a Catholic university, highlights the need for "aha" moments:

> When you have mixed audiences and you make people feel guilty and blame them, it is not conducive to learning. I have been to a few of those sessions. They were uncomfortable for me. You have to bring people along with you. . . . Shaming doesn't always work. And you have to get to that aha moment. (quoted in Chun & Evans, 2018, p. 157)

Voluntary programs tend to be more effective and reduce active resistance, but due to the tendency for the so-called choir to attend such programs, the active

endorsement of administrative and academic leadership provides a strong impetus for participation.

Specific types of offerings include symposia and events with speakers, learning modules within a given professional development series, and new employee/student orientation programs. In recent years, a number of universities have begun to offer Diversity and Inclusion Certificate Programs (DICPs). Take, for example, the DICP at the University of California, Santa Cruz that addresses social justice and is designed to improve campus climate and foster inclusion throughout the university. Required courses include Power, Privilege, and Oppression; Developing Diversity Change Agents; Supporting Queer and Trans Communities; Race: A Brief History of an Idea; Disability 101; and Class Matters (UC Santa Cruz, 2017). Another seminal organizational learning initiative is the creation of the Truth, Racial Healing & Transformation (TRHT) Campus Centers at 10 universities sponsored by the Kellogg Foundation. The goal of the centers is to dismantle racial hierarchies of human value and catalyze efforts to overcome inequities (Association of American Colleges & Universities, 2018).

Although online courses may represent a way to widely disseminate information and keep an institutional record of participation, such courses alone do not offer the depth and interaction needed to unpack complex diversity issues. Blended formats are another way to address program delivery. Regardless of format, opportunities for interactive discussion, relationship-building, and experiential learning are an essential aspect of program delivery.

"The framework for truth, racial healing and transformation leads with narrative change. And then we look at racial healing and relationship building. The racial healing circles are an important part of actualizing that component of the framework. Symbolically the circle sets aside the notion of hierarchy, there is a sense of being equal as well as connected; . . . methodologies are used which allow for deep affirmation, deep listening."

Gail Christopher, National Center for Healing and Nature (Association of American Colleges & Universities, 2018)

The Link Between Diversity Education and Accreditation

We next consider specific references to diversity professional development in accreditation criteria. Of particular note is the New England Association of Schools and Colleges (NEASC), which includes a specific criterion involving board development. As shown in Table 7.1, accreditation criteria clearly focus on ongoing professional development efforts for faculty and staff that support institutional mission and advance student learning outcomes through curricular and cocurricular programs.

TABLE 7.1. Accreditation and Diversity Education

Accrediting Agency	Criteria	Definition
Higher Learning Commission (HLC)	Criterion 3: Teaching and learning: Quality, resources, and support	3.C. Institution supports faculty professional development.
		3.E. Institution demonstrates claims to student educational experience through specific aspects of its mission.
	Criterion 5: Resources, planning, and institutional effectiveness	5.A. Staff are qualified and trained (Higher Learning Commission, 2014).
Southern Association of Colleges and Schools (SACS)	Section 6: Faculty	Institution provides professional development opportunities for faculty in alignment with institutional mission.
	Section 12: Academic and student support services	Institution provides student support programs consistent with mission (Southern Association of Colleges and Schools Commission on Colleges, 2017).
Western Association of Schools and Colleges (WASC)	Standard 1: Defining institutional purposes and ensuring educational objectives 1.4 Integrity and transparency	Institution responds appropriately to diversity in society through educational and cocurricular programs and commitment to WSCUC Diversity Policy.
	Standard 3: Developing and applying resources and organizational structures to ensure quality and sustainability 3.3 Faculty and staff	Institution supports faculty and staff development activities that enhance learning, teaching, and assessment of learning outcomes (WASC Senior College and University Commission, 2015).
New England Association of Schools and Colleges (NEASC)	Standard Three: Organization and governance	3.8 The board systematically develops and enhances its effectiveness through professional development.
	Standard Seven: Institutional resources	7.3 Institution provides opportunities for professional development of faculty, administrators, and staff (New England Commission of Higher Education, 2016).
Middle States Commission on Higher Education	Standard V: Educational Effectiveness Assessment	Consistent with mission, the institution plans, conducts, and supports a range of professional development progrms.
	Standard VI: Planning, Resources, and Institutional Improvement	The institution provides fiscal and human resource infrastructure to support operations and programs (Middle States Commission on Higher Education, 2014).

References for Further Study

A number of campuses and university systems have developed diversity asset inventories as part of the diversity audit process. For example, see

Jackson, J. F. L., & Charleston, L. J. (2014). *Iowa State Uni-versity's diversity audit and asset inventory*. Available from http://weilab.wceruw.org/CBCFALC/ISU%20 Comprehensive%20Report.pdf

University of Missouri System. (2016a). *DEI asset inventory*. Available from https://www.umsystem.edu/media/ president/deioffice/dei-asset-inventory-ums.pdf

In addition, see

Loden, M. (1995). *Implementing diversity: Best practices for making diversity work in your organization*. New York, NY: McGraw-Hill.

Audit Questionnaire Step 6: Inventory of Diversity Education Programs

This dimension of the diversity audit provides the opportunity to gauge the systematic implementation and integration of diversity education programs across the institutional spectrum. Although a listing of programs offered across the university or college is a useful first step, the inventory also needs to address whether and how university leadership has articulated the importance, urgency, and focus of diversity education. From this vantage point, the audit then considers how specific offerings advance the process of diversity organizational learning.

Vision and Focus

1. Are diversity education programs informed by a common vision for diversity and inclusion?

   ____Yes ____No

2. Has the president/chancellor articulated the vision, urgency, and focus of diversity education programs in official statements?

   a. ____Yes ____No

   b. If yes, please identify the specific ways this vision has been communicated:

   _____

   _____

   _____

3. Have vice presidents and deans communicated the vision, focus, and urgency of diversity education to the areas they oversee?

   a. ____Yes _____No ____In some divisions and colleges

   b. If yes, please identify the specific ways this vision has been communicated:

   _____

   _____

   _____

   _____

4. In what ways does the diversity officer(s) work collaboratively with academic and nonacademic areas to promote a common vision, urgency, and focus in diversity education programming?

   _____

   _____

   _____

5. What steps would help infuse the vision, urgency, and focus of diversity education more consistently across all organizational areas?

a. _____

b. _____

c. _____

Diversity Education Infrastructure

1. What staffing (FTE) has been allocated for diversity professional development of faculty, administrators, staff, and students? What is the level of the staff and where is the staffing located?

a. Responsible office _____ FTE _____ Title(s) _____

b. Responsible office _____ FTE _____ Title(s) _____

c. Responsible office _____ FTE _____ Title(s) _____

d. Responsible office _____ FTE _____ Title(s) _____

2. Besides salary compensation, what is the recurring budget for diversity professional development in each of the offices designated in question 1?

Budget allocation   Office

a. _____   _____

b. _____   _____

c. _____   _____

d. _____   _____

Specific Types of Diversity Education

1. Is diversity education provided for the board of trustees?

a. ____Yes ____No

b. How often is diversity education provided?

_____Every semester

_____Annually

_____On demand

_____Other

2. Is diversity education provided for academic and administrative leadership, including vice presidents and deans?

a. ____Yes ____No

b. How often is diversity education provided?

_____Every semester

_____Annually

_____On demand

_____Other

3. Is diversity education provided for managers and supervisors?

   a. ____Yes ____No

   b. How often is diversity education provided?

   _____Every semester

   _____Annually

   _____On demand

   _____Other

4. Is diversity education provided for faculty?

   a. ____Yes ____No

   b. How often is diversity education provided?

   _____Every semester

   _____Annually

   _____On demand

   _____Other

5. Is diversity education provided for staff?

   a. ____Yes ____No

   b. How often is diversity education provided?

   _____Every semester

   _____Annually

   _____On demand

   _____Other

6. Is diversity education provided for graduate assistants?

   a. ____Yes ____No

   b. How often is diversity education provided?

   _____Every semester

   _____Annually

   _____On demand

   _____Other

7. Is diversity education provided for students?

    a. _____Yes _____No

    b. How often is diversity education provided?

          _____Every semester

          _____Annually

          _____On demand

          _____Other

Content of Diversity Education

1. Does the institution offer a DICP?

    _____Yes _____No

2. Please assess the primary themes covered in diversity organizational learning in Table 7.2. Multiple elements can occur within a single course or seminar and there may be some overlap of topical areas among different offerings. Space is provided to include other topical areas.

TABLE 7.2. Topics Covered in Diversity Education Programs

Diversity-Related Policies and Processes	*Responsible Area(s)*
☐ Affirmative Action/Equal Opportunity	
☐ Appointment Policies	
☐ Discrimination Complaint Process	
☐ Disciplinary/Termination Process	
☐ Diversity Policy/Statement	
☐ Ethics	
☐ Federal and State Civil Rights Laws	
☐ Preventing Discrimination	
☐ Promotion and Tenure Guidelines	
☐ Recruitment and Hiring	
☐ Search Committee Training	
☐ Sexual Harassment	
☐ Whistleblower Protections	
☐ Other	
Strategic Diversity Leadership	
☐ Administrative Diversity Leadership	
☐ Board Diversity Leadership	

(Continues)

TABLE 7.2. (Continued)

Diversity-Related Policies and Processes	Responsible Area(s)
☐ Collaborative/Integrative Leadership	
☐ Cultural Change	
☐ Department Chair Leadership	
☐ Executive Diversity Leadership	
☐ Other	
Intergroup Relations	
☐ Conflict Resolution	
☐ Community Relations and Outreach	
☐ Diversity Dialogues	
☐ Intergroup Dialogue	
☐ Gender and Sexual Orientation	
☐ Racial/Ethnic Diversity	
☐ Religious Diversity	
☐ Social Identity and Intersectionality	
☐ Other	
Workplace Climate	
☐ Behavioral and Organizational Barriers	
☐ Empowerment	
☐ Inclusive Communication	
☐ Overcoming Stereotypes	
☐ Respect and Civility in the Workplace	
☐ Valuing Diversity	
☐ Workplace Bullying	
☐ Other	
Campus Climate	
☐ Green Zone (Veterans to Civilian Life)	
☐ Safe Zone	
☐ Other	
Diversity Awareness/Competencies	
☐ Cultural Competence	
☐ Disability Awareness	
☐ Gender and Sexual Orientation	
☐ Implicit/Explicit Bias	

(Continues)

TABLE 7.2. (Continued)

Diversity-Related Policies and Processes	*Responsible Area(s)*
☐ Mentoring/Coaching	
☐ Micro Inequities, Micro Aggressions	
☐ Multiculturalism	
☐ Other	
Sociohistorical Awareness	
☐ Antiracism	
☐ Privilege/Oppression	
☐ Social Justice Education	
☐ Other	
Pedagogy, Research, and Curriculum	
☐ Facilitating Classroom Discussion	
☐ First-Generation Students	
☐ Inclusive Teaching	
☐ Infusing Diversity in the Curriculum	
☐ Research in Diversity	
☐ Other	
Citizenship and International Issues	
☐ Civic Engagement	
☐ Cross-Cultural Issues	
☐ Diversity and Democracy	
☐ Global Citizenship and Perspective-Taking	
☐ National Trends and Issues	
☐ Other	
Diversity Assessment	
☐ Accreditation	
☐ AI	
☐ Climate Surveys	
☐ Metrics, Measurement, and Evaluation	
☐ Other	

Summative Evaluation: Please provide a summative evaluation of the results of this questionnaire and concrete steps for enhancement:

_____

_____

_____

_____

_____

Goals for enhancement:

1. _____

2. _____

3. _____

CHAPTER **8**

Assessing the Climate, Culture, and Readiness for Diversity Transformation

The measure of inclusivity of our campus has to be judged through the perceptions of those who are vulnerable.

Kumble R. Subbaswamy, chancellor,
University of Massachusetts, Amherst (2017a)

ONE OF THE MOST salient problems facing institutions of higher education is the creation of a welcoming and inclusive climate. Although strategic diversity plans may articulate a clear direction and set of aspirational goals for a campus, these plans often do not trickle down to affect day-to-day interactions, impact power relations, or influence divisional and departmental microclimates.

To address this sense of disconnection, campus climate surveys have evolved as an important vehicle for feedback from campus constituencies on everyday experiences of diversity. Their value lies in the ability to gauge perceptions about the campus environment and determine the degree to which campus stakeholders view their campuses as respectful, inclusive, safe, and welcoming. As such, climate surveys will benefit from the differentiated perspectives of groups including tenure- and non-tenure-track faculty, administrators, staff, students, and postgraduate researchers from different social identity groups. Periodic evaluation of campus climate over a defined time period will allow assessment of longitudinal progress as well as comparative review of results. Climate studies also offer support for accreditation requirements that focus on collaborative self-reflection and inquiry in service of continuous improvement.

Due to the political precariousness that accompanies the implementation of climate studies, commitment by the president and institutional leadership to ensure confidentiality, psychological safety, honest feedback, and transparency throughout the survey process is vital. This commitment will enable researchers to ask difficult questions, analyze data, and report results. Institutional leadership will also need to communicate the findings and develop an action plan to effect change with specific time frames and designation of accountability.

Collaboration of campus leadership with boards of trustees and governance bodies can help facilitate an understanding of the goals of the climate study and its relation to institutional improvement and effectiveness. In light of recent student demonstrations related to racial equity and social justice, the Association of Governing Boards of Universities and Colleges (AGB) has issued a comprehensive statement on governing board accountability for campus climate, inclusion, and civility. Specific recommendations include the need for the following:

- Collaboration and transparency by chief executives in working with the governing board on campus climate issues and informing the board of instances when efforts to advance diversity, equity, and inclusion are successful as well as unsuccessful
- Periodic review by boards of campus climate policies in relation to institutional mission
- Active leadership of boards in addressing campus climate through effective governance practices that include appointment of one or more board committees to review campus climate issues; definition and measurement of campus climate goals; and sponsoring of education and training on campus climate for the board, chief executive, and senior administrators

- Ensuring that chief executives meet board expectations on diversity and inclusion and demonstrate leadership in staff development (Association of Governing Boards of Universities and Colleges, 2016)

Before proceeding further, a definition of the related terms of *campus climate* and *culture* will bring further clarity to this aspect of the diversity audit.

Defining *Campus Climate* and *Culture*

The concepts of campus culture and climate have been viewed as two separate but interlocking constructs. The two constructs have, however, been used interchangeably. The culture of higher education has been described as an invisible tapestry that reflects deeply embedded values, norms, and ways of thinking and defines an institution's character (Kuh & Whitt, 1988; Peterson & Spencer, 1990). Due to the decentralized nature of colleges and universities, culture is not a unitary phenomenon but varies in different divisions, schools, colleges, and departments. Paired with the concept of culture is the notion of campus climate as a more transient, fluctuating phenomenon that reflects underlying cultural norms and can create a chilly environment for members of nondominant groups (D.G. Smith & Wolf-Wendel, 2005).

The emergence of a significant research literature over the past five decades recognizes the importance of climate in student success and learning outcomes. As articulated in research findings, campus climate is a multidimensional construct consisting of five major components:

1. Structural or compositional diversity
2. The institution's historical legacy of inclusion/exclusion
3. Psychological climate, including attitudes and perceptions among different identity groups
4. Behavioral climate
5. Organizational diversity that pertains to structures, policies, and processes (see Chun & Evans, 2016, for review; also see Hurtado, Alvarado, & Guillermo-Wann, 2012; Hurtado et al., 1998; Hurtado et al., 1999)

Climate studies not only examine perceptions relating to intergroup dynamics but also address the impact of organizational practices on the psychosocial environment (D.G. Smith, 1995).

More recently, the term *campus racial climate* has been used to describe the behaviors and expectations of the campus community in relation to issues of diversity, race, and ethnicity (e.g., Harper & Hurtado, 2007; Hurtado, 1992). For example, the University of Massachusetts, Amherst, climate study in 2017 revealed that White students were more likely to respond that they were "very satisfied" with the climate, whereas 55% of Black students and nearly one-third of Latino students reported that they were very or somewhat dissatisfied with the campus climate. One undergraduate student wrote the following:

> Simply being the only black student in a room brings on discomfort for me. At times, when things happen, although they are mundane and seemingly typical, I'm made to wonder, is it because of the color of my skin? I've also been disgusted by the way people in this community have engaged in discussing the results of the election by distancing themselves and the issues from white supremacy and racism. (quoted in University of Massachusetts, Amherst, 2017a, p. 22)

Confirming this perspective, consider the data gathered through focus groups and interviews of 36 Black juniors and seniors and 41 parents in a study of a predominantly White southern university. The accounts chronicle the unwelcoming atmosphere in dormitories and other campus spaces for minority students, such as the following description by the father of a Black student:

> The first time I rode through it looked like Ku Klux Klan country. . . . State University . . . just looked cold when I rode there, and I didn't like it, and I had already heard negative things before I went there. [What did you hear?] They were racist. (quoted in Feagin et al., 1996, p. 35)

Or take the commentary of a Black father bringing his daughter to a dorm:

> My daughter attended State University, and when I went there with her a couple of times—when she came (for) a weekend, we took her back. . . . You could feel it (prejudice), I mean, I went in the building with her. . . . It's like a thing that you can feel. I mean, black people have (antennae). No,

nothing, happened. It's just an atmosphere. The prejudice is the thing that nobody has to say nothing to you, to a black person. We know when it's in operation. (quoted in Feagin et al., 1996, p. 73)

As can be seen from these descriptions of campus climate, surveys can provide significant insight into the day-to-day experiences of members of minoritized groups on predominantly White campuses. Assessment of these experiences needs to disaggregate data based on factors that include race/ethnicity, age, gender, sexual orientation, gender identification, and disability and the intersectionality of these dimensions. In addition, survey data may address specific student attributes that include first-generation student status, religious affiliation, political orientation, and socioeconomic background.

Surveys can offer a window into overall campus climate as well as proximal campus climate in terms of experiences within a work unit, department, or classroom settings (Diermeier, 2016). Caution needs to be exercised in developing questions relating to work climate to ensure careful and meaningful definitions, relevant constructs, and valid criteria for evaluating responses. For example, a 2015 engagement survey at Harvard found that the majority of staff do not trust their supervisors. The description of this result in a presidential taskforce report, however, does not clarify the meaning of *trust* or how this construct is defined (Harvard University Presidential Task Force on Inclusion and Belonging, n.d.).

Types of Survey Instruments

In recent years, survey mechanisms have proliferated through professional associations, research arms of universities, and private consulting companies. As a result, the options for climate studies have increased dramatically. Discrete surveys can be administered to different cohorts of students, faculty, and administrators and staff. Alternatively, surveys can address multiple constituencies simultaneously.

With the emphasis on the prevention of sexual misconduct ensuing from Title IX requirements, specific climate surveys have been developed to gather student input in relation to sexual harassment, violence, misconduct, and assault. Among these vehicles are the Association of American Universities Campus Climate Survey on Sexual Assault and Sexual Misconduct as

well as the Department of Justice's draft instrument for measuring campus climate related to sexual assault (Bureau of Justice Statistics, 2016; Cantor et al., 2017). At some institutions, such as the University of Chicago, separate survey instruments have been developed for diversity and inclusion and sexual assault and misconduct (University of Chicago, 2016).

Climate surveys that center on diversity and inclusion and contribute to the process of diversity transformation are integral to the diversity audit. Examples of in-house surveys include the University of Wisconsin, Madison's 2016 Campus Climate Survey for students which addresses perceptions of the institutional commitment to diversity, as well as the University of Massachusetts, Amherst's Campus Climate Survey of faculty, staff, and students (University of Massachusetts, Amherst, 2017b; University of Wisconsin, Madison, 2018). The latter creates a framework for analysis that draws on the five research-based dimensions cited earlier in the chapter (University of Massachusetts, Amherst, 2017b). Both institutions have created extensive reports published online and have also engaged in significant pre- and postsurvey planning.

An example of a large-scale survey conducted with the assistance of an external consultant is the University of California's (UC) system-wide campus climate study at 10 campuses and 3 UC locations. The survey was the largest university system survey conducted to date. Findings gathered during 2012 and 2013 from 104,208 surveys were reviewed by a system-wide campus climate workgroup (University of California Office of the President, 2014) and resulted in the completion of campus action plans in 2015.

Cultural assessments are another vehicle for probing more deeply rooted cultural assumptions and unspoken cultural norms. Due to the difficulty of surfacing such assumptions, a qualitative approach is needed, with individual interviews and focus groups led by a skilled facilitator (Schein, 2006). A starting point for a cultural assessment can be a comparison of the institution's espoused values versus the degree to which diversity is actualized in day-to-day practices (see Chun & Evans, 2009; Foley, 2006).

Selection of Climate Survey Methods

Rather than stand-alone initiatives, climate surveys need to integrate both quantitative and qualitative data with existing campus data sets. From a methodological perspective, effective climate surveys "go beyond the numbers" in order to document perceptions and behaviors that affect nondominant groups. Because the climate for diversity is not an isolated phenomenon, such data can include, for example, evaluations of classroom climate that draw upon student evaluations (Hurtado & Halualani, 2014). Through the medium of open-ended questions, comments by faculty, administrators, staff, and students can yield substantial insights about perceived experiences. If final survey reports fail to include qualitative data, they will not capture nuanced feedback and may comprise purely quantitative findings gathered from Likert scales. However, great care must be exercised in reporting qualitative feedback to prevent identification of specific individuals or situations that are readily recognizable to internal audiences.

> *"Some issues regarding diversity and inclusion that affect me . . . [include] the inability to see myself represented more. . . . I do not feel as though my race and ethnic background are highly represented or the efforts to recruit more individuals like me are a high priority."*
> *Graduate student survey respondent, University of Michigan (Flaherty, 2016)*

The climate survey process is intimately connected with institutional context. The college's, or university's historical legacy, geographic location, size, mission, vision, and goals provide a framework for the climate survey process and will help determine appropriate areas of consideration. For example, the diversity mission and goals of a private, residential research-extensive university will differ from those of a public, nonresidential community college. Because some external surveys are designed for large institutions, these surveys may not be tailored to a smaller institution's organizational structure.

A number of survey instruments approach climate issues from different frameworks, such as IE, power and privilege, and social justice. These frameworks will necessarily guide questions and interpretation of data results. The use of a research-based framework will invoke appropriate social psychological constructs that include, for example, identity theory, social

identity theory, and the relation to these theories of identity salience and stereotype threat/vulnerability (Briesacher, 2014).

Selection of a climate survey consultant requires due diligence that includes close review of survey methodology. The validity and reliability of survey questions is a critical concern and requires that researchers interrogate the premises and assumptions that underpin survey questions. Questions and concerns regarding validity and reliability of survey construction include the following (e.g., Hart & Fellabaum, 2008; Klemenčič & Chirikov, 2015):

- Do surveys measure what they are designed to measure?
- Are the premises of the survey research based?
- Are reliability tests in an acceptable range?
- Have factor analyses been used?
- Is the framework for survey questions research based?
- Were terms such as *diversity, inclusion,* and *campus climate* defined clearly?
- Are the format and questions contextualized to the specific university or college environment?
- What type of investigator was used (internal, external, or both)?
- Was a representative sample obtained?
- Was consideration given to factors that might skew results?
- What methods are used (mixed methods, qualitative, quantitative)?
- Does the methodology probe beyond Likert scales and quantitative metrics?
- Are questions clear and unambiguous?
- Do questions seek to gauge prevailing cultural norms, assumptions, and behaviors?
- Are mechanisms in place to ensure one response per individual?
- If results are compared to those at other institutions, are these institutions comparable in terms of structure, size, mission, student population, and other factors?
- Does the data-gathering process include focus groups of stakeholders?

Advantages of in-house survey development include building greater engagement in the survey process through working groups, drawing on faculty research expertise, facilitating links with internal data sets, and customizing survey questions to the specific mission, goals, and historical legacy of a given campus. Cost can be a determining and overriding factor in decision-making relating to the selection of in-house developers versus external consultants.

Advantages of using an external consulting firm include increased perception of objectivity and independence as well as the ability to provide comparative benchmarking data through use of large data samples. One option for consideration in the use of externally developed resources is the rich array of research-based surveys developed by the Higher Education Research Institute (HERI) of the University of California, Los Angeles. HERI offers separate surveys for student cohorts such as freshmen and seniors, administrators and staff, and faculty. The faculty survey contains an optional climate module (HERI, 2017).

HERI's Diverse Learning Environments (DLE) survey for students is particularly relevant to the goals of a diversity audit. Piloted in 2010 at 14 institutions, the DLE survey is based on the MMDLE referenced in chapter 2 (see Hurtado, Alvarez, Guillermo-Wann, Cuellar, & Arellano, 2012; Hurtado & Guillermo-Wann, 2013). As noted earlier, this model seeks to gauge how campus environments create an integrated ecosystem that values the diversity of social identities and yields the educational benefits of diversity for all students. The interrelationship among campus diversity climate, educational practices, and learning outcomes is central to the MMDLE. The DLE survey includes factors measuring civic engagement, pluralistic orientation, awareness of privilege, and critical consciousness and action in terms of challenging one's own and others' biases (Hurtado & Guillermo-Wann, 2013).

As mentioned in chapter 2, the CECE project is now housed under the National Institute for Transformation and Equity at Indiana University, Bloomington. It has expanded its focus and now offers a range of distinct surveys: a two-year and four-year college survey, a graduate school survey, a faculty survey, and a staff survey. An alumni survey is now under development. The surveys are designed to diagnose campus environments and determine how these environments can be improved in terms of programs and practices. Most questions are based on a Likert-type response scale and can be completed fairly rapidly.

The surveys gauge experiences related to the concept of the cultural community or communities with which an individual identifies. This conceptual foundation may or may not be the desired framework for social psychological analysis at a given campus (see Briesacher, 2014). The student survey includes questions related to sense of belonging, cultural appreciation, academic self-efficacy, and academic motivation. Nine indicators are organized to yield information on cultural relevance and cultural responsiveness. These indicators measure the degree to which the group in question perceives the campus environment to be characterized by cultural factors including validation and holistic support (*CECE Surveys at a Glance*, 2018).

Phases in the Climate Survey Process

Institutions often form climate survey taskforces and commissions to help in formulating questions, developing outreach to stakeholders, reviewing results, and providing recommendations for change. The timing of the survey is critical and consideration needs to be given as to which groups will be surveyed and at what point in the academic year.

At the outset of the survey process, focus groups of faculty, administrator, staff, and student stakeholders can help identify salient issues and areas of consideration for the campus. For example, a process of meeting with student stakeholders at the University of New Hampshire engaged students as ambassadors to provide outreach and information to other students and build support for the survey effort (U.S. Department of Justice Office on Violence Against Women, 2016). Similarly, creating faculty and staff working groups can serve as a form of action inquiry that promotes ownership of results and generates greater responsibility and accountability (Bensimon et al., 2004; Clayton-Pedersen, Parker, Smith, Moreno, & Teraguchi, 2007).

Focus groups can also be used to gather qualitative data during the survey process. This aspect of the climate survey process will require confidential settings to ensure psychological safety as well as the guidance of a skilled facilitator. These groups can be specifically constructed for members of nondominant groups such as minority students and parents to allow facilitators to gain in-depth insights regarding the campus environment (e.g., Feagin et al., 1996).

Obtaining institutional review board (IRB) approval for human subjects is a necessary step. A sample

IRB notice is among the materials provided in an extensive toolkit with sample communication documents and administration guidelines on the HERI website (HERI, 2017).

A periodic communication process will need to be established to ensure transparency and keep stakeholders informed of progress. A letter from the president will help establish the goals of the survey and encourage participation. The communication process will need to indicate how and when results will be shared and the ways in which results will be used. Typical communication formats include the establishment of a website and dissemination of timelines, updates,

"Our Campus Climate Survey is a study of ourselves, for ourselves. . . . We welcome feedback and commentary and look forward to engaging in conversations about how diversity is lived and experienced by different campus community members" (University of Puget Sound, 2018).

reports, PowerPoint presentations, and analyses. Town halls are also effective ways of gathering feedback and discussing results.

Finally, preparation of a comprehensive report with recommendations will solidify the findings and identify concrete action steps. We next consider the ways in which climate surveys provide evidence of internal reflection, collaborative self-improvement, and institutional effectiveness in the accreditation process.

The Relation of Climate Surveys to Accreditation Criteria

Climate surveys offer evidence to accrediting agencies of systematic planning, transparency, and collaborative input. As shown in Table 8.1, accreditation requirements agencies emphasize the value of participatory input and valid assessment methods based on both quantitative and qualitative evaluation.

We now proceed to Audit Questionnaire Step 7, which addresses the measures taken to assess campus climate to date as well as future planning for evaluation of the climate.

TABLE 8.1. Campus Climate Surveys and Accreditation Criteria

Accrediting Agency	Criteria	Definition
Higher Learning Commission (HLC)	Criterion 5: Resources, Planning, and Institutional Effectiveness	5.B. Governance and administrative structures support collaborative processes to fulfill mission. 5.C. Institution conducts systematic, integrated planning. 5.D. Institution works systematically to improve performance. 5.D.2 Institution learns from operational performance and uses learning to improve effectiveness and capabilities (Higher Learning Commission, 2014).

(Continues)

TABLE 8.1. (Continued)

Accrediting Agency	Criteria	Definition
Southern Association of Colleges and Schools (SACS)	Section 7: Institutional Planning and Effectiveness	Commitment to principles of continuous improvement with a process for institutional effectiveness and planning for all programs and services linked to decision-making at all levels (Southern Association of Colleges and Schools Commission on Colleges, 2017).
Western Association of Schools and Colleges (WASC)	Standard 1: "Defining institutional purposes and ensuring educational objectives"	Integrity and Transparency: 1.4 "Consistent with its purposes and character, the institution demonstrates an appropriate response to the increasing diversity in society" through policies, curriculum and cocurriculum, hiring, admissions, and organizational practices. Diversity policy: Demonstrated commitment to the WSCUC Diversity Policy (WASC Senior College and University Commission, 2015).
New England Association of Schools and Colleges (NEASC)	Standard 2: Planning and Evaluation	Planning 2.1. Planning is broad based and involves the participation of both individuals and groups responsible for institutional outcomes. Evaluation 2.6. The institution systematically evaluates the attainment of mission and purposes with a focus on educational objectives. The system of evaluation supports institutional improvement using valid information using both quantitative and qualitative data methods (New England Commission of Higher Education, 2016).
Middle States Commission on Higher Education	Standard II: Ethics and Integrity Standard VI: Planning, Resources, and Institutional Improvement	The institution creates a climate of respect among faculty, administrators, staff, and students from diverse backgrounds and perspectives The institution continuously assesses and improves programs and services through planning and improvement processes that provide for participation and incorporate assessment results (Middle States Commission on Higher Education, 2014)

References for Further Study

Hurtado, S., Alvarez, C. L., Guillermo-Wann, C., Cuellar, M., & Arellano, L. (2012). A model for diverse learning environments: The scholarship on creating and assessing conditions for student success. In J. C. Smart & M. B. Paulsen (Eds.), *Higher education: Handbook of theory and research* (Vol. 27, pp. 41–122). New York, NY: Springer.

Hurtado, S., & Ruiz, A. (2012). The climate for underrepresented groups and diversity on campus. *HERI Research Brief.* Available from https://www.heri.ucla.edu/briefs/URMBriefReport.pdf

Museus, S. D. (2014). The culturally engaging campus environments (CECE) model: A new theory of success among racially diverse college student populations. In M. B. Paulsen (Ed.), *Higher education: Handbook of theory and research* (Vol. 29, pp. 189–227). New York, NY: Springer.

Audit Questionnaire Step 7: Self-Study Through Climate Surveys

A. For Campuses That Have Not Previously Conducted a Climate Survey:

1. Has consideration been given to conducting a campus climate survey?

    ____Yes   ____No

2. If the campus has not conducted a campus climate survey to date, what specific issues would benefit from information gained from this type of survey?

    ☐ Behavioral climate (sense of belonging, empowerment and support, mutual respect)

    ☐ Cross-racial interactions and campus racial climate

    ☐ Disaggregated data in relation to the campus experience

    ☐ Educational practices (curricula and cocurricula)

    ☐ Learning environment and classroom experiences

    ☐ Leadership and organizational culture

    ☐ Organizational equity and processes

    ☐ Psychological climate (attitudes, perceptions of institutional commitment to diversity)

    ☐ Safety

    ☐ Social identity and diversity experiences

    ☐ Student success

    ☐ Training needs

    ☐ Valuing diversity

    ☐ Working environment and job satisfaction

    ☐ Other (please specify):

    _____

3. What other measures have been used to assess institutional climate?

    _____

4. If a climate survey is undertaken, consideration should be given to development of surveys for different groups (i.e., students, faculty, staff) with a number of common items (Williams, 2013). Which surveys should be undertaken?

    ☐ Undergraduate students

    ☐ Graduate students

☐ Graduate assistants

☐ Postdocs

☐ Full-time faculty

☐ Part-time faculty

☐ Administrators

☐ Staff

5. What are the principal barriers to conducting a climate study?

☐ Financial

☐ Lack of internal support

☐ External pressures

☐ Other (please specify):

_____

6. Should it be determined that a study will be undertaken, what types of consultation would help determine the needed areas of focus in survey development?

☐ Dean's council

☐ Department chairs

☐ Diversity committee

☐ Focus groups

☐ Governance bodies

☐ HR

☐ Interviews

☐ President's cabinet

☐ Student affairs

☐ Town halls

☐ Other (please specify):

_____

B. For Campuses That Have Previously Conducted a Climate Survey:

1. Has a campus climate study been conducted within the last three years?

_____Yes   _____No

2. If not, what other measures have been used to assess institutional climate?

_____

3. If yes, indicate the year(s) of the most recent climate survey(s):

_____

a. Was this the first survey conducted?

_____Yes _____No

b. If no, what year(s) were prior survey(s) conducted?

_____

_____

c. What groups were included in the survey(s)? (Check all that apply)

☐ Undergraduate students

☐ Graduate students

☐ Graduate assistants

☐ Postdocs

☐ Full-time faculty

☐ Part-time faculty

☐ Administrators

☐ Staff

☐ Other (please specify):

_____

4. What type of survey instrument was used?

☐ In-house

☐ External consultant (please specify):

_____

☐ Other (please specify):

_____

5. Please indicate your level of satisfaction with the survey instrument:

☐ Highly satisfied

☐ Satisfied

☐ Neither satisfied nor dissatisfied

☐ Dissatisfied

6. Please explain the basis for your rating of the survey instrument:

_____

7. Was a committee formed to oversee survey development, dissemination, and analysis of results?

_____Yes _____No

8. Did the survey(s) link qualitative and quantitative findings with existing data sets?

_____Yes _____No

9. Did the survey(s) achieve an acceptable level of reliability?

_____Yes _____No

10. Were focus groups of stakeholders conducted?

_____Yes _____No

11. What types of focus groups were held to gather data? Please list:

a. _____

b. _____

c. _____

d. _____

e. _____

12. Were focus groups conducted that included only members of minoritized groups?

_____Yes _____No

Please explain:

_____

13. How were survey findings disseminated? Check all that apply.

☐ Campus-wide e-mails

☐ Department heads and chairs

☐ Executive officers

☐ Governance bodies

☐ Published report

☐ Town hall(s) and forums

☐ Website

☐ Other (please specify):

_____

14. Were survey results compared to other benchmarks such as best practices in peer institutions?

_____Yes _____No

15. Was comparison made with previous survey results?

_____Yes _____No _____N/A

16. Were specific goals, steps, and time lines for improvement specified based on survey results?

    _____Yes _____No

17. Which groups or constituencies have been involved in the review of findings of the campus climate study and establishment of future goals and measures?

    ☐ Alumni

    ☐ Board of trustees

    ☐ CDO

    ☐ Department heads and chairs

    ☐ Executive officers

    ☐ Faculty senate

    ☐ Managers and supervisors

    ☐ Staff council or senate

    ☐ Student governance

    ☐ Faculty

    ☐ Staff

    ☐ Other (please specify):

    _____

18. To what degree have processes and policies been implemented that respond to survey findings?

    ☐ To a high degree

    ☐ Changes in progress with some steps taken

    ☐ Initial phases

Summative Evaluation: Please provide a summative evaluation of the results of this questionnaire and concrete steps for enhancement:

_____

_____

_____

_____

_____

Goals for enhancement:

1. _____

2. _____

3. _____

CHAPTER 9

Building an Inclusive Talent Proposition

Recruitment, Hiring, and Search Committee Development

To enact the value of diversity in search and hiring processes, decision-makers must go beyond incorporating a question about diversity into an interview protocol. . . . Such actions represent tokenized treatment of the nation of diversity, rather than serious commitments.

S.D. Museus and F. Harris (2010, p. 35)

SLOW PROGRESS IN DIVERSIFYING both administrative and tenure-track faculty ranks indicates that much work still needs to be done in the systems and structures related to diversity recruitment and hiring. Over the last few decades, with the implementation of affirmative action programs for federal contractors, White female faculty have fared far better than their minority counterparts in terms of their increased representation, whereas the percentage of Black faculty has plateaued at about 5% (Rai & Critzer, 2000). As shown in Table 9.1, between 2003 and 2016, the percentage of African American faculty remained unchanged at 5%, whereas the representation of White women rose from 29% to 32%.

Rather than applying temporary fixes to the problem, systematic change in recruitment and hiring will facilitate the attainment of a more diverse administrative and faculty workforce in predominantly White institutions (PWIs).

Even though research on faculty hiring is more extensive than for staff and administrators, even for faculty greater attention has been paid to gender issues than to race/ethnicity or sexual orientation (e.g., Clauset, Arbesman, & Larremore, 2015). In fact, studies on the impact of race and ethnicity on hiring in higher education are limited (Derous, Pepermans, & Ryan, 2017).

This chapter is designed to assist in the evaluation of systems, structures, and processes that create a winning diversity talent strategy through recruitment, hiring, and search committee development. Although much practically oriented literature exists on this subject, research-based approaches to talent development in higher education are notably rare. For example, little is known regarding selection processes for tenure-track faculty in terms of search committee screening (Tomlinson & Freeman, 2017). The triadic gap among policy, research, and practice is a likely reason for the lack of success in diversity recruitment and hiring. The causal disconnection between scholarly research and practices fosters stagnation in the development of beneficial strategies that build an inclusive ecosystem (Bocanegra, 2012). To help overcome this gap, we share research findings that identify approaches to ensure equitable consideration of diverse candidates.

Recruitment and hiring in higher education are highly decentralized. Hiring recommendations typically take place within departments, with review by an additional tier of academic or administrative management such as deans or division heads. Although the need to recognize disciplinary and departmental needs is critical, decentralization can yield disparate results

TABLE 9.1. White Female, Minority Female, and African American Full-Time Faculty 2003–2016

	2016	*2015*	*2013*	*2011*	*2009*	*2007*	*2005*	*2003*
White Women	32%	32%	32%	30%	30%	30%	29%	29%
Minority Women	10%	9%	9%	9%	9%	8%	7%	7%
African Americans	5%	5%	5%	5%	5%	5%	5%	5%

Source. National Center for Education Statistics (2003, 2005, 2007, 2009, 2011, 2013, 2015, 2016). Analysis by authors.

in terms of diversity hiring. To add complexity to the picture, the localized nature of hiring decisions is subject to shifts in institutional decision-making and goals. In this regard, a disconnect can occur among decision-makers who may not take into account the impact of policy shifts on workforce demands, especially when budgetary reductions come into play (Cross & Goldenberg, 2009).

Because HR departments typically do not have responsibility for academic units, review of the phases of recruitment and hiring in faculty searches tends to be limited to compliance requirements. Furthermore, search committees are often powerful advocates in the decision-making process. Once committees have narrowed the slate of candidates, intervention by upper-level management tends to be viewed negatively, even if only to suggest consideration of an additional qualified, diverse applicant.

For these reasons, attentiveness at each stage of the search is necessary to ensure the inclusion of candidates from nondominant groups. Decision-making processes actually occur during each phase of the search, from the screening of applicants to recommending a short list for campus interviews to the final selection. To ensure equity in the review process, some institutions appoint diversity representatives or liaisons to serve on search committees. For example, at Oregon State University, the appointment of search advocates and training programs for these advocates resulted in the hiring of 25% of the candidates from underrepresented groups compared to 11% when committees did not have advocates (McMurtrie, 2016b). The diversity officer or other ex officio members may participate in the search committee for top administrative positions. Other universities may appoint a special position to help build faculty such as the University of Rhode Island's position titled director of diverse faculty and staff recruitment and retention that focuses explicitly on hiring and retaining diverse faculty and staff (McMurtrie, 2016a).

In order to set expectations for the search process, hiring authorities frequently will charge search committees and identify the need for inclusion of diverse candidates. In addition, the diversity or affirmative action officer typically will monitor search progress, including review of the advertising plan (sourcing), composition of the search committee, creation of the short list of interview candidates, and the hiring proposal. Despite these process-based reviews, Mary Beth Gasman (2016) identifies five reasons why more minority faculty are not hired in PWIs: (a) diversity and quality are viewed as antithetical and candidates who did not attend elite institutions or were not mentored by notable scholars are dismissed; (b) the lack of minorities in the pipeline is often cited despite the growing number of minority PhDs; (c) exceptions are made for White candidates, whereas playing by the rules is invoked for minority candidates; (d) search committees are not trained in recruitment, are not diverse, and often invoke the importance of the "right fit" for the department; and (e) contacts are not made with minority-serving institutions to seek potential candidates.

An increasing number of institutions have invested in diversity capacity through initiatives to recruit a diverse faculty, with 45% of 1,500 institutions in a 2017 survey reporting that initiatives were in place to attract women and minority faculty (Gagliardi et al., 2017). Some institutions provide direct funding support to departments for faculty hires who enhance diversity. For example, at Columbia University, the university has invested $85 million in faculty diversity recruitment and retention initiatives that have permitted the recruitment of over 54 underrepresented and female faculty (Chun & Evans, 2018).

Psychosocial Factors in the Search Process

With a view to creating inclusive hiring practices, we now examine several underlying psychosocial factors identified in the research literature that impact search processes. Chief among these factors is homophily, or the preference for similar others. Homophily is likely to produce homogeneity and to perpetuate the social reproduction of inequality. Due to the relatively limited participation of racial minorities in higher level positions, White males have increased opportunity to exercise self-similar preferences and reproduce advantage (Elliott & Smith, 2004; R. A. Smith & Elliott, 2002). Practices that reinforce glass ceilings in academe are sustained through cultural clones or groups of individuals who represent similar demographic characteristics such as gender and race/ethnicity (Essed, 2004).

The impact of homophily can be seen in all phases of the recruitment and hiring process. For example, in the recruitment process, job referrals are often informal and result from networking. Because networking is an important entry point for positions in higher education, the tendency for job referral and opportunity networks to be homophilous in relation to race can limit opportunities for members of nondominant groups (Elliott, 2001; Hartlep et al., 2017).

Homophily may also be exercised when faculty search committees favor candidates from elite or prestigious institutions, a practice that can limit opportunities for minority graduates from public research universities and less prestigious institutions. Informal networks can also favor internal hires and perpetuate academic inbreeding (Chun & Evans, 2012).

> *"When you're looking for people who might be good for positions, it's the same names that come up over and over again and they are usually sort of senior White male."*
> *Caroline, a White female provost in a prominent research university (quoted in Chun & Evans, 2012, p. 117)*

The preferential hiring of an institution's own graduates results when members of committees informally engage in practices that limit the hiring of external candidates (Altbach, Yudkevich, & Rumbley, 2015). In fact, a study of 200 faculty working at top-ranked programs found that 70% earned their doctorates from those programs (DiRamio, Theroux, & Guarino, 2009). These research findings suggest the lack of balanced representation and inclusive criteria in search pools as well as the impact of informal networks on hiring processes.

Another perspective that can undermine the objective scrutiny of applicants in search processes is the discourse of "fit" (Aguirre, 2000; Sensoy & DiAngelo, 2017). Underlying norms and prescriptive stereotypes regarding "fit" may affect the expectations of a search committee in the interview process and even provoke backlash when candidates violate the assumptions associated with their group (Berdahl & Min, 2012). When seen as a weak fit in relation to prevailing norms, minorities and women may be viewed as tokens or anomalies and their accomplishments and research may be devalued or viewed as outside the mainstream (Aguirre, 2000).

Research findings also indicate that when decisions involved more ambiguity and qualifications for a given position were less obvious, White participants recommended Black candidates with the same credentials less frequently. The benefit of the doubt extended to White candidates was not given similarly to Black applicants (Dovidio & Gaertner, 2000; Dovidio, Gaertner, Kawakami, & Hodson, 2002). Given these concerns, we next identify issues at each stage of the recruitment and hiring process that require systematic attention.

Formulation of the Job Description

The creation of the job description presents the opportunity to define a position broadly in order to attract a diverse applicant pool. A study of 689 searches conducted between 1995 and 1998 from 3 large public research universities found that underrepresented hires were more likely to occur when a diversity indicator such as education or scholarly work related to diversity was included in the job description or when a specific intervention strategy such as a search waiver enhanced or bypassed the traditional search process. Diversity indicators encompassed departments and subfields within a department. The study also noted the importance of examining field distribution of minority hires because, for example, Asian Americans face "legitimate challenges" (p, 153) due to their concentration in science, technology, engineering, and mathematics (STEM) fields but less common representation in social sciences and humanities (D.G. Smith, Turner, Osei-Kofi, & Richards, 2004).

In crafting an inclusive job description, greater flexibility in articulating job requirements can help diversify the applicant pool. Consider, for example, the approach of a White chair of psychology in an urban research university in recruiting faculty:

> One of the things that the research shows because minorities are, by definition, a smaller number, the odds just of finding a person who is underrepresented who studies exactly what you might set out to find, statistically is just less because there are fewer people. So if we, for example, . . . wanted to hire a cognitive psychology professor who studies reading . . . we might find plenty of individuals who study that, but the odds of finding an underrepresented minority who studies that particular topic are going to be less statistically. You might find someone who studies not reading, but psychology of language comprehension. So I would argue, that's close enough to what we're interested in: we need to be flexible about the topics. So maybe we find someone who studies language comprehension but not necessarily in a reading setting. (quoted in Chun & Evans, 2015, pp. 112–113)

As can be seen from the preceding quote, overcoming the argument that only a specific subfield should be considered within a discipline will permit consideration of a broader and more diverse talent pool.

Sourcing and Outreach

The creation of the advertising and sourcing or advertising plan requires proactive rather than passive strategies to build a diverse talent pool. Consider, for example, a survey of 638 faculty members that found that 82.3% had been involved in a search that lacked diversity in the applicant pool, and 81.4% had served on a search committee that lacked ethnic diversity (Buller, 2017).

The language in the job advertisement and the way that an institution presents the priority it gives to diversity are important factors in attracting diverse applicants. Yet the relation of applicant race and gender in terms of organizational attractiveness in the higher education workplace has received scant research attention. Job advertisements that portray organizational equity in a positive manner may be seen as more attractive to applicants from nondominant groups (see, e.g., Malinen & Johnston, 2007; K. M. Thomas & Wise, 1999). Although the inclusion of an equity statement has become routine at most universities and colleges, tailoring this statement specifically to institutional context including mission, vision, and values will help to defuse the perception that such statements are simply fulfilling an obligatory purpose.

Screening

Beginning with the initial phase of résumé screening, research indicates that stereotypes regarding social group membership can lead to exclusionary decisions (Derous et al., 2017). Take, for example, a study of invitations for interviews that found a White-sounding name was equal to eight years of additional experience on a résumé as compared to an ethnic-sounding name (Bertrand & Mullainathan, 2004).

The role of stereotyping in relation to sexual orientation during the application review process is documented in a large-scale audit study with 3,538 résumés submitted to 1,769 job postings by private employers in 7 states. The résumés of openly gay applicants resulted in significantly fewer callbacks in certain geographic areas including Texas and Ohio, but not in California, New York, Nevada, and Pennsylvania. When employers at the city, county, or state level were subject to relevant antidiscrimination laws, callback gaps were less prominent (Tilcsik, 2011).

Gender-specific stereotypes also impact the screening process. An audit study of 2,106 fictional applications submitted for 1,053 job openings used GPA to denote level of achievement for recent college graduates. The study found that high-achieving men received callbacks at a rate of nearly 2 to 1 in comparison with high-achieving women. This finding supports research indicating that although women are often perceived as less competent than men, when viewed as too competent or overqualified, they may be penalized by the assumption that they lack warmth and likeability. By contrast, women with moderate levels of achievement did not receive fewer callbacks, likely due to the perception that these candidates conformed to the stereotype of women as more sociable and outgoing. The differential callback rates applied only to the field of math and did not apply to business and English, due to the expectation that women will perform poorly in STEM fields (Quadlin, 2018). In addition, a randomized double-blind study of 127 male and female science faculty undertaken in a research-intensive university found that male student applicants for a laboratory position were rated as more competent and worthy of being hired than identical female applicants (Moss-Racusin, Dovidio, Brescoll, Graham, & Handelsman, 2012).

The systematic role of gender inequality in faculty placement has also been documented broadly in the scientific fields (Clauset et al., 2015). A study of 19,000 tenure-track or tenured faculty in 461 department- or school-level academic units in computer science, business, and history found observable statistical differences in the quality of institutional placement by gender in both computer science and business (Clauset et al., 2015).

Finally, despite assumptions about declining discrimination, a meta-analytic study of 55,842 applications submitted for 26,326 positions in 24 field experiments reveals that the level of hiring discrimination against African Americans has not improved over the last quarter century. On average Whites received 36% more callbacks than African Americans and 24% more than Latinos, even when accounting for education, gender, study method, local labor market, and other variables. The study concludes that levels of discrimination remain basically unchanged over time at the point of hire (Quillian, Pager, Hexel, & Midtbøen, 2017).

> *"In three years of applying to undergraduate teaching positions at the reduced rank of assistant professor, I have had only one interview and no offers. Two search-committee members honestly informed me that my age ruled me out of consideration."*
>
> *Michael Jon Stoil, associate professor of political science and military science, University of Guam (quoted in Stoil, 2014, para. 3)*

The results of multiple studies reveal ongoing and long-standing exclusion of diverse candidates in the screening process based on demographic characteristics. Such exclusion often involves stereotypical assumptions about candidates based on race/ethnicity, gender, disability, sexual orientation, and age. Moreover, as we have noted earlier, when a single diverse individual is hired into a predominantly White workplace setting, the individual can be tokenized and subject to greater scrutiny, increased performance expectations, and magnification of mistakes (Evans & Chun, 2007).

Search Committee Composition and Training

In recent years, colleges and universities have devoted greater attention to the influence of search committee composition on the recruitment process. When nondiverse committees represent microcosms of the existing administrative or faculty population, the committees can clone themselves in the recruitment process (Bilimoria & Buch, 2010; Hartlep et al., 2017). As Sensoy and DiAngelo (2017) emphasize, even when a minority is appointed to a search committee, the token member can be racialized by being the individual expected to bring a racial perspective to the committee. Furthermore, the tendency to expect the minority individual to have expertise on race and racial issues, but only these issues, can prevail. Similarly, the committee can assume that if the academic unit feels welcoming to majority members it will feel the same for minority group members.

Many universities have placed increasing emphasis on search committee training and development in order to enhance the potential for diversity hiring. For example, the National Science Foundation's (NSF) ADVANCE Program has fostered research and practices that will enhance the participation of women and minorities in academic STEM fields (see *ADVANCE Initiatives*, n.d.). The NSF ADVANCE website offers examples of institutional programs designed to enhance the inclusiveness of search committee processes.

Interviewing

The effectiveness of interviews as valid selection procedures is dependent on the individuals conducting them and can be affected by initial impressions based on subjective factors such as attractiveness and personal liking as well as stereotypical perceptions and bias (Dipboye & Jackson, 1999). For example, in a study based on a sample of 193 professional interviewers that compared interviewer reactions to a facially stigmatized White male in blind conditions using a curtain versus nonblind conditions, stigmatized candidates were rated lower and with greater confidence (Buijsrogge, Derous, & Duyck, 2016).

Structured interviews ensure that candidates are evaluated in a similar way by asking a standard set of predetermined questions and evaluating the responses comparatively. On occasion, a candidate may meet with subgroups from different constituencies who may not devise structured questions in advance. Coordination of the interview process requires attention to each interview that a candidate may experience. Behavioral-based questions provide a mechanism for determining how a candidate's past experience might bear on future performance, whereas purely hypothetical questions without reference to past experience do not provide a basis for evaluation of a candidate's past performance.

Negotiating the Offer

Negotiating the terms and conditions of employment can vary with more leeway given to attract candidates perceived as more desirable. For example, a study in a high technology company of 3,000 salary offers found that minority group members received significantly lower salaries than majority group members in the hiring process, although this difference was reduced if they had internal social ties within the organization (Seidel, Polzer, & Stewart, 2000). Women may be more conservative in seeking higher salaries and may be penalized from a compensation perspective for time out from the workplace or for lower salary histories.

Data on full-time workers in 2016 shows that Hispanic or Latina, African American, Indian or Alaska Native, and Native Hawaiian or other Pacific Islander women had lower median earnings than non-Hispanic White and Asian women. Asian American women had the smallest gender pay gap at 87% of White men's earnings, whereas Hispanic women experienced the largest gap, paid at only 54% of White men's earnings. In addition, the gender pay gap increased with age, with larger gaps for women between 55 and 64 years old paid 74% of men's earnings (Miller, 2018).

Recent legislation in certain states including California, Delaware, Massachusetts, New York, and Oregon and cities such as Pittsburgh and New Orleans has banned questions regarding prior salary history in the job application and interview process. Under California's salary history ban, employers cannot seek salary history or benefits information about an applicant either "personally or through an agent" such as an outside recruiter. In addition, upon request, employers must provide a pay scale for positions applied for by an applicant (Nichols, de Leon, & Withers, 2018).

The job offer for tenure-track faculty may include a number of other components such as start-up funds and general research support, course release time, equipment and lab space, summer salary, assistance with spouse placement, research assistance, and related components. For administrators, negotiable areas include moving costs and, when available, duration of hiring contract. Given that the greatest amount of leverage is possible at the outset of hiring, these considerations require careful attention by diverse candidates to help ensure job success.

Inclusive Hiring Strategies and Accreditation Criteria

References to hiring processes in accreditation criteria are somewhat limited. Standard 1.4 of the Western Association of Schools and Colleges on integrity and transparency refers to the importance of reflecting the diversity of society in hiring criteria (see Table 3.2). The Middle States criterion of Ethics and Integrity addresses the need for fair and impartial processes in hiring, promotion, and evaluation (Middle States Commission on Higher Education, 2014). The NEASC in Standard 6.4 (Teaching, Learning, and Scholarship) refers to the importance of "an open and orderly process" for faculty recruitment and appointment and under Standard 9 (Integrity, Transparency, and Public Disclosures) addresses the need for "non-discriminatory policies and practices" in recruitment and employment (Standard 9.5). Standard 9.5 further emphasizes the creation of an inclusive climate" that values and respects individuals with diverse backgrounds and characteristics (New England Commission of Higher Education, 2016).

We now proceed to Audit Questionnaire Step 8, which addresses institutional processes and policies related to recruitment and hiring.

References for Further Study

Columbia University. (2016). *Guide to best practices in faculty search and hiring.* Available from http://facultydiversity .columbia.edu/files/viceprovost/guide_to_best_practices _in_faculty_search_and_hiring_july_2016.pdf

Lee, C. (2014). *Search committees: A comprehensive guide to successful faculty, staff, and administrative searches.* Sterling, VA: Stylus.

Romero, A. Jr. (2017). *Best practices for recruiting and retaining diverse faculty for institutions of higher education.* Available from https://www.ccas.net/files/public/ Publications/Best%20Practices%20CCAS_March%20 2017_FINAL.pdf

Audit Questionnaire Step 8: Building an Inclusive Talent Proposition Through Recruitment, Hiring, and Search Committee Development

1. Do university or college policies and/or procedures address the importance of considering diversity and equity in hiring processes?

    ____Yes   ____No   ____For certain types of positions

    Please explain:

    _____

    Please provide the specific policy references:

    _____
    _____
    _____
    _____

    a. What aspects of the hiring process in relation to diversity are included in policies and/or procedures?
        ☐ Affirmative action goals
        ☐ Appointment processes
        ☐ Advertising plans
        ☐ Diversity mission, strategic plan, and goals
        ☐ Search committee composition
        ☐ Search committee training
        ☐ Search waivers
        ☐ Other (please specify):

        _____

        Are search committees charged by the hiring authority?

        ____Yes   ____No   ____For certain types of positions

        Please explain:

        _____

    b. Does the charging process refer to university or college diversity mission, vision, and goals?

        ____Yes   ____No

        Please explain:

        _____

    c. Do search committees receive department-specific data on the race/ethnicity and gender of incumbents and related affirmative action goals?

    ____Yes _____No

    d. Are search plans reviewed for broad outreach including specific publications that might reach diverse audiences?

    ____Yes _____No

    e. Are funds available for enhanced outreach, when departments are seeking to address underrepresentation, particularly in fields where the availability of women and minorities may be limited?

    ____Yes _____No

2. Is language included in job postings that reflects an interest in candidates who contribute to diversity priorities of the institution and department?

    ____Yes _____No

    Please explain:

    _____

3. Do search committees receive training related to search processes and equitable consideration of candidates?

    ____Yes _____No

    a. Please indicate the types of training offered:

    _____

    b. Does the training address common errors or biases that can impact search outcomes?

    ____Yes _____No

    c. Does the training provide examples of standardized, job-related evaluation criteria for screening and interviewing?

    ____Yes ____No

    d. Does the training include information on structured interviewing including behaviorally based questions?

    ____Yes ____No

4. Does the institution appoint diversity liaisons to search committees to ensure consistency in search processes?

    ____Yes ____No

    Please explain:

    _____

5. Does the hiring authority or institutional diversity officer periodically review aggregate applicant pools to determine the need for additional advertising or outreach?

    ____Yes ____No

6. Are evidence-based, job-related evaluation criteria established for screening applications?

   ____Yes ____No

7. Are short lists for on-campus interviews reviewed by the diversity liaison or hiring authority to ensure inclusion of members of underrepresented groups whenever possible?

   ____Yes ____No

8. Does the institution provide interview guidelines that address interview protocols, illegal questions, and the types of questions that lead to fair evaluation?

   ____Yes ____No

9. Does the institution provide guidelines and sample reference-checking forms that address the need for job-related inquiries, possible evaluative biases, and avoidance of unsuitable questions?

   ____Yes ____No

10. Does submission of the final candidates recommended for hire include a statement of the efforts made to recruit and interview women and underrepresented minorities?

    ____Yes ____No

11. Is the salary offer reviewed by the hiring authority for considerations of internal and external equity?

    ____Yes ____No

Summative Evaluation: Please provide a summative evaluation of the results of this questionnaire and concrete steps for enhancement:

_____

_____

_____

_____

_____

Goals for enhancement:

1. _____

2. _____

3. _____

CHAPTER 10

Total Rewards Strategy and Talent Retention

When Americans of color are oppressed or marginalized in the country's major institutions not only do they suffer personally and in their families and communities, but also numerous white-controlled institutions suffer significantly—and some may eventually deteriorate and decline as a result. Excluding or marginalizing a great many people of color has meant excluding much human knowledge, creativity, and understanding. . . . A society that ignores such a great store of knowledge and ability irresponsibly risks its future.

Joe Feagin (2013, p. 213)

ALTHOUGH HIRING DIVERSE AND talented faculty and staff is an essential driver of innovation, the sustainability of talent resources is integral to institutional survival and viability. As the opening quotation for this chapter emphasizes, undervaluing diverse talent wastes a valuable resource. In recognition of the competitive edge provided by human capital assets, the private sector has devoted greater attention to the development of strategic practices that enhance the retention of diverse and talented employees. Academic research conducted on talent practices has focused on the private sector, likely due to the more immediate correlation between high-performance talent systems and the bottom line. By contrast, the research literature pertaining to higher education talent practices has been limited for the most part to analysis of discrete functions such as faculty compensation (Evans & Chun, 2012).

Organizational Capabilities and Talent Practices

From a holistic standpoint, the organizational capabilities that enable an institution to reach its goals and define its identity are linked to institutional success. These capabilities are, in essence, intangible assets that identify what an institution is good at doing and its distinctive identity (Ulrich & Smallwood, 2004). By definition, intangible assets are difficult to quantify. Because roughly two-thirds of college and university budgets represent salary and benefits, human capital assets are the most important investment an institution can make. Extensive research studies by Dave Ulrich and others at the University of Michigan have identified 14 prominent organizational capabilities that characterize well-managed organizations. These capabilities are as follows (Ulrich & Brockbank, 2005; Ulrich et al., 2009; Ulrich & Smallwood, 2004):

1. Talent
2. Speed
3. Shared mind-set
4. Accountability
5. Collaboration
6. Learning
7. Leadership
8. Client connectivity
9. Strategic unity
10. Innovation
11. Efficiency

12. Simplicity
13. Social responsibility
14. Managing and anticipating risk

To this list we add diversity capability as a critical organizational asset in terms of building a culture of IE (Evans & Chun, 2012). In considering these capabilities, key questions for consideration include the following:

- In what ways does the institution foster collaboration and communication across organizational silos and among diverse constituencies?
- How is innovation rewarded and recognized?
- Do diverse leaders receive equitable institutional support and resources?
- How is social responsibility cultivated?
- Are strategic unity and shared diversity mind-set understood and cultivated within organizational culture?

With reference to these questions, HR, more than any other institutional function, is responsible for processes that develop and sustain organizational capabilities (Ulrich et al., 2008). Yet in higher education, one of the predominant drawbacks in institutional talent strategy is the bifurcation of HR practices between academic and administrative/staff functions. Typically, HR departments report through the financial side of the house, and the responsibility for faculty functions is often limited to benefits, retirement programs, and certain aspects of faculty professional development. This bifurcation becomes problematic in the effort to create a cohesive talent strategy. Rethinking the role of HR as integrative talent strategists in collaboration with academic affairs will enhance the potential for the participation, engagement, and retention of diverse talent (Chun & Evans, 2014a).

In addressing retention, a comprehensive total rewards strategy (TRS) will enable an institution to strengthen organizational capabilities through both financial and nonfinancial components. The employee value proposition (EVP) is key to understanding employee turnover because it addresses the full range of intrinsic and extrinsic rewards that an organization offers to employees in return for their continued employment (Dore, 2004; Kochanski & Ledford, 2001). The EVP strengthens retention through five principal elements: (a) direct compensation, (b) work content, (c) affiliation, (d) benefits, and (e) career development (Ledford, 2002, 2003). Other significant aspects of an effective TRS include employment security, promotion and advancement, recognition programs, professional development, health and work/life benefits, job design and content, workload, and flexible schedules (Evans & Chun, 2012). Each component has exit drivers that can lead to turnover. For example, although working at a college or university offers a significant benefit in terms of the pride that derives from institutional affiliation, an adverse working climate will undermine that affiliation and lead to turnover. Institutions also need to develop their own differentiated EVP, since all types of rewards cannot receive the same emphasis (Ledford, 2003).

Climate and Retention

The climate and culture of the institution and the division/department play an integral role in the retention of diverse talent. *Diversity climate* refers to the way employees perceive that diversity is valued within organizational life and supported by equitable employment practices. Research indicates that diversity climate perceptions vary by racial group (D.M. Kaplan, Wiley, & Maertz, 2011; Mor Barak, Cherin, & Berkman, 1998).

In chapter 8, we introduced the concept of campus racial climate to address the broad perspective of how race and ethnicity are valued in the overall university or college environment. Although the concepts of campus racial climate and diversity climate may seem redundant, institutional racial climate and departmental diversity climate are interlocking spheres. Take, for example, a study of the relation between the macro-level racial climate and individual faculty satisfaction based on a 2004–2005 faculty survey with 172,051 participants at 511 two- and four-year colleges and universities. The study found a strong, positive relationship between perceptions of a positive campus racial climate and individual faculty job satisfaction (Victorino, Nylund-Gibson, & Conley, 2013). Similarly, a literature review of issues relating to minoritized faculty in 252 publications from 1988 to 2007 supports the bridge between institutional and departmental contexts. The macro context of a lack of campus diversity and micro level practices of tokenism and marginalization within the department have been shown to contribute negatively to the experiences of faculty of color (Turner, González, & Wood, 2008).

> *"I've since found that one way to support myself as an African American faculty member in a program of which I am the only one of two Black women, is to find other women of color and White women to write with. The process of writing with other women who share similar struggles with me around racism or sexism supports me" (Fries-Britt & Kelly, 2005, p. 234)*

An interview study of 107 non-tenure-track faculty in 25 departments in 3 institutions identified 4 prototypes of departmental cultures: (a) destructive, (b) neutral, (c) inclusive, and (d) learning (Kezar, 2013). Destructive cultures had a negative effect on faculty performance and were characterized by nonsupportive leadership, whereas inclusive cultures were characterized by respect that, in turn, engendered faculty's willingness to go beyond what was expected. At the opposite end of the continuum, learning cultures offered policies and practices that enabled faculty to support student learning and provided professional knowledge that strengthened capacity (Kezar, 2013).

The persistence of members of nondominant groups can be impeded by a variety of workplace factors such as inhospitable microclimates, lack of supervisory support, marginalization and tokenism, limited opportunities for participation and advancement, social or interpersonal factors, absence of formal and informal mentoring, and inequitable personnel practices. As noted in chapter 4, forms of behavioral asymmetry between supervisor and employee can embody biases, stereotypes, differential expectations, and even forms of psychological abuse (Evans & Chun, 2007; Sidanius & Pratto, 1999).

Due to the fact that perceived competence is an important ingredient of power, stereotypes of incompetence, weakness, or lack of initiative relating to minority groups can preclude the development and maintenance of power commensurate with positional authority (Ragins, 1997). Consider, for example, a study of 5 African American women faculty that reveals how the myth of presumed incompetence can be perpetuated through lack of mentoring, isolation, and covert racism (Wallace, Moore, Wilson, & Hart, 2012). One part-time African American faculty member was summarily notified that she had been transferred from her administrative position in student affairs in a career of more than 20 years to another position off campus. She writes that "others would presume my transfer was due to incompetence." She further describes the constant scrutiny she faced in the new off-campus location to which she was transferred and "the mounting anxieties from ostracism, isolation, stress, and the lack of professional support and interaction." She adds, "I knew there was no incompetence involved, only administrative politics." Another colleague had suffered a similar fate resulting in a damaged career and reputation (quoted in Wallace et al., 2012, p. 435).

In another example, as documented in a study conducted by several women faculty at the Massachusetts Institute of Technology (MIT), disparities can exist in the assignment of office and laboratory space, teaching obligations, committee responsibilities, and awards (Hart, Brigham, Good, Mills, & Monk, 2009). Faculty from underrepresented backgrounds are often expected to mentor minoritized students and serve on committees as the diversity representative, on top of teaching and research obligations. Such forms of cultural taxation have increased with the demographic shifts in minority student enrollment, and often minority faculty are needed as role models to support the hurdles faced by students from nondominant groups (June, 2015). At the University of Southern Illinois, Carbondale, for example, there are only 31 Black tenure-track or tenured professors, whereas there are 3,000 undergraduate, graduate, and professional school Black students (June, 2015). The end result, in some cases, is to detract from junior faculty's ability to conduct research for tenure attainment.

> *"I was naïve enough to think that I had been hired as an assistant professor, but I really was there to be a one-person minority-affairs office."*
>
> *Janice Hamlet, associate professor of communications at Northern Illinois University, describing her first teaching appointment at a different research university while completing her dissertation (quoted in June, 2015, para. 30)*

The phenomenon of *calculative attachment* or the employee's perception of the possibility of attaining values and goals in a workplace setting can mediate elements of job satisfaction such as compensation and supervisory effectiveness and affect the potential for voluntary turnover (D. M. Kaplan et al., 2011). Inequitable environments diminish attachment and the view that the workplace will offer a satisfactory experience. The organizational commitment or affective attachment of the employee also mediates the relation of race and diversity climate to workplace goals and impacts the choice to remain with an institution (McKay et al., 2007). Take, for example, a study of 5,370 managers in a large national retail organization that found a prodiversity work climate correlated with increased organizational commitment and resulted in lower turnover intentions among Blacks, although it did not demonstrate similar results for Hispanics (McKay et al., 2007).

The revolving door for minority faculty in higher education has been well documented (see, e.g., Moreno, Smith, Clayton-Pedersen, & Teraguchi, 2006). A study of 28 California colleges and university campuses involved in the Campus Diversity Initiative sponsored by the James Irvine Foundation found that 58% of all new underrepresented hires between 2000 and 2004 were simply replacing underrepresented faculty who had left their institutions (Moreno et al., 2006). (In this study, the term *underrepresented* was used to apply to African American, Latino, and American Indian/Alaska Native populations.) The turnover rate among Asian Americans and Pacific Islanders was 50%. The high turnover rate of underrepresented faculty undercut the proactive efforts of these colleges and universities to diversify their faculty. The authors emphasize that, as with student populations, "for there to be true access, there must be success" (Moreno et al., 2006, p. 12). Interestingly, however, institutional mission, size, selectivity, and wealth were not differentiators in the turnover rate. Campuses with the most significant gains in diverse faculty linked their efforts to institutional mission and deployed multiple strategies to ensure success (Moreno et al., 2006).

Prevalent norms of success can influence retention, as in the STEM fields, which tend to favor characteristics associated with White male scientists such as competitive and individualistic practices (Ong, Smith, & Ko, 2018). Interviews with 39 professionals and undergraduates in STEM reinforce the isolation of women in the field, counteracted by the creation of "counterspaces" such as one participant's description of a monthly women-in-astronomy dinner. Counterspaces are not only physical spaces but also psychological, conceptual, and even ideological spaces within a university or college setting (Ong et al., 2018). A longitudinal study of female faculty that involved interviews of 87 faculty women in the second phase found that most of the women in STEM were the only females in their departments and were called on for increased involvement in service. Even during leave related to family commitments, they faced challenges in keeping labs operational and getting grants (Wolf-Wendel & Ward, 2015).

With these concerns in mind, this section of the diversity audit focuses on the creation of an integrated talent retention strategy rather than a set of isolated practices. It highlights the crucial role of HR departments in building a systematic talent strategy in collaboration with academic affairs that enhances retention for faculty, administrators, and staff. When cohesive talent practices are not part of an institution's overall HR strategy, organizational synapses can occur. And when HR is viewed as a transaction-based function rather than a strategic partner, HR can become mired in day-to-day processing activities rather than being proactive in the design of future-oriented initiatives. As shown in a study sample of over 20,000 participants from 3 data sets from 1988, 1992, and 1997, HR's evolution can be mapped in 4 phases: (a) operationally reactive in responding to everyday business demands, (b) operationally proactive in designing fundamental HR programs, (c) strategically reactive in support of current business strategies, and (d) strategically proactive in projecting future alternative strategies (Brockbank, 1999). With a strategically proactive and integrated HR talent strategy, an institution can enhance engagement and job attachment.

In the next sections, we focus on discrete elements of the EVP and the ways that these components contribute to high-performance talent systems.

Direct Compensation

Maintaining market competitiveness and internal inequity represent substantial challenges for universities and colleges in an era of shrinking resources and with the downturn in state-funded appropriations for public institutions. In the effort to attract diverse talent, problems arise when new hire salaries cause compression with existing salaries for long-term employees. Given these concerns, a cohesive compensation strategy will address both internal and external equity in order to align pay practices with institutional values and goals. Two components of this strategy include systematic compensation analysis that includes benchmarking with market through salary surveys as well as developing the institution's compensation philosophy.

Compensation Analysis

A systematic, comparative analysis of compensation levels based on race/ethnicity and gender coupled with rank, longevity, and related factors will help identify internal disparities. Many institutions undertake pay equity studies to address salient issues for minoritized groups and benchmark the results against peer institutions. Consider, for example, the College and University Professional Association's (CUPA-HR) comprehensive study of representation and pay equity for women and minority administrators from 2001 through 2016. Drawing on a sample of institutions with 10 or more years of history in the CUPA-HR survey of 2,270 colleges and universities, the study revealed that few institutions were top performers in both equitable pay and structural representation of women and minority administrators. Interestingly, associate's institutions dominated the list of 11 most successful institutions in terms of minority pay. But the gap in the representation of minority administrators has not narrowed. Over the last 15 years the gap has actually widened. At the same time, minority pay rankings were similar across all types of institutions, with minority pay close to parity with compensation for White administrators (Bichsel & McChesney, 2017b). Nonetheless, the results of this survey indicate that the lack of minority representation remains a persistent issue in university and college administration.

A 2007 study of 18,000 faculty members at 819 positions using data from the 1999 National Survey of Postsecondary Faculty demonstrated the interactional effects of race/ethnicity, gender, and marital status. The study found differences in pay based on gender, with negative effects for being female and positive effects for being married or cohabiting (Toutkoushian, Bellas, & Moore, 2007). Faculty men tended to be married at a higher rate than faculty women, and women may sometimes be limited geographically due to the

frequent assumption that female careers follow those of spouses or are shared with roles as family caregivers. Geographic area was a factor, with higher salaries in mideastern and far western locations (Toutkoushian et al., 2007). As a result, salary equity cannot be determined by single factors but needs consideration with multiple components that affect pay. An update of this study indicates the continuing need for women's salaries to reach greater parity with men's salaries (Finkelstein, Conley, & Schuster, 2016).

From an overall perspective, salaries for faculty are higher at doctoral universities compared to master's or baccalaureate institutions and community colleges, with an average premium rising from 16% in 1969 to 29% in 2013–2014 (Finkelstein et al., 2016). Research conducted by Finkelstein and colleagues reveals that whereas in 1979 salaries barely differed between the private and public sectors, by 2013–2014, the public sector disadvantage had increased, with full professor salaries at a 37% disadvantage at public doctoral universities. This gap has made recruitment of talent even more difficult. By 2014, field-based disparities had also accelerated markedly, with the greatest salary spread in business (62.8%) and law (57.3%). Seven fields exceed English by over 20%. Faculty salaries in the fine arts and particularly music have lagged considerably (83.1%); an effect is also seen in foreign languages (96.5%). This trend reflects demand in the economy at large for fields such as computer science, accounting, and engineering (Finkelstein et al., 2016).

Salary data for full-time non-tenure-track faculty and part-time faculty are also part of the salary equation, as approximately 70% of the faculty labor force today are contingent faculty, with 50% of this group employed part-time and 29% full-time (Yakoboski & Foster, 2014). On a per course basis, recent data indicate that most institutions pay less than $3,000 for a 3-credit course, with $4,000 offered at some research universities. Because approximately 25% to 30% of the contingent faculty workforce piece together a living through multiple institutions, sometimes their total income does not even surpass the federal poverty level (Finkelstein et al., 2016).

Development of a Compensation Philosophy

An institution compensation philosophy can provide a prominent vehicle for articulating the institution's strategic compensation-related goals. Ideally, it will identify the relation of compensation practices to institutional mission, vision and values, desired market position, and commitment to internal equity. Institutions have increasingly addressed the need to attract and retain talented and diverse employees in their compensation philosophy statements. These statements have often emanated from HR departments and may or may not address faculty compensation.

Consider, for example, Kansas State University's (2018) compensation philosophy that articulates the importance of "a fair and competitive total rewards program" that will retain and recognize "a high-performing and diverse employee community at all levels" (para. 1). The University of Iowa's (n.d.) HR compensation philosophy identifies the importance of total rewards as essential in recruiting and retaining a diverse workforce that will fulfill the institution's mission and goals. Creighton University's (n.d.) compensation philosophy is articulated in a *Compensation Guide* that links compensation to specific values and goals.

The award of merit-based pay can vary considerably in terms of the percentage of the pay increase and the individuals who receive it. Pay decisions need to be reviewed carefully for differential impact and adverse impact. Due to the different types of salary structures for faculty, administrators, and staff, the analysis needs to focus on components of the pay process that include compa-ratio (relation to the salary range midpoint), rank (for faculty positions), length of time in position, experience, educational qualifications, evaluative criteria, and other relevant variables. This analysis also requires review of equity and the comparative progress of women and minorities in the specific area or discipline.

Indirect Compensation

The configuration of benefits and retirement packages represents drivers of retention, although they usually have less impact than direct compensation in attracting new talent. A 2017 Willis Towers Watson study of over 30,000 private sector employees in 22 countries with nearly 5,000 U.S. participants found that 65% of those surveyed indicated that managing their health is a top priority, whereas 61% expressed dissatisfaction with well-being initiatives offered by their employers. The survey also indicated that employees are seeking greater choice and flexibility in benefits plans (Willis Towers Watson, 2018). This trend suggests the need for caution in trimming benefits programs that impact employee satisfaction and the importance of wellness initiatives. One approach to identifying programs that are most meaningful to employees is to seek their input by conducting focus groups and town halls prior to the selection of belt-tightening initiatives that impact benefits programs.

A 2017 CUPA-HR survey of 358 institutions found that the percentage of institutions offering wellness-related programs had risen in 2017, with 59% now offering these programs. For institutions that do not have a program in place, nearly one-third have plans to institute a wellness program in the next year (CUPA-HR, 2017).

Due to budgetary constraints and rising health care costs, institutions have sought to streamline benefits offerings through changes to deductibles, increased employee premiums, and decreased subsidies for dependents. The CUPA-HR report also identifies a steady increase in the percentage of institutions that offer high-deductible health plans, a trend that had increased steadily over the past three years. Another finding of the report with implications for hiring of diverse talent is that despite the 2015 Supreme Court determination that same-sex couples have the right to marry (*Obergefell v. Hodges*), this decision has not had an impact on health-care benefits for same-sex or opposite-sex domestic partners (Bichsel & McChesney, 2017).

On the retirement side, some state systems have moved from defined benefit retirement plans that provide a monthly salary following retirement based on a formula using age, salary, and years of service to defined contribution plans. Defined contribution plans are tax-deferred annuities using a 401(k), 403(b), or 457(k) model that involve monthly contributions during employment that are supplemented by the employer. Other aspects of indirect compensation include tuition reimbursement plans for the individual employee and, in some cases, family members, as well as sabbaticals and leave programs.

Work/Life Balance

Perceived work/life balance is a holistic concept that encompasses practices and policies as well as institutional/departmental support. A work/life integration model recognizes the interdependence of multiple spheres for both male and female employees (Sallee & Lester, 2009). For minoritized faculty, administrators, and staff, work/life balance has particular significance because a lack of balance between professional and personal responsibilities can add to stress and pressure caused by workplace inequities (Denson, Szelényi, & Bresonis, 2018). Imbalance in these spheres can indeed be the tipping point causing a decision to leave or stay at an institution. A study of 2,953 faculty members from 69 institutions found that institutional support for personal/family responsibilities and an academic career was the most positive predictor of perceived work/life balance (Denson et al., 2018). Yet the prevalence of unsupportive work/life cultures in higher education can create stigma against parental caregiving in favor of an institutional emphasis on prestige and research productivity (Denson et al., 2018).

In higher education, a hierarchy of importance foregrounds faculty over staff and has resulted in greater value being placed on work/life balance for full-time tenure-track or tenured faculty (Lester, 2013). This imbalance creates an inequitable range of policy offerings implemented across employment groups (Lester, 2013). Family-friendly policies such as stop-the-clock tenure programs for childbirth and adoption, part-time appointments, reduction in teaching loads for family care, and recognition of the needs of dual-career spouses are among the options available to tenure-track and tenured faculty at a number of institutions. But even when such programs exist, a culture of fear may inhibit use of available options such as tenure extension programs and require institutional safeguards to ensure appropriate implementation (Ward & Wolf-Wendel, 2004). For example, interviews with 120 female tenure-track faculty members conducted in 2002 found that the ability to manage family and work was not facilitated by institutional policies and required negotiating individual solutions (Ward & Wolf-Wendel, 2004). Consider the example of Lorna, a faculty member at a land-grant institution who was told by her chair that academic leaves and maternity leave were viewed as abusing the system. Or Melanie, who could not afford to take unpaid leave during childbirth:

> Another issue that I had while I was there is that I did have a child and that was the worst experience of my life. My husband didn't have a job so I couldn't take the 12 weeks of unpaid leave

without losing my house. (quoted in Gardner, 2013, p. 363)

The primacy of the departmental and divisional culture impacts the ability of faculty and staff to utilize existing programs. The discretion of supervisors including department heads and executives comes into play in determining the availability of options (Lester, 2013).

Policies that offer flexibility in work hours for staff can help offset limited financial resources and enhance employee commitment and engagement. Take, for example, the pilot program at MIT where a team of 35 employees worked on a remote work pilot for at least 2 to 3 days per week. The program reduced the stress of commuting and is expected to result in increased productivity even during record-breaking Boston winter snowfalls (Hirst, 2016).

Finally, rewards and recognition for contributions to diversity will help institutionalize the value of diversity within the culture of the organization, leading to retention of diverse talent. Increasingly a number of universities and colleges have framed these awards in terms of the goal of IE.

Accreditation and Retention

There are few explicit references to retention of faculty, administrators, and staff in regional accreditation criteria. The need for retention is implied in resource requirements and adequacy of faculty to support the educational mission. Although accreditation criteria emphasize processes that support strategic planning, stated mission, governance, and resource allocation, the sustainability of human capital investments has received considerably less attention. The Western Association of Schools and Colleges does address sustainability as well as organizational commitment of faculty and staff. Middle States Commission on Higher Education ties employment processes to institutional integrity. Table 10.1 provides relevant criteria that pertain to investments in human capital and retention practices.

In consideration of the five key aspects of the EVP, Audit Questionnaire Step 9 examines programs and practices that comprise the institution's TRS and contribute to faculty, administrator, and staff retention.

TABLE 10.1. The Relation of Accreditation Criteria to Total Rewards and Retention

Accrediting Agency	*Criteria*	*Definition*
Western Association of Schools and Colleges (WASC)	Standard 3: Developing and Applying Resources and Organizational Structures to Ensure Quality and Sustainability	"The institution sustains its operations" in support of educational objectives through investments in human and other resources and through decision-making structures. 3.1. "The institution employs faculty and staff with substantial and continuing commitment to the institution" (WASC Senior College and University Commission, 2015).
New England Association of Schools and Colleges (NEASC)	Standard 6: Teaching, Learning, and Scholarship	6.8. Criteria for faculty retention are addressed in a faculty handbook or other written documents. 6.10. The institution uses effective procedures for appointments, performance, and retention (New England Commission of Higher Education, 2016).
Middle States Commission on Higher Education	Standard II: Ethics and Integrity	"Fair and impartial practices" (Middle States Commission on Higher Education, 2014, p. 5) are employed in hiring, evaluation, and promotion. The institution establishes fair and impartial policies and procedures.

References for Further Study

Gutiérrez y Muhs, G., Niemann, Y. F., Gonzalez, C. G., & Harris, A. P. (Eds.). (2012). *Presumed incompetent: The intersections of race and class for women in academia.* Boulder, CO: University Press of Colorado.

McCormick, H. (2015). *Rethinking total rewards.* UNC Kenan-Flagler Business School. Available from https://www.kenan-flagler.unc.edu/~/media/Files/documents/executive-development/unc-white-paper-rethinking-total-rewards-final.pdf?_ga=2.114191367.1644975339.1542940716-1693999363.1457219091&_ga=2.114191367.1644975339.1542940716-1693999363.1457219091

Audit Questionnaire Step 9: TRS and Retention Practices

1. Does the institution have a stated compensation philosophy linked to institutional mission, vision, and values?

   ____Yes ____No

   a. Does the compensation philosophy identify the need to retain and sustain a talented and diverse workforce?

   ____Yes ____No

   b. Does the compensation philosophy address both internal and external equity?

   ____Yes ____No

2. Does the compensation program involve regular review of the comparative progress of women and minorities?

   a. For administrators?

   ____Yes ____No

   b. For faculty?

   ____Yes ____No

   c. For managers and supervisors?

   ____Yes ____No

   d. For professional staff?

   ____Yes ____No

   e. For support staff?

   ____Yes ____No

3. Are formal guidelines issued for discretionary salary increases such as the distribution of merit pools?

   a. For administrators?

   ____Yes ____No

   b. For full-time faculty?

   ____Yes ____No

   c. For staff?

   ____Yes ____No

   d. Please explain:

   _____

4. What positions initiate and approve discretionary salary adjustments?

   a. For faculty?

      Initiates_____

      Approves_____

   b. For administrators?

      Initiates_____

      Approves_____

   c. For staff?

      Initiates_____

      Approves_____

5. Are discretionary increase recommendations reviewed for equity and potential disparities for women and minorities?

   ____Yes ____No

   a. Which offices review these recommendations for equity?

      _____

6. Does the institution have a benefits strategy that links benefits packages and leave programs to a total rewards approach and EVP?

   ____Yes ____No

7. Has the institution sought employee input on benefits, wellness, and work/life offerings through surveys, studies, or focus groups/town halls?

   ____Yes ____No

   Please describe:

   _____

8. Were the results of benefits, wellness, and work/life surveys communicated to employees?

   ____Yes ____No

9. Does the institution have a wellness program and plan?

   ____Yes ____No

   a. Is there staffing for the wellness function?

      ____Yes ____No

   b. Are incentives offered for wellness goals?

      ____Yes ____No

10. Does the institution produce written materials describing work/life and wellness benefits and policies?

    ____Yes ____No

Please describe:

_____

_____

11. Does the institution have a flex-time policy?

     ____Yes ____No

12. Does the institution have a telecommuting policy?

     ____Yes ____No

13. Does the institution offer stop-the-clock tenure and reduced workload policies for parents of newborn children or adoptive parents?

     ____Yes ____No

     Please list the policies here:

     1. _____

     2. _____

     3. _____

14. Is regular review conducted of the implementation of stop-the-clock and parental leave policies in terms of accessibility across divisions and departments?

     ____Yes ____No

15. Does the institution have a dual-career program that assists with spousal placement?

     ____Yes ____No

16. Does the institution have formal mentoring programs?

     a. For junior faculty?

        ____Yes ____No

     b. For administrators?

        ____Yes ____No

     c. For staff?

        ____Yes ____No

     Please describe these programs:

     _____

     _____

17. Does the institution have a confidential employee assistance program (EAP)?

     ____Yes ____No

     a. Does the EAP provide regular utilization statistics to HR?

        ____Yes ____No

b. Is the EAP program identified in policy and shared in benefits materials disseminated to employees?

____Yes ____No

c. Does the program offer counseling to employees?

____Yes ____No

18. Is regular review conducted of promotion and advancement statistics in terms of the participation of women and minorities?

____Yes ____No

a. Which offices and positions conduct this review?

_____

_____

_____

b. How are findings communicated?

_____

c. Does the board of trustees receive periodic updates on promotion and advancement with analysis of the participation of women and minorities by employment group and division/department?

____Yes ____No

d. Does the board of trustees discuss these statistics at their meetings?

____Yes ____No

19. Is regular review conducted of turnover statistics in terms of women and minorities?

____Yes ____No

a. Which offices conduct this review?

_____

_____

_____

b. Does the board of trustees receive periodic updates on turnover with analysis of the participation of women and minorities by employment group and division/department?

____Yes ____No

c. Does the board of trustees discuss these statistics at their meetings?

____Yes ____No

20. Are exit interviews conducted to determine the reasons for lack of retention?

____Yes ____No

a. Which positions conduct these interviews?

_____

b. Is confidential analysis of the results of exit interviews presented in summary format to administration?

____Yes ____No

c. Does the analysis address turnover reasons for women and minorities?

____Yes ____No

d. Is the analysis shared with the board of trustees?

____Yes ____No

21. Does the institution have a diversity recognition program?

_____Yes _____ No

Please describe:

_____

_____

_____

Summative Evaluation: Please provide a summative evaluation of the results of this questionnaire and concrete steps for enhancement:

_____

_____

_____

_____

_____

Goals for enhancement:

1. _____

2. _____

3. _____

CHAPTER 11

Implementation Guide

THIS CHAPTER OFFERS A step-by-step guide to the implementation of the diversity audit that addresses successive phases of the process and identifies key participants in each dimension. It provides a planning matrix to track milestones, time lines, and expected outcomes. As emphasized in the introduction, there is no single implementation model for the audit. Due to significant differences in college/university missions, organizational structures and contexts, and institutional history, the most appropriate configuration of responsibilities for the audit process will need to be determined locally. Some campuses may not have appointed a CDO. Others may deploy a decentralized network of diversity personnel. As a result, the guidelines in this chapter can be adapted and modified based on organizational needs.

Phase 1: Planning for the Audit

Before introducing the campus-wide diversity audit, initial discussions would typically occur in the president's cabinet to address goals, the link to diversity strategic planning, the estimated time frame for completion, and expected outcomes. The initial discussion would establish the process for reviewing audit findings and the implementation of audit findings.

Leadership of the Audit Process
During the planning phase, the leadership and responsibilities for oversight of the audit process would be finalized. We have suggested possible alternatives in the introduction that include the CDO in coordination with a subset of the campus-wide diversity committee or the appointment of a steering committee that could be led by academic and nonacademic partners. At this point in time, needed resources for the audit such as institutional research, technological support, and staffing would be identified.

Communication Plan
During the initial phase, a campus-wide communication plan would be developed with a multifaceted communication strategy. In order to disseminate clear and concise information about the audit, the communication strategy would use tools such as internal e-mail and regular updates via e-blasts, in-person briefings to key constituencies, videos, and web portals with customized calendars and announcements.

The communication strategy would emphasize executive commitment and link the diversity audit to strategic diversity planning goals as well as the accreditation process. It would address the importance of diversity assessment in light of research-based frameworks such as IE and stress the effort to enhance a welcoming community that engages diversity in support of the educational process and organizational learning. It would highlight the specific dimensions of the audit and describe the benefits and expected outcomes of institutional diversity assessment. The communication strategy would establish the leadership for the audit process with an emphasis on broad-based collaboration of representative stakeholders from academic and nonacademic areas.

Examples of communication strategies include the University of Missouri's home page for the Diversity, Equity, and Inclusion Audit, which includes the what, why, how, and who of the audit process; audit goals and FAQs; important dates; messages to the university community from the president and chancellors; and links to resources (University of Missouri System, 2016b).

Key Participants

- President/chancellor and provost, who will provide strategic leadership for the audit in terms of communicating its purpose, relation to strategic institutional goals, urgency, and expected outcomes
- President's cabinet, who will review the overall plan for the audit
- CDO and college diversity officers, who will provide guidance and coordination in the audit process
- Campus-wide diversity committee of faculty, administrators, staff, and students, who will provide input regarding ways to communicate with the campus and build support for the audit in terms of their respective constituencies
- University communications officer in partnership with the chief information officer, who can provide strategic guidance and assistance in the development and dissemination of the communication plan

Action Steps

- Discuss the overall framework for the audit and guiding vision/values based on university/college mission.
- Finalize audit leadership/coordination responsibilities.
- Discuss expectations for the audit and how findings will be reviewed.
- Determine projected time frame for audit completion.
- Discuss top-level communication strategies about the audit including communication with the board of trustees and campus-wide communication.
- Discuss communication strategies across decentralized university/college culture to build engagement and ensure success of audit.
- Discuss time commitments for audit leadership.
- Review/determine needed staffing or technological support.

Phase 2: Complete Foundational Dimensions of the Audit

During the initial implementation phase, audit leadership such as the steering committee or diversity research team will work collaboratively to plan and oversee the implementation process. The committee can map the sequence for completion of the dimensions and determine estimated time frames using the Audit Planning Matrix (see Table 11.1 later in this chapter).

It is recommended that the first five dimensions be undertaken first to establish the foundational data for the audit. During this phase, engagement with the campus community will set the tone for the audit by seeking feedback on the first two dimensions (i.e., the meaning of *diversity* and *inclusion* and the academic/mission-centered case for diversity and inclusion). In addition, this phase will lay the groundwork for demographic analysis and provide baseline and longitudinal data regarding structural diversity. It will further include an assessment of the diversity infrastructure in terms of its centrality, pervasiveness, and integration.

1. *Defining* Diversity *and* Inclusion

This dimension of the audit offers the opportunity to begin a campus-wide, collective conversation with faculty, administrators, staff, and students about the meaning of *diversity* and *inclusion*. Rather than a polarizing debate, developing a common definition can bring together stakeholders from across the college/university spectrum. This work cannot be taken for granted. A survey found that 63% of the CDOs polled felt that their work was hindered by a lack of a widely accepted definition of *diversity* (Williams, 2013).

To begin the analysis, the different definitions of *diversity* and *inclusion* currently used throughout the institution are compiled. The audit team includes definitions from university/college mission statements and strategic planning documents as well as from the mission statements of divisions, colleges, and schools. This background work will surface predominant themes, commonalities, and nuances in the definitions of *diversity* and *inclusion*.

Williams (2013) provides five suggestions for initiating the campus-wide discussion on the meaning of diversity and inclusion: (a) include primary and secondary dimensions of diversity rather than a singular emphasis on race/ethnicity, (b) encourage feedback from multiple constituencies, (c) embrace the complexity of diversity in relation to institutional excellence and the learning process, (d) highlight the educational benefits of diversity and meeting the needs of diverse groups, and (e) draft and redraft the definitions to reflect the values and priorities of the institution.

Key Participants

- CDOs and college diversity officers who will collaborate with the diversity committee or diversity research team in compiling existing definitions
- Dean's council for discussion of definitions in concert with department heads/chairs
- Governance bodies such as faculty senate and student government who will discuss their perspectives on the definitions
- Nonacademic areas including finance, HR, facilities, student affairs, and multicultural centers

Action Steps

- Gather feedback from constituent groups.
- Review and compile existing definitional variations.
- Identify the major themes and domains referenced in these definitions.
- Link definitions to the institution's educational mission and purpose.
- Determine which elements can be strengthened or modified.
- Collaboratively draft working definitions for finalization by the president's cabinet and dissemination on the college/university web page.

2. The Academic/Mission-Centered Case for Diversity and Inclusion

This audit dimension examines the way the academic/mission-centered case for diversity is referenced in the university/college mission, vision, and values statements, as well as in the strategic plan, policies, and processes. It also addresses public communication of the academic/mission-centered case for diversity and the extent to which faculty and staff are familiar with it. The analysis addresses the number of colleges and schools that have diversity plans and whether the

academic case for diversity and inclusion is reflected in these plans.

This aspect of the audit can generate discussion with stakeholders such as deans, department chairs, and department heads across the institutional landscape in clarifying the relation of diversity and inclusion to institutional mission. The conversation can serve as a companion topic in campus-wide discussions related to the meaning of diversity and inclusion. Reflecting on the mission-centered case for diversity and inclusion will strengthen engagement with the academic community, particularly in relation to the paradigm of IE and its focus on student intellectual and social development. It will also solidify the role of nonacademic areas that may not have a direct connection to the overall academic mission and to the student experience in their day-to-day work. Final review will necessarily involve the president and president's cabinet to reflect further on needed enhancements to official university statements.

Key Participants

- CDO and college diversity officers, who will collaborate with the diversity committee or diversity research team to compile references to the academic/mission-centered case for diversity and inclusion
- Input from dean's council and department heads and chairs regarding college diversity plans and references to the academic/mission-centered case for diversity and inclusion in these plans
- Review and discussion of compiled information by president and president's cabinet
- Discussion with HR and student affairs for input in relation to diversity education programs

Action Steps

- Review official university/college mission, vision, and values statements and policies/processes for references to the academic/mission-centered case for diversity and inclusion.
- Identify policies that may benefit from references to the academic/mission-centered case for diversity and inclusion.
- Identify references to the academic case for diversity and inclusion in official processes.

- Compile references to the case for diversity in college and school diversity plans.
- Initiate discussions with academic stakeholders such as the provost's staff, deans, and department heads and chairs.
- Initiate discussions with nonacademic areas to solidify the reasoning behind the case for diversity and inclusion.
- Review findings with president and president's cabinet, particularly in relation to accreditation criteria.

3. The Building Blocks of Compositional and Relational Demography

The module of the audit establishes baseline metrics of structural diversity and optimally will include longitudinal analysis of progress. The findings in this dimension will serve as a communication tool in identifying specific employment groups that would benefit from greater diversity. The first aspect, the depth of this analysis, will depend on availability of data resources and technical staff. Much of the local data may be available in institutional research fact books and interactive university/college websites. To compare structural diversity with peer institutions, technical facility in extracting data from the IPEDS database is needed, as well as the ability to extract, merge, and compare fields from institutional databases.

The second aspect of the analysis in this dimension focuses on process-based outcomes. In concert with HR and academic affairs, the research team can compile analyses of process-based outcomes related to race/ethnicity and gender such as faculty and staff turnover, merit-based pay programs, tenure attainment, and performance evaluations. In addition to quantitative data snapshots, sources of qualitative data will enable the research team to cross-check and validate results.

Key Participants

- Members of the diversity research team with expertise in data analysis
- Institutional research staff, who will provide access to data resources
- Information technology staff, who will help compile data and merge results in tables
- HR and academic affairs personnel, who will provide access to process-based outcomes

- Affirmative action officer, who will share data from the affirmative action plan
- CDO and members of the diversity committee or diversity research team, who will analyze and summarize overall results

Action Steps

- Work with institutional research to compile longitudinal data on representation and progress of women and minorities in all employment groups (administrators, faculty, and staff).
- Review affirmative action plan on incumbency and goals for representation of women and minorities in employment groups and at the departmental level (including by academic discipline).
- Analyze undergraduate and graduate student demographic information.
- Compare findings with peer institutions using IPEDS data.
- Compare ratio of women and minority faculty to student demographics.
- Compile process-based findings in compensation, promotion, advancement, and turnover for minorities and women.
- Analyze representation and compensation of women and minorities in tenure ranks.

4. Strategic Diversity Infrastructure

This dimension of the diversity audit addresses the organizational architecture for diversity in terms of leadership and integration across the decentralized campus landscape. Because diversity officers often have limited staffing and resources coupled with a tendency to view their roles as symbolic positions, the analysis will provide the opportunity to assess ways that the diversity infrastructure leadership would benefit from enhanced institutional support.

Key Participants

- CDO and divisional or college diversity officers, who will assess the current architecture
- Affirmative action officer, who will provide input as needed on compliance-related functions
- President and provost, who will review the intermediate findings

Action Steps
- Analyze current organizational design, staffing, research capability, budgetary resources, and employment status for diversity leadership functions.
- Review integration and coordination of diversity positions on campus.
- Identify diversity taskforces and decentralized structures.
- Discuss structural integration of diversity efforts.

5. The Strengths and Pitfalls of Diversity Strategic Planning

This module builds on the findings of the previous dimension of strategic diversity infrastructure. It addresses the planning process for institutions that have incorporated diversity strategic planning into overall university or college strategic plans as well as those that have also created separate diversity strategic plans. This dimension will allow engagement in further discussions regarding the merits of different diversity strategic planning approaches. It also addresses systemic planning in terms of the relation of centralized diversity plans to those of decentralized units.

Key Participants
- CDO and divisional or college diversity officers, who will analyze the current diversity strategic planning process and review networked planning processes
- President and provost, who will review the intermediate findings

Action Steps
- Review and analyze diversity strategic planning process.
- Identify areas of focus and approaches that would enhance diversity strategic planning.

Phase 3: Coordination and Implementation of Remaining Modules

The four remaining modules of the audit can be addressed in the order desired by the campus or undertaken simultaneously with related modules, depending on the availability of staffing resources and stakeholder participation. As with the first two modules of the diversity audit, these modules can be used to strengthen stakeholder engagement and ensure greater integration of diversity efforts.

6. Creating a Comprehensive Inventory of Diversity Education Programs

This dimension provides the opportunity to strengthen the coalition of stakeholders involved in diversity education programs across the university. It seeks to ascertain whether diversity education programs are informed by a common vision, urgency, and focus in relation to institutional mission and goals. For this reason, study of this dimension brings into play the importance of partnerships among key offices, including academic affairs, student affairs, and HR, working collaboratively to provide integrated programming. In addition, the audit seeks to ascertain whether diversity education is provided for all organizational levels.

Key Participants
- CDO and divisional or college diversity officers, who will analyze institutional prioritization given to diversity programs and the relation of diversity education programs to mission
- Institutional offices that present diversity education programs, including those referenced previously, that will discuss the integration of these programs in order to eliminate redundancy and capitalize on existing resources

Action Steps
- Review and compile leadership statements regarding the urgency and focus of diversity education programs.
- Catalogue existing diversity education programs and topics covered.
- Convene key institutional stakeholders to discuss the integration of diversity education programs in order to avoid reduplication and create greater programmatic synergy.

7. Assessing the Climate, Culture, and Readiness for Diversity Transformation

This dimension of the audit is designed to help campuses assess whether to conduct a climate survey or, if the institution has already done so, to determine satisfaction with the instrumentation and implementation of the findings. As the number of options for climate surveys increases, informed selection of alternatives will allow greater customization to campus needs. Factors to consider in survey selection include the underlying assumptions of the model, the variables measured in terms of quantitative and qualitative data, reliability and validity of the instrument, costs, and potential for data benchmarking with peer institutions. Analysis of these factors will help campuses determine next steps and the most appropriate choice of survey methodology.

Key Participants
- Members of the diversity research team with expertise in data analysis, who will review data variables, analysis, and options for survey development and may enlist additional faculty expertise to assist with evaluation of survey options
- CDO in collaboration with college diversity officers, who will review potential for a new or additional climate survey, selection of methodology, and how findings will be communicated and implemented
- President and provost, who will review the recommendations of the audit team

Action Steps
- If a past climate survey has been conducted, review satisfaction with results, overall findings, and steps implemented, including how results were incorporated in diversity strategic planning.
- For future survey development, conduct cost/benefit analysis of survey options as needed in light of campus mission, priorities, and needs; review different models available and the types of data they will yield.
- Review other institutional data sources that may yield information on campus climate.

8. Building an Inclusive Talent Proposition: Recruitment, Hiring, and Search Committee Development

This dimension of the audit focuses on building an inclusive pipeline of diverse and talented faculty and staff and enhancing the structured and equitable review of candidates at each stage of the hiring process. As such, evaluation of current systems, policies, and processes related to diversity recruitment and hiring will benefit from the active participation and partnership of academic affairs, HR, affirmative action, and the office of diversity and inclusion. The collaborative work of these offices in providing diversity recruitment guidelines and training as well as working with stakeholders to ensure broad outreach and diverse applicant pools will enhance the possibility of concrete gains in diversifying the faculty and staff workforce. This dimension can also be paired with the next aspect of the audit, as both dimensions involve cross-divisional programmatic collaboration.

Key Participants
- Academic affairs, HR, and affirmative action officers in collaboration with the CDO and diversity officers

Action Steps
- Evaluate references to diversity mind-set and competencies in search, hiring, and appointment policies and processes.
- Review charging processes for both academic and nonacademic search committees in terms of diversity and inclusion.
- Address the process for reviewing outreach/advertising plans to reach underrepresented candidates, particularly in disciplines with few minorities and women.
- Evaluate content, consistency, and scope of search committee training.
- Identify target of opportunity or cluster hire opportunities.
- Highlight innovative approaches that will enhance equity and inclusion in recruitment and hiring processes across academic and nonacademic units.

9. TRS and Talent Retention

This module is designed to address factors that strengthen the retention of talent through a comprehensive TRS. The TRS encompasses both intrinsic and extrinsic rewards that strengthen the EVP. The audit will provide an overview of programs that contribute to the five elements of the EVP: (a) direct compensation, (b) benefits, (c) work content, (d) affiliation, and (e) career development. The analysis is designed to help identify the main components of a campus TRS; however, it can be further elaborated to address the full scope of current offerings unique to a campus and to identify desired future programmatic enhancements. This dimension will benefit from the synergy and collaboration of HR and academic affairs to determine ways to develop greater strategy unity across decentralized campus departments and ensure equitable organizational processes and support for diverse talent.

Key Participants
- Academic affairs and HR officers in collaboration with the CDO and diversity officers

Action Steps
- Conduct analysis of current TRS and retention practices in light of the components of the EVP; identify current programs that promote retention, affiliation, and job satisfaction.
- Review current processes for reviewing the compensation, advancement, retention, and turnover of women and minorities.
- Address potential opportunities for enhancement of the TRS strategy that will strengthen retention of diverse and talented faculty and staff.

To assist in the implementation of the nine audit dimensions, the Diversity Audit Planning Matrix (Table 11.1, following page) will allow the diversity research team to set time lines and determine resource needs and accountability. Following the completion of all nine audit questionnaires, the holistic overview presented in the last chapter summarizes diversity systems maturity in each of the dimensions, identifies future enhancements, and provides an integrated perspective for campus planning.

TABLE 11.1. Diversity Audit Planning Matrix

Dimension	Responsible Stakeholders for Completion	Strategies/Actions Needed	Resources Needed	Key Milestones	Institutional Accountability for Review	Estimated Time line
Developing a common definition of *diversity* and *inclusion*						
Building the academic/ mission-centered case for diversity						
Structural and compositional diversity						
Strategic diversity infrastructure						
Diversity strategic planning						
Diversity education and professional development programs						
Climate, culture, and readiness for diversity transformation						
Recruitment, hiring, and search committee development						
TRS and talent retention						

CHAPTER **12**

A Holistic Overview

*The greatest challenge today . . . is the accurate and
complete description of complex systems.*
Edward O. Wilson (1998, p. 93)

THIS FINAL CHAPTER LOOKS proactively toward the
future by creating a holistic overview that will
allow campuses to gauge the degree of interaction and
integration across the nine diversity dimensions. The
overview addresses the complexity and tension among
horizontal and vertical elements of the campus infrastructure and generates greater horizontal integration
for the whole campus as a learning community for
diversity (Keeling, Underhile, & Wall, 2007).

Each chapter's summative evaluation will provide
a window into an important aspect of diversity and
inclusion on campus. Although at first glance data
mining may appear to be a methodical and tedious
undertaking, its value lies in the insight it yields in
terms of structural flaws in programs and services
(Gagliardi, 2018). The discipline of data analysis coupled with diagnostic reflection will allow prioritization
of institutional goals and planning for future improvement. In synthesizing the nine facets of the diversity
audit, campuses can ascertain the degree to which
diversity and inclusion are operationalized through
organizational infrastructure, resource allocation, policies, processes, programs, organizational culture, and
day-to-day interactions. Consistent with accreditation
criteria, the audit will document concrete advances
and provide a vehicle for longitudinal assessment.

To gain insight into how different types of institutions have implemented diversity audits, we share
here several best practice examples. These examples
offer strategies for conducting an institution-wide

diversity audit that will inform overall planning and
enable concrete enhancements in support of diversity
and inclusion.

Best Practice Examples

Although the emphasis in each of these examples
varies based on institutional size and type, all three
institutions cited here implemented a broad-based
assessment process with the goal of establishing a
baseline diversity and inclusion metrics to inform day-
to-day operations. Tactical strategies include piloting
the audit process over a defined time period, building ownership at the unit level by engagement with
stakeholders, and creating research teams from diversity councils to analyze results. Both qualitative and
quantitative data were gathered by all three campuses
to capture the nuances of everyday experience and the
quality of relationships across difference.

University of Denver
At the University of Denver (DU), a private doctoral
research university with nearly 12,000 students, Frank
Tuitt, senior adviser to the president and chancellor on
diversity and inclusion and professor of higher education, embarked on a 2-year pilot diversity audit beginning in 2016. In consultation with a leading expert
from AAC&U, an online survey was developed and
the audit was undertaken in all academic and business units. The goal of the audit was to understand
the needs of faculty and staff in relation to their ability
to advance the university's commitment to IE. The 4
principal components of the survey are (a) leadership,

139

(b) resources, (c) capacity, and (d) goals. The analysis of quantitative findings was led by an internal collaborative team drawn from the university's Chancellor's Diversity and Equity Advisory Committee. Tuitt indicated that rather than conducting another campus climate assessment, DU sought to set a baseline for the institution in terms of its ability to embed IE in its day-to-day operations.

The audit process is an integral step in realizing the university's objective of creating IE plans for each academic and administrative unit and the institution as a whole as articulated in the strategic plan DU Impact 2025. The provost set expectations for unit attainment, and resources were made available from strategic planning implementation funds to provide diversity infrastructure at the department level. As Tuitt explained, the unit-based focus is designed to provide departments with a greater sense of ownership in advancing IE goals and priorities. He emphasized that the Office of Diversity and Inclusion has moved from a focus on program delivery to creating partnerships with departments in order to embed IE within the systems and structures that drive university life.

Hodges University

From 2013 to 2014, Hodges University, a private, master's-level university in southwest Florida with an enrollment of approximately 1,600 students, undertook an in-house diversity audit. According to Gail Williams, the CDO appointed in 2011, the university explored hiring an external consultant but determined that hiring a consultant would be too expensive. In addition to budgetary concerns, working with a consultant would have caused potential disruption to year-round academic course schedules.

As a result, Williams worked closely with the Hodges University Diversity Committee (HUDC) and the Office of Institutional Effectiveness to design an extensive online survey. Feedback was sought from stakeholders in terms of desired questions. Survey development took place over approximately three months. In addition to quantitative metrics, the survey included open-ended questions in order to gather qualitative feedback from faculty, staff, and students. Survey questions sought to ascertain demonstrable and measurable ways that diversity is valued in different aspects of campus life and integrated within the educational process. Following the completion of the audit and analysis of the findings, Williams identified opportunities for improvement and

mapped the university's diversity progress on a stage-based diversity development continuum.

Davenport University

Davenport University, a private nonprofit university located in Grand Rapids, Michigan, with 7,000 students and 11 campuses, conducted a diversity audit over a 9-month period from 2010 to 2011 with the assistance of an external consultant. The university serves a high percentage of first-generation and minority students and the audit was initiated in order to understand how the institution could respond more effectively to the needs of its diverse student population. The audit was selected as a vehicle for assessment because it is broader than a climate survey and could provide a baseline evaluation of diversity-related programs, policies, procedures, and curricula.

Davenport's president, Richard J. Pappas, and the executive vice president for organizational development, Dave Veneklase, launched an initiative in which surveys and focus groups were conducted on every campus and data were compiled into a series of recommendations. As a result of the audit, the university established a diversity officer position, now held by Rhae-Ann Booker, and formed a cross-functional grassroots Diversity, Equity, and Inclusion Council. The data subcommittee of the council has been particularly instrumental in reviewing institutional data from a diversity lens ranging from the highest level performance indicators to disaggregated data and qualitative climate data. Booker indicated that the audit findings have guided her work and informed the process of diversity strategic planning that will be incorporated into the university's forthcoming strategic plan, Vision 2025. Veneklase emphasized that the key to institutional success is talent. Unlike institutions that have subsumed HR under financial leadership, Davenport's elevation of organizational development to a cabinet-level position recognizes the priority given to nurturing diverse talent and leveraging diversity and inclusion as institutional assets.

Alignment of Audit Findings With Accreditation Criteria

Given these representative best practice examples, the audit concludes with an overall summation of the findings of all nine dimensions of the audit. This summation addresses the goals of accreditation and provides an evaluation of diversity systems maturity based on the AQIP model.

The diversity audit aligns with accreditation criteria in four important ways: (a) it focuses on self-reflection, (b) it documents areas of performance strength, (c) it relies on a systems-based analysis, and (d) it builds proactively on areas of strength to chart a path for continuous self-improvement. The interrelationship of components in a systems-based format allows the college or university to identify opportunities for greater synergy and establish a common reference point for future improvement (see Higher Learning Commission, 2017).

The AQIP Systems Portfolio and its method of evaluation based on the Baldrige Excellence Framework provides an important point of reference for the audit results. The portfolio identifies four phases leading to systems maturity: (a) reacting, (b) systematization, (c) alignment, and (d) integration. This phase-based methodology is particularly pertinent to evaluation of progress in diversity and inclusion because it focuses on processes and results as evidence of system maturity (Higher Learning Commission, 2017). The emphasis on processes is critical because inequity unfolds within the context of organizational processes and is often overlooked. An analysis of processes and results will identify the degree to which inclusion has been

attained through equitable participation of diverse individuals in the life of the institution.

Rather than discrete, piecemeal activities, the AQIP model requires formal definition of well-understood, documented, and repeatable diversity processes that are measurable and subject to improvement. In this way, the results of the audit can contribute to the ongoing process of diversity transformation. With each facet of the audit, colleges and universities can assess the existing institutional context and areas for improvement. Although the nine factors set the table for diversity, in-depth process reviews that address supervisory discretion and disparate outcomes need to occur. In other words, organizational checks and balances are needed as processes unfold and decisions are made. Tables 12.1 and 12.2 represent an adaptation of the AQIP portfolio model for evaluating the stages of diversity systems maturity in terms of processes and results.

With this model as a guide, campus professionals can review the findings of each chapter and evaluate progress on each dimension using the criteria from the AQIP Systems Portfolio in Tables 12.1 and 12.2. To help with the evaluation, the Systems Portfolio guide identifies the following desirable attributes of organizational processes that have been adapted with specific reference to diversity and inclusion (Higher Learning Commission, 2013):

TABLE 12.1. Evaluation of Processes

Reacting	*Systemization*	*Alignment*	*Integration*
Diversity initiatives respond to immediate needs rather than in anticipation of future requirements. Goals have not been clearly defined and diversity-related procedures are largely informal.	The institution has started to operate using well-understood, repeatable, documented diversity processes with the goal of making activities measurable. Diversity goals are generally understood. Coordination across units is evident and silos are eroding.	The institution operates using diversity processes that are explicit, repeatable, and evaluated regularly. Processes are focused on key diversity goals with an emphasis on coordination and communication across units in light of institutional goals.	Diversity processes are predictable, repeatable, and explicit. They are evaluated regularly for effectiveness and integrated across units through analysis, innovation, and sharing. Progress is tracked on key strategic and tactical goals.

Note. Adapted from Higher Learning Commission (2013).

TABLE 12.2. Evaluation of Results

Reacting	Systematic	Aligned	Integrated
Institutional diversity goals lack metrics and benchmarks for assessing progress. Data on diversity-related initiatives and operational processes have not been collected, disaggregated, or analyzed. Data have not been distributed or segmented in order to inform decision-making.	Institutional diversity data have been collected and are analyzed at various levels. Results have been shared and started to erode institutional silos and build improvement initiatives across units.	Diversity metrics and benchmarks are used by all affected stakeholders and reported. Trends are beneficial and sustainable. Results are distributed to ensure effective planning and decision-making.	Diversity data are analyzed to optimize performance and monitored relative to appropriate benchmarks. Trend data are analyzed and results are shared in ways that encourage collaboration. The measures and metrics for diversity goals are used in decision-making and resource allocation.

Note. Adapted from Higher Learning Commission (2013).

- Are formally defined in policy
- Are clearly aligned with mission-based diversity goals
- Have separate activities connected into larger processes that contribute to diversity progress
- Are managed by an individual or group responsible for improving them
- Are efficient yet inclusive without cumbersome and unnecessary steps

In gauging the level of results, campuses can do the following:

- Develop measures to determine achievement of diversity and inclusion goals.
- Identify the absence of effective processes that promote progress toward equity goals.
- Strengthen existing process reviews to address the potential for inequitable outcomes.
- Ensure that results are benchmarked to peer institutions in terms of effectiveness.
- Measure results over time to allow understanding of variations in performance.

Although ratings may be approximations, they will allow campuses to identify broad areas for improvement. With these criteria in mind, please review the criteria in Tables 12.1 and 12.2 and complete the overall evaluation in Table 12.3.

Concluding Perspectives

In concluding the diversity audit, we draw once more on "the woke academy" as an appropriate metaphor for the active collaboration of campus constituencies in the difficult work of diversity transformation. The diversity audit calls for the active engagement of all stakeholders in the diversity enterprise. With its critical analysis of equity and inclusion in organizational processes, the audit transcends the tendency toward periodic statistical reports. It will guide institutional planning efforts designed to promote diversity organizational learning and enhance diversity capacity. By implementing audit findings, the institution demonstrates its commitment to continuous improvement in the realization of diversity and inclusion in both processes and results.

Through the medium of institutional mission and values, institutions can implement concrete approaches that will ensure the creation of an inclusive learning, living, and working environment. Such an environment is characterized by participation, collaboration, and empowerment in supervisory relationships, collegial discourse, scholarly research, classrooms, and campus spaces. Universities and colleges may, in essence, be torchbearers in a divisive national climate by modeling the power of democratic principles and values. In this sense, the ongoing project of diversity and inclusion seeks to challenge the status quo, shine a light on exclusionary power systems and structures, and develop an actionable agenda that promotes inclusivity in every aspect of campus life.

TABLE 12.3. Diversity Audit Summary Table

Use the following ratings: Reacting – R, Systematic – S, Aligned – A, Integrated – I

Dimension	Evaluation of Processes	Evaluation of Results	Specific Goals for Enhancement
Defining *diversity* and *inclusion*			1. 2. 3.
The academic/ mission-centered case for diversity			1. 2. 3.
Compositional and relational demography			1. 2. 3.
Strategic diversity infrastructure			1. 2. 3.
The strengths and pitfalls of diversity			1. 2. 3.
Creating a comprehensive inventory of diversity education programs			1. 2. 3.
Assessing the climate, culture, and readiness for diversity transformation			1. 2. 3.
Recruitment, hiring, and search committee develop-ment			1. 2. 3.
TRS and talent retention			1. 2. 3.

References

Abigail Noel Fisher v. University of Texas at Austin; David B. Pryor. (2014). Available from https://www.ca5.uscourts .gov/opinions%5Cpub%5C09/09-50822-CV2.pdf

Adserias, R. P., Charleston, L. J., & Jackson, J. F. L. (2017). What style of leadership is best suited to direct organizational change to fuel institutional diversity in higher education? *Race Ethnicity and Education, 20*(3), 315–331.

ADVANCE initiatives. (n.d.). Available from https://www .portal.advance.vt.edu/index.php/categories/initiatives

Aguirre, A. Jr. (2000). *Women and minority faculty in the academic workplace.* San Francisco, CA: Jossey-Bass.

Ahonen, P., Tienari, J., Merilainen, S., & Pullen, A. (2014). Hidden contexts and invisible power relations: A Foucauldian reading of diversity research. *Human Relations, 67*(3), 263–286.

Altbach, P., Yudkevich, M., & Rumbley, L. E. (2015). *Academic inbreeding: Local challenge, global problem.* In M. Yudkevich, P. G. Altbach, & L. E. Rumbley (Eds.), *Academic inbreeding and mobility in higher education: Global perspectives* (pp. 1–16). New York, NY: Palgrave Macmillan.

American Association of University Professors. (n.d.). *1966 statement on government of colleges and universities.* Available from http://www.aaup.org/report/1966-statement-government-colleges-and-universities

American Council on Education. (2013). *On the pathway to the presidency 2013: Characteristics of higher education's senior leadership.* Washington DC: American Council on Education.

American Council on Education. (2017). *Comprehensive demographic profile of American college presidents shows slow progress in diversifying leadership ranks, concerns about funding.* Available from http://www.acenet .edu/news-room/Pages/Comprehensive-Demographic-Profile-of-American-College-Presidents-Shows-Slow-Progress-in-Diversifying-Leadership-Ranks.aspx

American University. (2018). *American University's Plan for Inclusive Excellence.* Available from https://www.american .edu/president/diversity/inclusive-excellence/

Amherst College. (n.d.a). *Diversity & inclusion.* Available from https://www.amherst.edu/amherst-story/diversity

Amherst College. (n.d.b). *Trustee's statement on diversity: Statement on diversity.* Available from https://www.amherst .edu/amherst-story/diversity/trustee-s-statement-on-diversity

Amherst College. (2015). *Strategic plan for Amherst College.* Available from https://www.amherst.edu/system/ files/media/Amherst-College-06-09-2015-strategic-plan.pdf

Antonio, A. L., & Clarke, C. G. (2011). The official organization of diversity in American higher education: A retreat from race? In L. M. Stulberg & S. L. Weinberg (Eds.), *Diversity in American higher education: Toward a more comprehensive approach* (pp. 87–103). New York, NY: Routledge.

Aoun, J. E. (2017). *Robot-proof: Higher education in the age of artificial intelligence.* Cambridge, MA: MIT Press.

Argyris, C. (1993). Education for leading-learning. *Organizational Dynamics, 21*(3), 5–17.

Argyris, C. (1997). Learning and teaching: A theory of action perspective. *Journal of Management Education, 21*(1), 19–26.

Argyris, C., & Schon, D. A. (1996). *Organizational learning II: Theory, method, and practice.* Reading, MA: Addison-Wesley.

Armstrong, P. (2018). *Bloom's taxonomy.* Available from https://cft.vanderbilt.edu/guides-sub-pages/blooms -taxonomy/

Association of American Colleges & Universities. (2018). *Introducing the truth, racial healing & transformation campus centers.* Available from https://www.aacu .org/campus-model/introducing-truth-racial-healing-transformation-campus-centers

Association of Governing Boards of Universities and Colleges. (2016). *Governing board accountability for campus climate, inclusion, and civility.* Available from http://agb .org/sites/default/files/agb-statements/statement_2016_ campus_climate.pdf

Auburn University. (2006). *Auburn University strategic diversity plan.* Available from https://cws.auburn.edu/ diversity/files/diversityplanfinal.pdf

Bensimon, E. M. (2004). The diversity scorecard: A learning approach to institutional change. *Change, 36*(1), 44–52.

Bensimon, E. M. (2012). The Equity Scorecard: Theory of change. In E. M. Bensimon & E. Malcom (Eds.), *Confronting equity issues on campus: Implementing the Equity Scorecard in theory and practice* (pp. 17–44). Sterling, VA: Stylus.

Bensimon, E. M., Dowd, A. C., and Witham, K. (2016). Five principles for enacting equity by design. *Diversity & Democracy 19*(1). Available from https://www.aacu.org/diversitydemocracy/2016/winter/bensimon

Bensimon, E. M., & Malcom, E. (Eds.). (2012a). *Confronting equity issues on campus: Implementing the Equity Scorecard in theory and practice*. Sterling, VA: Stylus.

Bensimon, E. M., & Malcom, E. (2012b). Introduction. In E. M. Bensimon & E. Malcom (Eds.), *Confronting equity issues on campus: Implementing the Equity Scorecard in theory and practice* (pp. 1–14). Sterling, VA: Stylus.

Bensimon, E. M., Polkinghorne, D. E., Bauman, G. L., & Vallejo, E. (2004). Doing research that makes a difference. *The Journal of Higher Education, 75*(1), 104–126.

Berdahl, J. L., & Min, J. A. (2012). Prescriptive stereotypes and workplace consequences for East Asians in North America. *Cultural Diversity and Ethnic Minority Psychology, 18*(2), 141–152.

Berrey, E. (2015). *The enigma of diversity: The language of race and the limits of racial justice*. Chicago, IL: University of Chicago Press.

Bertrand, M., & Mullainathan, S. (2004). Are Emily and Greg more employable than Lakisha and Jamal? A field experiment on labor market discrimination. *The American Economic Review, 94*(4), 991–1013.

Bezrukova, K., Jehn, K. A., & Spell, C. S. (2012). Reviewing diversity training: Where we have been and where we should go. *Academy of Management Learning and Education, 11*(2), 207–227.

Bichsel, J., & McChesney, J. (2017, August). *Employee healthcare benefits in higher education: Key findings and summary tables for the 2016–17 academic year*. Available from https://www.cupahr.org/wp=content/uploads/surveys/publications/2017/Benefits17_Overview.pdf

Bilimoria, D., & Buch, K. K. (2010). The search is on: Engendering faculty diversity through more effective search and recruitment. *Change, 42*(4), 27–32.

Bocanegra, J. O. (2012). Overcoming the gap between diversity recruitment research and practice. *Communique, 40*(8), 28–29.

Bohanon, M. (2018, June 25). The Mizzou effect: Some colleges struggle to recover from protests sparked by racial tensions. *Insight Into Diversity*. Available from http://www.insightintodiversity.com/the-mizzou-effect-some-colleges-struggle-to-recover-from-protests-sparked-by-racial-tensions/

Bowman, N. A. (2011). Promoting participation in a diverse democracy: A meta-analysis of college diversity experiences and civic engagement. *Review of Educational Research, 81*(1), 29–68.

Bowman, N. A. (2012). Promoting sustained engagement with diversity: The reciprocal relationships between informal and formal college diversity experiences. *The Review of Higher Education, 36*(1), 1–24.

Briesacher, A. (2014). *Integrating stereotype threat into identity and social identity theory* (Unpublished doctoral dissertation). Kent State University, Kent, OH.

Brimhall-Vargas, M. (2012). The myth of institutionalizing diversity: Structures and the covert decisions they make. In C. Clark, K. Fasching-Varner, & M. Brimhall-Vargas (Eds.), *Occupying the academy: Just how important is diversity in higher education?* (pp. 85–95). Lanham, MD: Rowman & Littlefield.

Brockbank, W. (1999). If HR were really strategically proactive: Present and future directions in HR's contribution to competitive advantage. *Human Resource Management, 38*(4), 337–352.

Brown, S. (2016, May 15). Auditing diversity: An interest in assessments is rising as officials strive to show they are committed. *The Chronicle of Higher Education*. Available from http://www.chronicle.com/article/Auditing-Diversity/236428

Brown-Glaude, W. R. (Ed.). (2009). *Doing diversity in higher education: Faculty leaders share challenges and strategies*. New Brunswick, NJ: Rutgers University.

Brown University. (2016). *Pathways to diversity and inclusion: An action plan for Brown University*. Available from https://brown.edu/web/documents/diversity/actionplan/diap-full.pdf

Buijsrogge, A., Derous, E., & Duyck, W. (2016). Often biased but rarely in doubt: How initial reactions to stigmatized applicants affect interviewer confidence. *Human Performance, 29*(4), 275–290.

Buller, J. L. (2015). *Change leadership in higher education: A practical guide to academic transformation*. San Francisco, CA: Jossey-Bass.

Buller, J. L. (2017). *Hire the right faculty member every time: Best practices in recruiting, selecting, and onboarding college professors*. Lanham, MD: Rowman & Littlefield.

Bureau of Justice Statistics. (2016). *Draft instrument for measuring campus climate related to sexual assault*. Available from https://www.bjs.gov/content/pub/pdf/RevisedInstrumentModules_1_21_16_cleanCombined_psg.pdf

Burnes, B. (2009). Kurt Lewin and the planned approach to change: A reappraisal. In W. W. Burke, D. G. Lake, & J. W. Paine (Eds.), *Organization change: A comprehensive reader* (pp. 226–254). San Francisco, CA: Wiley.

Cantor, D., Fisher, B., Chibnall, S., Townsend, R., Lee, H., Bruce, C., & Thomas, G. (2017). *Report on the AAU Campus Climate Survey on Sexual Assault and Sexual*

Misconduct. Available from https://www.aau.edu/sites/default/files/AAU-Files/Key-Issues/Campus-Safety/AAU-Campus-Climate-Survey-FINAL-10-20-17.pdf

Carnegie Classification of Institutions of Higher Education. (2017). *News & announcements: 2018 classification update.* Available from http://carnegieclassifications.iu.edu/index.php

Carroll, L. (1897). *Through the looking-glass, and what Alice found there.* Philadelphia, PA: Henry Altemus Press

Catalyst. (2005). *Making change: Creating a business-aligned diversity scorecard.* Available from https://www.bentley.edu/files/2015/09/04/Catalyst%20Scorecard.pdf

CECE surveys at a glance: A new generation of diversity surveys. (2018). Available from https://www.indiana.edu/~cece/wordpress/surveys-at-a-glance/

Chang, M. J. (2011). *Quality matters: Achieving benefits associated with racial diversity.* Available from http://kirwaninstitute.osu.edu/wp-content/uploads/2012/09/Mitchell-Chang_final_Nov.-1-2011_design_3.pdf

Chang, M. J., Chang, J. C., & Ledesma, M. C. (2005). Beyond magical thinking: Doing the real work of diversifying our institutions. *About Campus, 10*(2), 9–16.

Chang, M. J., & Ledesma, M. C. (2011). The diversity rationale: Its limitations for educational practice. In L. M. Stulberg & S. L. Weinberg (Eds.), *Diversity in American higher education: Toward a more comprehensive approach* (pp. 74–86). New York, NY: Routledge.

Chen, D. W. (2017, June 20). At colleges, demographic changes everywhere but the top. *New York Times.* Available from https://www.nytimes.com/2017/06/20/nyregion/college-president-survey-demographic-changes.html?smprod=nytcore-iphone&smid=nytcore-iphone-share

Chun, E. (2009). *Dramatizing diversity.* Available from http://ednachun.com/Dramatizing%20Diversity%20-%20Chun.pdf

Chun, E. (2017a). Cultural competence matters for department chairs. *The Department Chair, 28*(1), 7–8.

Chun, E. B. (2017b). Diversity and inclusion: The balancing act between governing boards and college or university administration. In R. Thompson-Miller & K. Ducey (Eds.), *Systemic racism: Making liberty, justice, and democracy real* (pp. 79–110). New York, NY: Palgrave Macmillan.

Chun, E., & Evans, A. (2009). *Bridging the diversity divide: Globalization and reciprocal empowerment in higher education* (ASHE-ERIC Higher Education Reports, Vol. 35, No. 1). San Francisco, CA: Jossey-Bass.

Chun, E., & Evans, A. (2012). *Diverse administrators in peril: The new indentured class in higher education.* Boulder, CO: Paradigm.

Chun, E., & Evans, A. (2014a). *Designing and implementing strategies for the development of a winning faculty workforce.* Available from https://www.tiaainstitute.org/publication/designing-and-implementing-strategies

Chun, E., & Evans, A. (2014b). *The new talent acquisition frontier: Integrating HR and diversity strategy in the private and public sectors and higher education.* Sterling, VA: Stylus.

Chun, E., & Evans, A. (2015a). *Affirmative action at a crossroads: Fisher and forward* (ASHE-ERIC Higher Education Reports, Vol. 41, No. 4). San Francisco, CA: Jossey-Bass.

Chun, E., & Evans, A. (2015b). *The department chair as transformative diversity leader: Building inclusive learning environments in higher education.* Sterling, VA: Stylus.

Chun, E. B., & Evans, A. (2018). *Leading a diversity culture shift in higher education: Comprehensive strategies for organizational leadership.* New York, NY: Routledge.

Clarke, C. G., & Antonio, A. L. (2012). Rethinking research on the impact of racial diversity in higher education. *The Review of Higher Education, 36*(1), 25–50.

Clauset, A., Arbesman, S., & Larremore, D. B. (2015). Systematic inequality and hierarchy in faculty hiring networks. *Science Advances, 1*(1), 1–6.

Clayton-Pedersen, A., & Musil, C. M. (2005). Introduction to the series. In D. A. Williams, J. B. Berger, & S. A. McClendon (Eds.), *Toward a model of Inclusive Excellence and change in postsecondary institutions* (pp. iii–ix). Available from http://www.aacu.org/inclusive_excellence/documents/williams_et_al.pdf

Clayton-Pedersen, A. R., Parker, S., Smith, D. G., Moreno, J. F., & Teraguchi, D. H. (2007). *Making a real difference with diversity: A guide to institutional change.* Washington, DC: Association of American Colleges & Universities.

CNN. *University of Missouri names interim president* [Video]. (2015). Available from https://www.youtube.com/watch?v=ck9tpnLS-Ds&app=desktop

Coates, T. (2017). *We were eight years in power: An American tragedy.* New York, NY: One World.

Coleman, A. L., Palmer, S. R., Lipper, K., & Milem, J. F. (2010). *A diversity action blueprint: Policy parameters and model practices for higher education institutions.* Available from https://secure-media.collegeboard.org/digital-Services/pdf/diversity/diversity-action-blueprint.pdf

College and University Professional Association for Human Resources. *Data on demand.* (2017). Available from http://www.cupahr.org/surveys/dataondemand/hr-benchmarking/

College Board, American Council on Education, & Education Council. (2015). *A policy and legal "syllabus" for diversity programs at colleges and universities.* Available from https://professionals.collegeboard.org/pdf/adc-diversity-syllabus-institutions.pdf

College of Business Administration. (2004). *Strategic diversity plan.* Available from http://www.usf.edu/business/documents/about/diversity-strategic-plan.pdf

Columbia University. (2016). *Guide to best practices in faculty search and hiring.* Available from http://faculty diversity.columbia.edu/files/viceprovost/guide_to_best_practices_in_faculty_search_and_hiring_july_2016.pdf

Cooper, M. (2016). Why women (sometimes) don't help other women. *Atlantic.* Available from https://www.theatlantic.com/business/archive/2016/06/queen-bee/488144/

Cooperrider, D., Srivastva, S. (1987). Appreciative inquiry in organizational life. *Research in Organizational Change and Development, 1,* 129–169.

Creighton University. (n.d.). *Compensation guide.* Available from https://www.creighton.edu/fileadmin/user/AdminFinance/HumanResources/Manager_Toolkit/Compensation/Creighton_Compensation_Guide.pdf

Cross, J. G., & Goldenberg, E. N. (2009). *Off-track profs: Nontenured teachers in higher education.* Cambridge, MA: Massachusetts Institute of Technology.

CUPA-HR. (2017, August 9). *5 noteworthy findings from CUPA-HR's healthcare benefits in higher ed survey.* Available from https://www.cupahr.org/press-releases/5-noteworthy-findings-cupa-hrs-healthcare-benefits-higher-ed-survey/

Danowitz, M. A. (2015). Rethinking higher education diversity studies through a diversity management frame. In R. Bendl, I. Bleijenbergh, E. Henttonen, & A. J. Mills (Eds.), *The Oxford handbook of diversity in organizations* (pp. 357–369). New York, NY: Oxford University Press.

Denson, N., Szelényi, K., & Bresonis, K. (2018). Correlates of work-life balance for faculty across racial/ethnic groups. *Research in Higher Education, 59*(2), 226–247.

Derous, E., Pepermans, R., & Ryan, A. M. (2017). Ethnic discrimination during resume screening: Interactive effects of applicants' ethnic salience with job context. *Human Relations, 70*(7), 860–882.

di Bartolo, A. N. (2015). Rethinking gender equity in higher education. *Diversity & Democracy.* Available from https://www.aacu.org/diversitydemocracy/2015/spring/dibartolo

Diaz, A., & Kirmmse, J. (2013). A new rubric for assessing institution-wide diversity. *Diversity and Democracy, 16*(3). Available from https://www.aacu.org/publications-research/periodicals/new-rubric-assessing-institution-wide-diversity

Diermeier, D. (2016). *The 2016 campus climate survey—Findings* (University of Chicago). Available from https://provost.uchicago.edu/announcements/2016-campus-climate-survey-findings

Dipboye, R. L., & Jackson, S. (1999). The influence of interviewer experience and expertise on selection decisions. In R. W. Eder & M. M. Harris (Eds.), *The employment interview: Theory, research, and practice* (pp. 259–278). Thousand Oaks, CA: Sage.

DiRamio, D., Theroux, R., & Guarino, A. J. (2009). Faculty hiring at top-ranked higher education administration programs: An examination using social network analysis. *Innovative Higher Education, 34*(3), 149–159.

Dore, T. (2004). *The relationships between job characteristics, job satisfaction, and turnover intention among software developers* (Unpublished doctoral dissertation). Argosy University, Chicago, IL.

Dovidio, J. F., & Gaertner, S. L. (2000). Aversive racism and selection decisions: 1989 and 1999. *Psychological Science, 11*(4), 315–319.

Dovidio, J. F., Gaertner, S. L., Kawakami, K., & Hodson, G. (2002). Why can't we just get along? Interpersonal biases and interracial distrust. *Cultural Diversity and Ethnic Minority Psychology, 8*(2), 88–102.

Dowd, A. C., & Bensimon, E. M. (2015). *Engaging the "race question": Accountability and equity in U.S. higher education.* New York, NY: Teachers College Press.

Elliott, J. R. (2001). Referral hiring and ethnically homogeneous jobs: How prevalent is the connection and for whom? *Social Science Research, 30*(3), 401–425.

Elliott, J. R., & Smith, R. A. (2001). Ethnic matching of supervisors to subordinate work groups: Findings on "bottom-up" ascription and social closure. *Social Problems, 48*(2), 258–276.

Elliott, J. R., & Smith, R. A. (2004). Race, gender, and workplace power. *American Sociological Review, 69*(3), 365–386.

Engberg, M. E., & Hurtado, S. (2011). Developing pluralistic skills and dispositions in college: Examining racial/ethnic group differences. *The Journal of Higher Education, 82*(4), 416–443.

Essed, P. (2004). Cloning amongst professors: Normativities and imagined homogeneities. *Nordic Journal of Feminist and Gender Research, 2,* 113–122.

Evans, A., & Chun, E. B. (2007). *Are the walls really down? Behavioral and organizational barriers to faculty and staff diversity* (ASHE-ERIC Higher Education Reports, Vol. 33, No. 1). San Francisco, CA: Jossey-Bass.

Evans, A., & Chun, E. (2012). *Creating a tipping point: Strategic human resources in higher education.* San Francisco, CA: Jossey-Bass.

Ewell, P. T., & Cumming, T. (2017). History and conceptual basis of assessment in higher education. In T. Cumming & M. D. Miller (Eds.), *Enhancing assessment in higher education: Putting psychometrics to work* (pp. 3–26). Sterling, VA: Stylus.

Faulk, M. (2018, June 7). Mizzou makes $45 million in cuts, including 185 jobs. *St. Louis Post-Dispatch.* Available from https://www.stltoday.com/news/local/education/mizzou-makes-million-in-cuts-including-jobs/article_64e77417-5c35-5ff9-a069-acbc5fe84d48.html

Feagin, J. R. (2006). *Systemic racism: A theory of oppression.* New York, NY: Routledge.

Feagin, J. R. (2013). *The white racial frame: Centuries of racial framing and counter-framing* (2nd ed.). New York, NY: Routledge.

Feagin, J. R., & Ducey, K. (2017). *Elite white men ruling: Who, what, when, where, and how.* New York, NY: Routledge.

Feagin, J. R., Vera, H., & Imani, N. (1996). *The agony of education: Black students at white colleges and universities.* New York, NY: Routledge.

Ferdman, B. M. (2013). The practice of inclusion in diverse organizations: Toward a systemic and inclusive framework. In B. M. Ferdman & B. R. Deane (Eds.), *Diversity at work: The practice of inclusion* (pp. 3–54). San Francisco, CA: Jossey-Bass.

Fincher, M., Katsinas, S., & Bush, V. B. (2010). Executive management team demography and minority student retention: Does executive team diversity influence the retention of minority students? *Journal of College Student Retention Research Theory and Practice, 11*(4), 459–481.

Finkelstein, M. J., Conley, V. M., & Schuster, J. H. (2016). *The faculty factor: Reassessing the American academy in a turbulent era.* Baltimore, MD: Johns Hopkins University Press.

Flaherty, C. (2016, October 20). Feeling isolated and excluded. *Inside Higher Ed.* Available from https://www.insidehighered.com/news/2016/10/20/surveys-graduate-students-reveal-campus-climate-issues-yale-michigan

Foley, J. (with Kendrick, J.). (2006). *Balanced brand: How to balance the stakeholder forces that can make or break your business.* San Francisco, CA: Jossey-Bass.

Fowler, M., Medenica, V. E., & Cohen, C. J. (2017, December 15). Why 41 percent of white millennials voted for Trump. *Washington Post.* Available from https://www.washingtonpost.com/news/monkey-cage/wp/2017/12/15/racial-resentment-is-why-41-percent-of-white-millennials-voted-for-trump-in-2016/?noredirect=on&utm_term=.852aa9962166

Fries-Britt, S., & Kelly, B. T. (2005). Retaining each other: Narratives of two African American women in the academy. *The Urban Review, 37*(3), 221–242.

Gagliardi, J. S. (2018). Unpacking the messiness of harnessing the analytics revolution. In J. S. Gagliardi, A. Parnell, & J. Carpenter-Hubin (Eds.), *The analytics revolution in higher education: Big data, organizational learning, and student success* (pp. 189–200). Sterling, VA: Stylus.

Gagliardi, J. S., Espinosa, L. L., Turk, J. M., & Taylor, M. (2017). *American college president study 2017.* Available from http://therivardreport.com/wp-content/uploads/2017/07/ACPS-Report-FINAL-web.pdf

Garces, L. M., & Jayakumar, U. M. (2014). Dynamic diversity: Toward a contextual understanding of critical mass. *Educational Researcher, 43*(3), 115–124.

Gardner, S. K. (2013). Women faculty departures from a striving institution: Between a rock and a hard place. *The Review of Higher Education, 36*(3), 349–370.

Gasman, M. (2016). *The five things no one will tell you about why colleges don't hire more faculty of color: It's time for higher ed to change its ways.* Available from http://hechingerreport.org/five-things-no-one-will-tell-colleges-dont-hire-faculty-color/

Gasman, M., Abiola, U., & Travers, C. (2015). Diversity and senior leadership at elite institutions of higher education. *Journal of Diversity in Higher Education, 8*(1), 1–14.

Grutter v. Bollinger. (2017). Available from http://caselaw.findlaw.com/us-supreme-court/539/306.html

Guitierrez y Muhs, G., Niemann, Y. F., Gonzalez, C. G., & Harris, A. P. (Eds.). (2012). *Presumed incompetent: The intersections of race and class for women in academia.* Boulder: University Press of Colorado.

Halualani, R. T., Haiker, H., & Lancaster, C. (2010). Mapping diversity efforts as inquiry. *Journal of Higher Education Policy and Management, 32*(2), 127–136.

Halualani, R. T., Haiker, H. L., Lancaster, C., & Morrison, J. H. (2015). *Diversity mapping data portrait.* Available from https://csumb.edu/sites/default/files/images/st-block-95-1429229970817-raw-csumbdiversitymappingdataportrait.pdf

Harper, S. R., & Hurtado, S. (2007). Nine themes in campus racial climates and implications for institutional transformation. *New Directions for Student Services, 120,* 7–24.

Harris, M. S. (2013). *Understanding institutional diversity in American higher education* (ASHE-ERIC Higher Education Reports, Vol. 39, No. 3). San Francisco, CA: Jossey-Bass.

Hart, J. (2009). Family-friendly activism. In J. Lester & M. Sallee (Eds.), *Establishing the family-friendly campus: Models for effective practice* (pp. 125–140). Sterling, VA: Stylus.

Hart, J., Brigham, L., Good, M. K., Mills, B. J., & Monk, J. (2009). Agents of change: Faculty leadership in initiating and sustaining diversity at the University of Arizona. In W. R. Brown-Glaude (Ed.), *Doing diversity in higher education: Faculty leaders share challenges and strategies* (pp. 166–183). New Brunswick, NJ: Rutgers University Press.

Hart, J., & Fellabaum, J. (2008). Analyzing campus climate studies: Seeking to define and understand. *Journal of Diversity in Higher Education, 1*(4), 222–234.

Hartlep, N. D., Hensley, B. O., Wells, K. E., Brewer, T. J., Ball, D., & McLaren, P. (2017). Homophily in higher education: Historicizing the AERA member-to-fellow pipeline using theories of social reproduction and social networks. *Policy Futures in Education, 15*(6), 670–694.

Harvard University Presidential Task Force on Inclusion and Belonging. (n.d.). *Pursuing excellence on a foundation of inclusion.* Available from http://inclusion andbelongingtaskforce.harvard.edu/files/inclusion/files/harvard_inclusion_belonging_task_force_final_report_full_web_180327.pdf

Heim, J. (2017, August 14). Recounting a day of rage, hate, violence and death. *Washington Post.* Available from https://www.washingtonpost.com/graphics/2017/local/charlottesville-timeline/?utm_term=.8d7c6832f218

HERI. (2017). *Overview of surveys.* Available from https://heri.ucla.edu/overview-of-surveys/2017/

Higher Learning Commission. (2013). *Systems portfolio guide: Academic quality improvement program.* Available from http://eac.edu/surveys/PortfolioGuide2014.pdf

Higher Learning Commission. (2014). *HLC policy: Criteria for accreditation.* Available from http://www.hlcommission.org/Policies/criteria-and-core-components.html

Higher Learning Commission. (2017). *AQIP pathway systems portfolio and appraisal.* Available from http://download.hlcommission.org/AQIPPathway-SystemsPortfolioAppraisal_PRC.pdf

Hirst, P. (2016, June 30). How a flex-time program at MIT improved productivity, resilience, and trust. *Harvard Business Review.* Available from https://hbr.org/2016/06/how-a-flex-time-program-at-mit-improved-productivity-resilience-and-trust

Hodson, R. (2001). *Dignity at work.* New York, NY: Cambridge University Press.

Horton, H. D. (1999). Critical demography: The paradigm of the future? *Sociological Forum, 14*(3), 363–367.

Hubbard, E. E. (2004). *The Diversity Scorecard: Evaluating the impact of diversity on organizational performance.* Burlington, MA: Elsevier Butterworth-Heinemann.

Huber, D. (2016, May 29). Despite drop in donations and enrollment, Mizzou finds over $1 million for "diversity audit." *The College Fix.* Available from https://www.thecollegefix.com/post/27635/

Hurtado, S. (1992). The campus racial climate: Contexts of conflict. *Journal of Higher Education, 63*(5), 539–569.

Hurtado, S., Alvarado, A. R., & Guillermo-Wann, C. (2012). *Inclusive learning environments: Modeling a relationship between validation, campus climate for diversity, and sense of belonging.* Available from https://www.heri.ucla.edu/ford/downloads/ASHE2012-Inclusive-Learning.pdf

Hurtado, S., Alvarez, C. L., Guillermo-Wann, C., Cuellar, M., & Arellano, L. (2012). A model for diverse learning environments: The scholarship on creating and assessing conditions for student success. In J. C. Smart & M. B. Paulsen (Eds.), *Higher education: Handbook of theory and research* (Vol. 27, pp. 41–122). New York, NY: Springer.

Hurtado, S., Clayton-Pedersen, A. R., Allen, W. R., & Milem, J. F. (1998). Enhancing campus climates for racial/ethnic diversity: Educational policy and practice. *The Review of Higher Education, 21*(3), 279–302.

Hurtado, S., Griffin, K. A., Arellano, L., & Cuellar, M. (2008). Assessing the value of climate assessments: Progress and future directions. *Journal of Diversity in Higher Education, 1*(4), 204–221.

Hurtado, S., & Guillermo-Wann, C. (2013). *Diverse learning environments: Assessing and creating conditions for student success—Final report to the Ford Foundation.* Available from https://www.heri.ucla.edu/ford/DiverseLearningEnvironments.pdf

Hurtado, S., & Halualani, R. (2014). Diversity assessment, accountability, and action: Going beyond the numbers. *Diversity and Democracy, 17*(4). Available from https://www.aacu.org/diversitydemocracy/2014/fall/hurtado-halualani

Hurtado, S., Milem, J., Clayton-Pedersen, A., & Allen, W. (1999). *Enacting diverse learning environments: Improving the climate for racial/ethnic diversity in higher education* (ASHE-ERIC Higher Education Report, Vol. 26, No. 8). Washington, DC: George Washington University Graduate School of Education and Human Development.

Hurtado, S., & Ruiz, A. (2012). The climate for underrepresented groups and diversity on campus. *HERI Research Brief.* Available from https://www.heri.ucla.edu/briefs/URMBriefReport.pdf/

IBIS Consulting. (2016). *Diversity, equity and inclusion: A roadmap for the future.* Available from https://www.umsystem.edu/media/president/deioffice/ibis-ums-deiaudit-report.pdf

Indiana University. (2014). *The bicentennial strategic plan for Indiana University.* Available from https://strategicplan.iu.edu/doc/plan.pdf

Indiana University, Bloomington. (2018). *Statement on diversity.* Available from https://bfc.indiana.edu/policies/statements-resolutions/diversity-inclusion/diversity-statement.html

Indiana University police hires chief diversity officer. (2017, September 12). *Diverse Issues in Higher Education.* Available from http://diverseeducation.com/article/101401/

Iowa State University Institutional Research. (2018). *2017–2018 fact book.* Available from https://www.ir.iastate.edu/factbk

It's Your Yale. (2017). *Diversity & inclusion.* Available from https://your.yale.edu/community/diversity-inclusion

Jackson, J. F. L. (2004). Introduction: Engaging, retaining, and advancing African Americans in executive-level positions: A descriptive and trend analysis of academic administrators in higher and postsecondary education. *The Journal of Negro Education, 73*(1), 4–20.

Jackson, J. F. L., & Charleston, L. J. (2014). *Iowa State University's diversity audit and asset inventory.* Available from http://weilab.wceruw.org/CBCFALC/ISU%20Comprehensive%20Report.pdf

Jackson, J. F. L., & O'Callaghan, E. M. (2009). What do we know about glass ceiling effects? A taxonomy and critical review to inform higher education research. *Research in Higher Education, 50*(5), 460–482.

Jackson, J. F. L., O'Callaghan, E. M., & Leon, R. A. (2014). *Measuring glass ceiling effects in higher education: Opportunities and challenges.* San Francisco, CA: Jossey-Bass.

Jardina, A. (2017, August 16). White identity politics isn't just about white supremacy: It's much bigger. *Washington Post.* Available from https://www.washingtonpost.com/news/monkey-cage/wp/2017/08/16/white-identity-politics-isnt-just-about-white-supremacy-its-much-bigger/?utm_term=.daefe2332700

June, A. W. (2015, November 8). The invisible labor of minority professors. *The Chronicle of Higher Education.* Available from https://www.chronicle.com/article/The-Invisible-Labor-of/234098

Kaiser, C. R., Major, B., Jurcevic, I., Dover, T. L., Brady, L. M., & Shapiro, J. R. (2013). Presumed fair: Ironic effects of organizational diversity structures. *Journal of Personality and Social Psychology, 104*(3), 504–519.

Kansas State University. (2018). *Compensation philosophy.* Available from https://www.k-state.edu/hcs/initiatives/compensation/philosophy.html

Kaplan, D. M., Wiley, J. W., & Maertz, C. P. Jr. (2011). The role of calculative attachment in the relationship between diversity climate and retention. *Human Resource Management, 50*(2), 271–287.

Kaplan, R. S., & Norton, D. (1992). The balanced scorecard: Measures that drive performance. *Harvard Business Review, 70*(1), 71–79.

Keeling, R. P., Underhile, R., & Wall, A. F. (2007). Horizontal and vertical structures: The dynamics of organization in higher education. *Liberal Education, 93*(4), 22–31.

Kent State University. (2018). *Equity action plan.* Available from https://www.kent.edu/diversity/equity-action-plan

Kezar, A. (2005). What campuses need to know about organizational learning and the learning organization. In A. J. Kezar (Ed.), *Organizational learning in higher education* (pp. 7–22). San Francisco, CA: Jossey-Bass.

Kezar, A. J. (2007). Tools for a time and place: Phased leadership strategies to institutionalize a diversity agenda. *The Review of Higher Education, 30*(4), 413–439.

Kezar, A. (2013). Departmental cultures and non-tenure-track faculty: Willingness, capacity, and opportunity to perform at four-year institutions. *The Journal of Higher Education, 84*(2), 153–188.

Kezar, A., & Carducci, R. (2009). Revolutionizing leadership development: Lessons from research and theory. In A. Kezar (Ed.), *Rethinking leadership in a complex, multicultural, and global environment: New concepts and models for higher education* (pp. 1–38). Sterling, VA: Stylus.

Kezar, A., & Eckel, P. (2002). Examining the institutional transformation process: The importance of sensemaking, interrelated strategies, and balance. *Research in Higher Education, 43*(3), 295–328.

Kezar, A., & Eckel, P. (2008). Advancing diversity agendas on campus: Examining transactional and transformational presidential leadership styles. *International Journal of Leadership in Education, 11*(4), 379–405.

Kezar, A., Glenn, W. J., Lester, J., & Nakamoto, J. (2008). Examining organizational contextual features that affect implementation of equity initiatives. *The Journal of Higher Education, 79*(2), 125–159.

Kezar, A., & Lester, J. (2011). *Enhancing campus capacity for leadership: An examination of grassroots leaders in higher education.* Stanford, CA: Stanford University Press.

Klemenčič, M., & Chirikov, I. (2015). *How do we know how students experience higher education? On the use of student surveys.* Available from https://link.springer.com/chapter/10.1007/978-3-319-20877-0_24

Knox, M. W., & Teraguchi, D. H. (2005). Institutional models that cultivate comprehensive change. *Diversity Digest, 9*(2), 10–11.

Kochanski, J., & Ledford, G. E. (2001). "How to keep me"—Retaining technical professionals. *Research Technology Management, 44*(3), 31–38.

Kuh, G. D., & Whitt, E. J. (1988). *The invisible tapestry: Culture in American colleges and universities* (ASHE-ERIC Higher Education Reports, Vol. 17, No. 1). San Francisco, CA: Jossey-Bass.

Ledford, G. E. Jr. (2002, October). *Attracting, retaining, and motivating employees: The rewards of work framework.* Paper presented at the meeting of the College & University Professional Association for Human Resources, Dallas, TX.

Ledford, G. E. Jr. (2003). The rewards of work framework: Attracting, retaining and motivating higher education employees. *CUPA-HR Journal, 54*(2), 22–26.

Lee, C. (2014). *Search committees: A comprehensive guide to successful faculty, staff, and administrative searches.* Sterling, VA: Stylus.

Lehigh University. (n.d.). *The principles of our equitable community.* Available from https://www.lehigh.edu/~inprv/initiatives/PrinciplesEquity_Sheet_v2_032212.pdf

Lester, J. (2013). Work-life balance and cultural change: A narrative of eligibility. *The Review of Higher Education, 38*(4), 463–488.

Loden, M. (1995). *Implementing diversity: Best practices for making diversity work in your organization.* New York, NY: McGraw-Hill.

Lomax, R. J., Moore, T. E., & Smith, C. B. (1995). *The Michigan Mandate: Promise and progress.* Available from http://umich.edu/~aaupum/affirm08.htm

Malinen, S., & Johnston, L. (2007). The influence of an equity statement on perceivers' implicit and explicit associations between males and science. *New Zealand Journal of Psychology, 36*(1), 18–24.

Maramba, D. C. (2011). Few and far between: Exploring the experiences of Asian American and Pacific Islander women in student affairs administration. In J.-M. Gaëtane & B. Lloyd-Jones (Eds.), *Women of color in higher education: Turbulent past, promising future* (pp. 337–359). Bingley, UK: Emerald Group.

McCormick, H. (2015). *Rethinking total rewards.* UNC Kenan-Flagler Business School. Available from https://www.kenan-flagler.unc.edu/~/media/Files/documents/executive-development/unc-white-paper-rethinking-total-rewards-final.pdf?_ga=2.114191367.1644975339.1542940716-1693999363.1457219091&_ga=2.114191367.1644975339.1542940716-1693999363.1457219091

McDonald, P., & Coleman, M. (1999). Deconstructing hierarchies of oppression and adopting a "multiple model" approach to anti-oppressive practice. *Social Work Education, 18*(1), 19–33.

McElwee, S., & McDaniel, J. (2017, March 14). Fear of diversity made people more likely to vote Trump: The 2016 election was really a battle about having an open society. *Nation.* Available from https://www.thenation.com/article/fear-of-diversity-made-people-more-likely-to-vote-trump/

McKay, P. F., Avery, D. R., Tonidandel, S., Morris, M. A., Hernandez, M., & Hebl, M. (2007). Racial differences in employee retention: Are diversity climate perceptions the key? *Personnel Psychology, 60*(1), 35–62.

McMurtrie, B. (2016a, September 11). Different strategies for diverse hiring. *The Chronicle of Higher Education.* Available from https://www.chronicle.com/article/Different-Strategies-for/237749

McMurtrie, B. (2016b, September 11). How to do a better job of searching for diversity. *The Chronicle of Higher Education.* Available from https://www.chronicle.com/article/How-to-Do-a-Better-Job-of/237750

McMurtrie, B. (2016c, September 16). What it will take for Missouri to meet its faculty-diversity goal. *The Chronicle of Higher Education.* Available from http://www.chronicle.com/article/What-It-Will-Take-for-Missouri/237816

Middle States Commission on Higher Education (2014). *Standards for accreditation and requirements for affiliation.* Available from http://www.msche.org/wp-content/uploads/2018/06/RevisedStandardsFINAL.pdf

Milem, J. F., Chang, M. J., & Antonio, A. L. (2005). *Making diversity work on campus: A research-based perspective.* Available from http://siher.stanford.edu/AntonioMilemChang_makingdiversitywork.pdf

Miller, K. (2018). *The simple truth about the gender pay gap.* Available from https://www.aauw.org/research/the-simple-truth-about-the-gender-pay-gap/

Mor Barak, M. E., Cherin, D. A., & Berkman, S. (1998). Organizational and personal dimensions in diversity climate: Ethnic and gender differences in employee perceptions. *The Journal of Applied Behavioral Science, 34*(1), 82–104.

Moreno, J. F., Smith, D. G., Clayton-Pedersen, A. R., & Teraguchi, D. H. (2006). *The revolving door for underrepresented minority faculty in higher education: An analysis from the Campus Diversity Initiative.* Washington, DC: Association of American Colleges & Universities; Claremont, CA: Claremont Graduate University. Available from https://www.slcc.edu/inclusivity/docs/the-revolving-door-for-underrepresented-minority-faculty-in-higher-education.pdf

Moss-Racusin, C. A., Dovidio, J. F., Brescoll, V. L., Graham, M. J., & Handelsman, J. (2012). Science faculty's subtle gender biases favor male students. *Proceedings of the National Academy of Sciences of the United States of America, 109*(41), 16474–16479.

Museus, S. D. (2014). The Culturally Engaging Campus Environments (CECE) model: A new theory of success among racially diverse college student populations. In M. B. Paulsen (Ed.), *Higher education: Handbook of theory and research* (Vol. 29, pp. 189–227). New York, NY: Springer.

Museus, S. D., & Harris, F. (2010). Success among college students of color: How institutional culture matters. In T. E. Dancy II (Ed.), *Managing diversity: (Re)visioning equity on college campuses* (pp. 25–44). New York, NY: Peter Lang.

Myers, S. L. Jr. (1997). Why diversity is a smoke screen for affirmative action. *Change, 29*(4), 24–32.

National Center for Education Statistics. (2003). *IPEDS survey of human resources.* Washington, DC: Author.

National Center for Education Statistics. (2005). *IPEDS survey of human resources.* Washington, DC: Author.

National Center for Education Statistics. (2007). *IPEDS survey of human resources.* Washington, DC: Author.

National Center for Education Statistics. (2009). *IPEDS survey of human resources.* Washington, DC: Author.

National Center for Education Statistics. (2011). *IPEDS survey of human resources.* Washington, DC: Author.

National Center for Education Statistics. (2013). *IPEDS survey of human resources.* Washington, DC: Author.

National Center for Education Statistics. (2015). *IPEDS survey of human resources.* Washington, DC: Author.

National Center for Education Statistics. (2016). *IPEDS survey of human resources.* Washington, DC: Author.

National Institute for Transformation and Equity. (2017). *Our story: Mission, history, and pillars.* Available from https://www.indiana.edu/~cece/wordpress/ourstory/

New England Association of Schools and Colleges. (2016). *Standard one: Mission and purposes.* Available from https://cihe.neasc.org/standards-policies/standards-accreditation/standards-effective-july-1-2016#standard_one

New England Commission of Higher Education Commission of Higher Education. (2016). *Standards (Effective July 1, 2016).* Available from https://cihe.neasc.org/standards-policies/standards-accreditation/standards-effective-july-1-2016

New England Resource Center for Higher Education (NERCHE). (n.d.a). *NERCHE self-assessment rubric for the institutionalization of diversity, equity, and inclusion in higher education.* Available from http://www.compactnh.org/wp-content/uploads/2016/09/NERCHEs-Self-Assessment-Rubric-for-the-Institutionalization-of-Diversity-Equity-and-Inclusion-in-Higher-Education.pdf

New England Resource Center for Higher Education (NERCHE). (n.d.b). *Self-assessment rubric for the institutionalization of diversity, equity, and inclusion in higher education. Colby College.* Available from http://www.colby.edu/president/wp-content/uploads/sites/108/2016/04/self-assessment-rubric-NERCHE.pdf

Nichols, S. R., de Leon, L. C., & Withers, H. A. (2018). *California's salary history ban: Answers to frequently asked questions.* Available from https://www.shrm.org/resourcesandtools/legal-and-compliance/state-and-local-updates/pages/california-salary-history-ban-questions.aspx

Office of Diversity, Equity & Community Engagement, University of Colorado, Boulder. (n.d.). *Defining and enacting diversity, equity, & inclusion.* Available from https://www.colorado.edu/odece/diversity-plan/resources/defining-and-enacting-diversity-equity-inclusion

Office of the President, University of Michigan. (2017). *Diversity, equity & inclusion.* Available from https://president.umich.edu/initiatives-and-focus-areas/diversity-equity-inclusion/

Ohio State. (n.d.). *Ohio State's strategic plan—Time and change: Enable, empower and inspire.* Available from https://president.osu.edu/assets/uploads/PDFs/WEB_Ohio%20State_Strategic_Plan_Narrative_.pdf

Ong, M., Smith, J. M., & Ko, L. T. (2018). Counterspaces for women of color in STEM higher education: Marginal and central spaces for persistence and success. *JRST, 55*(2), 206–245.

Orr, D. W. (2016). *Dangerous years: Climate change, the long emergency, and the way forward.* New Haven, CT: Yale University Press.

O'Sullivan, D., & Byers, D. (2017, September 28). Exclusive: Fake black activist accounts linked to Russian government. *CNN.* Available from http://money.cnn.com/2017/09/28/media/blacktivist-russia-facebook-twitter/index.html?sr=twCNN092817blacktivist-russia-facebook-twitter0917PMStory

Owen, D. S. (2009). Privileged social identities and diversity leadership in higher education. *The Review of Higher Education, 32*(2), 185–207.

Paluck, E. L., & Green, D. P. (2009). Prejudice reduction: What works? A review and assessment of research and practice. *Annual Review of Psychology, 60,* 339–367.

Penn State. (n.d.). *Our commitment to impact: The Pennsylvania State University's strategic plan for 2016 to 2020.* Available from http://strategicplan.psu.edu/executive-summary/

Penn State. (2016). *Penn State statement on diversity, equity, and inclusion.* Available from http://equity.psu.edu/diversity-statement

Penn State. (2018). *Historical archive of diversity strategic planning.* Available from http://equity.psu.edu/historical-archive-diversity-strategic-planning

Peterson, M. W., & Spencer, M. G. (1990). Understanding academic culture and climate. In W. G. Tierney (Ed.), *Assessing academic climates and cultures* (pp. 3–18). San Francisco, CA: Jossey-Bass.

Picca, L. H., & Feagin, J. R. (2007). *Two-faced racism: Whites in the backstage and frontstage.* New York, NY: Routledge.

Pike, G., & Kuh, G. D. (2006). Relationships among structural diversity, informal peer interactions and perceptions of the campus environment. *The Review of Higher Education, 29*(4), 425–450.

Pope, R. L., Mueller, J. A., & Reynolds, A. L. (2009). Looking back and moving forward: Future directions for diversity research in student affairs. *Journal of College Student Development, 50*(6), 640–658.

Pope, R. L., Reynolds, A. L., & Mueller, J. A. (2004). *Multicultural competence in student affairs.* San Francisco, CA: Jossey-Bass.

Prasad, A. (2001). Understanding workplace empowerment as inclusion: A historical investigation of the discourse of difference in the United States. *The Journal of Applied Behavioral Science, 37*(1), 51–69.

Prilleltensky, I., & Gonick, L. S. (1994). The discourse of oppression in the social sciences: Past, present, and future. In E. J. Trickett, R. J. Watts, & D. Birman (Eds.), *Human diversity: Perspectives on people in context* (pp. 145–177). San Francisco, CA: Jossey-Bass.

Quadlin, N. (2018). The mark of a woman's record: Gender and academic performance in hiring. *American Sociological Review, 83*(2), 331–360.

Quillian, L., Pager, D., Hexel, O., & Midtbøen, A. H. (2017). *Meta-analysis of field experiments shows no change in racial discrimination in hiring over time.* Available from http://www.pnas.org/content/early/2017/09/11/1706255114

Ragins, B. R. (1997). Diversified mentoring relationships in organizations: A power perspective. *The Academy of Management Review, 22*(2), 482–521.

Ragins, B. R. (2007). Diversity and workplace mentoring relationships: A review and positive social capital approach. In T. D. Allen & L. T. Eby (Eds.), *The Blackwell handbook of mentoring: A multiple perspectives approach* (pp. 281–300). Malden, MA: Blackwell.

Ragins, B. R., & Sundstrom, E. (1989). Gender and power in organizations: A longitudinal perspective. *Psychological Bulletin, 105*(1), 51–88.

Ragins, B. R., & Wiethoff, C. (2005). Understanding heterosexism at work: The straight problem. In R. L. Dipbov & A. Colella (Eds.), *Discrimination at work: The psychological and organizational bases* (pp. 177–201). New York, NY: Psychology Press.

Rai, K. B., & Critzer, J. W. (2000). *Affirmative action and the university: Race, ethnicity, and gender in higher education employment.* Lincoln: University of Nebraska Press.

Report on faculty diversity and inclusivity in FAS. (2016, May 19). Available from https://fassenate.yale.edu/sites/default/files/files/Reports/FAS%20Senate%20-%202016-05-19%20-%20Diversity%20and%20Inclusivity FINAL%20copy%202.pdf

Reyes, K. A. (n.d.). *Developing a strategic inclusion & diversity action plan: Lessons learned from research & practice.* Available from https://www.sreb.org/sites/main/files/file-attachments/diversity_and_inclusion_webinar.pdf

Roberts, C. J. (2007). *Opinion of Roberts, C. J.: Parents Involved in Community Schools, petitioner 05.908 v. Seattle School District No. 1 et al.* Available from http://www.law.cornell.edu/supct/pdf/05-908P.ZO

Robinson, C. (2015). Clashing with tradition: The chief diversity officer at white public institutions. In K. J. Fasching-Varner, K. A. Albert, R. W. Mitchell, & C. M. Allen (Eds.), *Racial battle fatigue in higher education:*

Exposing the myth of post-racial America (pp. 217–224). Lanham, MD: Rowman & Littlefield.

Robinson-Armstrong, A., King, D., Killoran, D., & Fissinger, M. X. (2009). The Equity Scorecard: An effective tool for assessing diversity initiatives. *International Journal of Diversity in Organizations, Communities and Nations, 8*(6), 31–40.

Romero, A. Jr. (2017). *Best practices for recruiting and retaining diverse faculty for institutions of higher education.* Available from https://www.ccas.net/files/public/Publications/Best%20Practices%20CCAS_March%202017_FINAL.pdf

Roscigno, V. J. (2007). *The face of discrimination: How race and gender impact work and home lives.* Lanham, MD: Rowman & Littlefield.

Roscigno, V. J., Garcia, L. M., & Bobbitt-Zeher, D. (2007). Social closure and processes of race/sex employment discrimination. *The Annals of the American Academy of Political and Social Science, 609*(1), 16–48.

Ruben, B. D. (2016). *Excellence in higher education guide: A framework for the design, assessment, and continuing improvement of institutions, departments, and programs* (8th ed.). Sterling, VA: Stylus.

Sallee, M., & Lester, J. (2009). The family-friendly campus in the 21st century. In J. Lester & M. Sallee (Eds.), *Establishing the family-friendly campus: Models for effective practice* (pp. 159–166). Sterling, VA: Stylus.

Schein, E. H. (2006). So how can you assess your corporate culture? In J. V. Gallos (Ed.), *Organization development: A Jossey-Bass reader* (pp. 614–633). San Francisco, CA: Jossey-Bass.

Seidel, M.-D. L., Polzer, J. T., & Stewart, K. J. (2000). Friends in high places: The effects of social networks on discrimination in salary negotiations. *Administrative Science Quarterly, 45*(1), 1–24.

Seltzer, R. (2017, March 2). Failing to keep up. *Inside Higher Ed.* Available from https://www.insidehighered.com/news/2017/03/02/racial-gap-among-senior-administrators-widens

Sensoy, O., & DiAngelo, R. (2017). "We are all for diversity, but . . .": How faculty hiring committees reproduce whiteness and practical suggestions for how they can change. *Harvard Educational Review, 87*(4), 557–580.

Sidanius, J., & Pratto, F. (1999). *Social dominance: An intergroup theory of social hierarchy and oppression.* New York, NY: Cambridge University Press.

Smith, D. G. (1990). Embracing diversity as a central campus goal. *Academe, 76*(6), 29–33.

Smith, D. G. (1995). Organizational implications of diversity in higher education. In M. M. Chemers, S. Oskamp, & M. Costanzo (Eds.), *Diversity in organizations: New* perspectives for a changing workplace (pp. 220–244). Thousand Oaks, CA: Sage.

Smith, D. G. (2009a). *Diversity's promise for higher education: Making it work.* Baltimore, MD: Johns Hopkins University Press.

Smith, D. G. (2009b, March 27). *How do you know you are making progress?* Available from http://equity.psu.edu/workshop/spring-2009/assets/pdf/sp09/smith_am.pdf

Smith, D. G. (2014). Identity and diversity. In D. G. Smith (Ed.), *Diversity and inclusion in higher education: Emerging perspectives on institutional transformation* (pp. 10–26). New York, NY: Routledge.

Smith, D. G., & Parker, S. (2005). Organizational learning: A tool for diversity and institutional effectiveness. In A. J. Kezar (Ed.), *Organizational learning in higher education* (pp. 113–125). San Francisco, CA: Jossey-Bass.

Smith, D. G., Turner, C. S., Osei-Kofi, N., & Richards, S. (2004). Interrupting the usual: Successful strategies for hiring diverse faculty. *The Journal of Higher Education, 75*(2), 133–160.

Smith, D. G., & Wolf-Wendel, L. E. (2005). *The challenge of diversity: Involvement or alienation in the academy?* (ASHE-ERIC Higher Education Report, Vol. 31, No. 1). San Francisco, CA: Jossey-Bass.

Smith, R. A., & Elliott, J. R. (2002). Does ethnic concentration influence employees' access to authority? An examination of contemporary urban labor markets. *Social Forces, 81*(1), 255–279.

Snipes, R. L., Oswald, S. L., & Caudill, S. B. (1998). Sex-role stereotyping, gender biases, and job selection: The use of ordinal logit in analyzing Likert scale data. *Employee Responsibilities and Rights Journal, 11*(2), 81–97.

Southern Association of Colleges and Schools Commission on Colleges. (2017). *Proposed revisions to the principles of accreditation: Foundations for quality enhancement.* Available from http://www.sacscoc.org/2017ProposedPrinc/Proposed%20Principles%20Adopted%20by%20BOT.pdf

Spina, E. (2017). *Why diversity matters.* Available from https://udayton.edu/blogs/president/2017/08/why_diversity_matters.php

Stage, F. K., & Wells, R. S. (2014). Critical quantitative inquiry in context. *New Directions for Institutional Research, 2013*(158), 1–7.

Stanley, C. A. (2014). The chief diversity officer: An examination of CDO models and strategies. *Journal of Diversity in Higher Education, 7*(2), 101–108.

State University of New York. (2016). *Campus guide for strategic diversity & inclusion plan development.* Available from https://www.newpaltz.edu/media/diversity/1%20-%20SUNY%20Guide%20-Strategic%20Diversity%20Plan%20Development%203-16.pdf

Stoil, M. J. (2014, May 15). "Blatant age discrimination" infests faculty hiring. *The Chronicle of Higher Education.* Available from https://www.chronicle.com/blogs/letters/blatant-age-discrimination-infests-faculty-hiring/

Sturm, S. (2010). Activating systemic change toward full participation: The pivotal role of boundary spanning institutional intermediaries. *Saint Louis University Law Journal, 54,* 1117–1137.

Subbaswamy, K. R. (2017). *Message from the chancellor* (University of Massachusetts, Amherst). Available from http://issuu.com/uofmassachusettsamherst/docs/17-633_climate_survey_abridged_repo/5?e=24352215/47926357

Swaak, T. (2018, January 17). Racist flyers calling African-Americans 'Stupid monkeys' found at South Carolina college. *Newsweek.* Available from http://www.newsweek.com/racist-flyers-found-university-south-carolina-campus-783775

Taylor, T., Milem, J., & Coleman, A. (2016). *Bridging the research to practice gap: Achieving mission-driven diversity and inclusion goals.* Available from http://www.aacu.org/sites/default/files/BridgingResearchPracticeGap.pdf

Thomas, K. M., & Wise, P. G. (1999). Organizational attractiveness and individual differences: Are diverse applicants attracted by different factors? *Journal of Business and Psychology, 13*(3), 375–390.

Thomas, R. R. Jr. (1990). From affirmative action to affirming diversity. *Harvard Business Review, 90*(2), 107–117.

Tilcsik, A. (2011). Pride and prejudice: Employment discrimination against openly gay men in the United States. *American Journal of Sociology, 117*(2), 586–626.

Tomlinson, G., & Freeman, S. Jr. (2017). Who really selected you? Insights into faculty selection processes in top-ranked higher education graduate programmes. *Journal of Further and Higher Education, 42*(6), 855–867.

Tosey, P., Visser, M., & Saunders, M. N. K. (2011). The origins and conceptualizations of "triple-loop" learning: A critical review. *Management Learning, 43*(3), 291–307.

Toutkoushian, R. K., Bellas, M. L., and Moore, J. V. (2007). The interaction effects of gender, race, and marital status on faculty salaries. *The Journal of Higher Education, 78*(5), 572–601.

Transforming Maryland: Expectations for excellence in diversity and inclusion. (2010). Available from https://www.provost.umd.edu/Documents/Strategic_Plan_for_Diversity.pdf

Tsui, A. S., & Gutek, B. A. (1999). *Demographic differences in organizations: Current research and future directions.* Lanham, MD: Lexington Books.

Tsui, A. S., Porter, L. W., & Egan, T. D. (2002). When both similarities and dissimilarities matter: Extending the concept of relational demography. *Human Relations, 55*(8), 899–929.

Tuitt, F. (2016). *Making excellence inclusive in challenging times.* Available from http://go.galegroup.com/ps/i.do?p=PROF&u=clic_hamline&id=GALE|A457562532&v=2.1&it=r&sid=PROF&asid=07f9372a

Turner, C. (2016, August 10). The business case for gender diversity. *HuffPost.* Available from https://www.huffingtonpost.com/caroline-turner/the-business-case-for-gen_b_7963006.html

Turner, C. S. V., González, J. C., & Wood, J. L. (2008). Faculty of color in academe: What 20 years of literature tells us. *Journal of Diversity in Higher Education, 1*(3), 139–168.

U. of Cincinnati shooting puts spotlight on campus police. (2015, July 31). *Chicago Tribune.* Available from http://www.chicagotribune.com/news/nationworld/ct-campus-police-20150731-story.html

UC Berkeley Division of Equity & Inclusion. (2018). *Planning toolkits and resources.* Available from https://diversity.berkeley.edu/programs-services/diversity-planning/toolkits-and-resources

UC Berkeley strategic plan for equity, inclusion, and diversity: Pathway to excellence. (2009). Available from https://diversity.berkeley.edu/sites/default/files/speid_final_webversion.pdf

UCLA Equity, Diversity and Inclusion. (2018a). *CrossCheck Live.* Available from https://equity.ucla.edu/crosscheck/crosscheck-live/

UCLA Equity, Diversity and Inclusion. (2018b). *Our Teams: BruinX.* Available from https://equity.ucla.edu/about-us/our-teams/bruinx/

UC San Diego Office for Equity, Diversity, and Inclusion. (2018). *Strategic plan for inclusive excellence: You have the power to transform.* Available from https://diversity.ucsd.edu/initiatives/strategic-plan.html

UC Santa Cruz. (2017). *DICP course listings & schedule.* Available from https://diversity.ucsc.edu/training/certificate_program/courses.html

Ulrich, D., Allen, J., Brockbank, W., Younger, J., & Nyman, M. (2009). *HR transformation: Building human resources from the outside in.* New York, NY: McGraw-Hill.

Ulrich, D., & Brockbank, W. (2005). *The HR value proposition.* Boston, MA: Harvard Business School.

Ulrich, D., Brockbank, W., Johnson, D., Sandholtz, K., & Younger, J. (2008). *HR competencies: Mastery at the intersection of people and business.* Alexandria, VA: Society for Human Resource Management.

Ulrich, D., & Smallwood, N. (2004). Capitalizing on capabilities. *Harvard Business Review, 82*(6), 119–127.

University of Arizona. (2002). *Diversity action plan for the University of Arizona.* Available from http://nca2010.arizona.edu/documents/Shared/Diversity/diversity%2520action%2520plan.pdf

University of California Board of Regents. (2010). *Regents policy 4400: Policy on University of California diversity statement.* Available from http://regents.universityofcalifornia.edu/governance/policies/4400.html

University of California Office of the President. (2014). *What is campus climate? Why does it matter?* Available from http://campusclimate.ucop.edu/what-is-campus-climate/

University of Chicago. (2016). *Climate survey.* Available from http://climatesurvey.uchicago.edu/

University of Colorado, Boulder, Office of Diversity, Equity, and Community Engagement. (n.d.). *Diversity plan: An update on making excellence inclusive.* Available from https://www.colorado.edu/odece/diversity-plan

University of Iowa. (n.d.). *Compensation philosophy.* Available from https://hr.uiowa.edu/dept-comp-class/philosophy

University of Louisville. (2016). *Kentucky policy for diversity, equity, and inclusion.* Available from http://louisville.edu/diversity/diversity-policy-planning/ky-cpe-diversity-policy

University of Louisville. (2017). *Diversity plan: 2017–2021.* Available from http://louisville.edu/diversity/diversity-policy-planning/diversity-plan/ULDiversityPlanOctober2017.pdf

University of Massachusetts, Amherst. (2015). *Diversity strategic plan.* Available from https://www.umass.edu/diversity/sites/default/files/diversity_strategic_plan_2015.pdf

University of Massachusetts, Amherst. (2017a). *Campus climate survey: Abridged report.* Available from http://issuu.com/uofmassachusettsamherst/docs/17-633_climate_survey_abridged_repo?e=24352215/47926357

University of Massachusetts, Amherst. (2017b). *Executive summary: Abridged campus climate report.* Available from https://www.umass.edu/diversity/sites/default/files/Abridged-Report-Executive-Summary.pdf

University of Michigan. (n.d.). *President Schlissel's charge to the U-M community for a strategic planning process on diversity, equity and inclusion.* Available from https://diversity.umich.edu/wp-content/uploads/2015/11/DSP-Charge-to-Community_FINAL.pdf

University of Michigan. (2016). *Diversity, equity & inclusion: Strategic plan.* Available from http://diversity.umich.edu/wp-content/uploads/2016/10/strategic-plan.pdf

University of Michigan. (2017). *Diversity, equity & inclusion: Strategic plan progress report.* Available from http://diversity.umich.edu/wp-content/uploads/2017/11/Diversity_Equity_and_Inclusion_Year_One_Progress_Report.pdf

University of Michigan. (2018). *Campuswide & unit plans.* Available from https://diversity.umich.edu/strategic -plan/unit-activities/

University of Missouri System. (2016a). *DEI asset inventory.* Available from https://www.umsystem.edu/media/ president/deioffice/dei-asset-inventory-ums.pdf

University of Missouri System. (2016b). *Diversity, equity, and inclusion audit.* Available from https:///www.um system.edu/deiaudit

University of New Hampshire. (2012). *2010–2020 inclusive excellence strategic plan.* Available from https://www .unh.edu/inclusive/sites/default/files/media/PDFs/10- 20_inclusiveexcellencestategicplan.pdf

University of Puget Sound (2018). *Campus climate survey.* Available from https://www.pugetsound.edu/about/ diversity-at-puget-sound/campus-climate-survey/

University of Washington. (2017). *UW diversity blueprint: 2017–2021.* Available from https://www.washington .edu/diversity/files/2017/01/17_DiversityBlueprint -010917.pdf

University of Wisconsin, Madison. (2014). Forward together: A framework for diversity and inclusive excellence. The Ad Hoc Diversity Planning Committee. Available from https://diversity.wisc.edu/wp-content/ uploads/2017/02/FrameworkforDiversityMay192014 _2.pdf

University of Wisconsin, Madison. (2015). Affecting R.E.E.L. change: Retain, equip, engage, lead, for diversity & inclusion. Available from https://diversity.wisc.edu/ wp-content/uploads/2017/04/Patricks-preferred-04.08 .15-DF-REEL-Report-FINAL_Updated.pdf

University of Wisconsin, Madison. (2018). *2016 campus climate survey at UW-Madison.* Available from https:// apir.wisc.edu/diversity/climate-study-surveys/

University of Wisconsin System. (n.d.). *Design for diversity.* Available from https://diversity.wisc.edu/wp-content/ uploads/2017/03/Design-for-Diversity-UW-System .pdf

University of Wisconsin System. (2018). *UW system accountability dashboard.* Available from https://www .wisconsin.edu/accountability/

U.S. Department of Justice Office on Violence Against Women. (2016). *An administrator's perspective on campus climate surveys.* Available from https://www.justice.gov/ ovw/file/902121/download

Victorino, C. A., Nylund-Gibson, K., & Conley, S. (2013). Campus racial climate: A litmus test for faculty satisfaction at four-year colleges and universities. *The Journal of Higher Education, 84*(6), 769–805.

Virginia Polytechnic Institute and State University. (2000). *The faces of change: University diversity plan 2000–2005.* Available from https://vtechworks.lib.vt .edu/bitstream/handle/10919/79581/dsp2000-2005 .pdf?sequence=1&isAllowed=y/

Virginia Polytechnic Institute and State University (n.d.) Toward an inclusive community: Diversity and inclusion at Virginia Tech. Diversity Strategic Plan 2013-2018. Available from https://www.inclusive.vt.edu/Initiatives/ dsp.html

Wallace, S. L., Moore, S. E., Wilson, L. L., & Hart, B. G. (2012). African American women in the academy: Quelling the myth of presumed incompetence. In G. Guitiérrez y Muhs, Y. F. Niemann, C. G. Gonzalez, & A. P. Harris. (Eds.), *Presumed incompetent: The intersections of race and class for women in academia* (pp. 421–438). Boulder: University Press of Colorado.

Ward, K., & Wolf-Wendel, L. (2004). Fear factor: How safe is it to make time for family? *Academe, 90*(6), 28–31.

WASC Senior College and University Commission. (2015). *Handbook of accreditation 2013 revised.* Available from https://www.wscuc.org/content/2013-handbook- accreditation

WASC Senior College and University Commission (2017). *Equity and Inclusion Policy.* Available from https://www .wscuc.org/content/equity-inclusion-policy

Williams, D. (2006). Overcoming the brutal facts: Building and implementing a relentless diversity change process. *The Diversity Factor, 14*(4), 10–18.

Williams, D. A. (2013). *Strategic diversity leadership: Activating change and transformation in higher education.* Sterling, VA: Stylus.

Williams, D. A., Berger, J. B., & McClendon, S. (2005). *Toward a model of inclusive excellence and change in postsecondary institutions.* Available from http://www .aacu.org/inclusive_excellence/documents/williams_ et_al.pdf

Williams, D. A., & Wade-Golden, K. C. (2013). *The chief diversity officer: Strategy, structure, and change management.* Sterling, VA: Stylus.

Willis Towers Watson (2018). *Employer health and wellbeing initiatives fall short with employees, Willis Towers Watson survey finds.* Available from https://www .willistowerswatson.com/en-US/press/2018/02/ employer-health-and-well-being-initiatives-fall-short- with-employees

Wilson, E. O. (1998). *Consilience: The unity of knowledge.* New York, NY: Vintage Books.

Wilson, J. L., Meyer, K. A., & McNeal, L. (2012). Mission and diversity statements: What they do and do not say. *Innovative Higher Education, 37*(2), 125–139.

Wolf-Wendel, L., & Ward, K. (2015). Academic mothers: Exploring disciplinary perspectives. *Innovative Higher Education, 40*(1), 19–35.

Woodard, Q. (2014). *Understanding the implications of organizational culture and organizational structure for the role of the Chief Diversity Officer in higher education* (Unpublished doctoral dissertation). University of Illinois, Urbana.

Yakoboski, P. J., & Foster, J. E. (2014, June). *Strategic utilization of adjunct and other contingent faculty. TIAA Institute.* Available from https://www.tiaainstitute.org/public/institute/research/strategic-utilization-of-adjunct-and-other-contingent-faculty

About the Authors

Edna Chun and Alvin Evans are award-winning authors and human resource (HR) and diversity thought leaders with extensive experience in complex, multicampus systems of higher education. Two of their books, *Are the Walls Really Down? Behavioral and Organizational Barriers to Faculty and Staff Diversity* (Jossey-Bass, 2007) and *Bridging the Diversity Divide: Globalization and Reciprocal Empowerment in Higher Education* (Jossey-Bass, 2009), were recipients of the prestigious Kathryn G. Hansen Publication Award by the College and University Professional Association for Human Resources. In addition, their coauthored book, *The New Talent Acquisition Frontier: Integrating HR and Diversity Strategy in the Private and Public Sectors and Higher Education* (Stylus, 2014), received a silver medal in the 2014 Axiom Business Book Awards and is the first book to provide a concrete roadmap to the integration of HR and diversity strategy.

Recent publications include *Leading a Diversity Culture Shift in Higher Education* (Routledge, 2018), which draws on extensive interviews with chief diversity officers and university leaders to provide a systematic approach to diversity organizational learning,

and *The Department Chair as Transformative Leader: Building Inclusive Learning Environments in Higher Education* (Stylus, 2015), the first research-based resource on the academic department chair's role in diversity transformation. Other publications include *Diverse Administrators in Peril: The New Indentured Class in Higher Education* (Paradigm, 2012), the first in-depth interview study of the work experiences of minority; female; and lesbian, gay, bisexual, and transgender (LGBT) administrators in higher education, and *Rethinking Cultural Competence in Higher Education: An Ecological Framework for Student Development* (Jossey-Bass, 2016), a study that draws on a survey of recent college graduates now working as professionals to offer leading-edge, integrative models for the attainment of diversity competence.

Both authors are sought-after plenary speakers and facilitators at national conferences and symposia. Their numerous journal articles in leading HR and diversity journals focus on talent management and diversity strategies. Edna Chun is chief learning officer, and Alvin Evans is higher education practice leader for HigherEd Talent, a national diversity and HR consulting firm.

Index

Race & Diversity books from Stylus Publishing

Building on Resilience
Models and Frameworks of Black Male Success Across the P-20 Pipeline
Edited by Fred A. Bonner II
Foreword by Tim King

Diverse Millennial Students in College
Implications for Faculty and Student Affairs
Edited by Fred A. Bonner II, Aretha F. Marbley, and Mary F. Howard-Hamilton

Answering the Call
African American Women in Higher Education Leadership
Beverly L. Bower and Mimi Wolverton

The Department Chair as Transformative Diversity Leader
Building Inclusive Learning Environments in Higher Education
Edna Chun and Alvin Evans
Foreword by Walter H. Gmelch

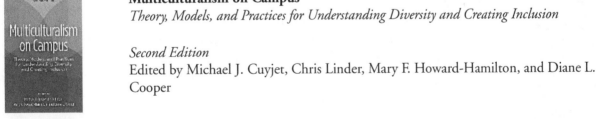

Multiculturalism on Campus
Theory, Models, and Practices for Understanding Diversity and Creating Inclusion

Second Edition
Edited by Michael J. Cuyjet, Chris Linder, Mary F. Howard-Hamilton, and Diane L. Cooper

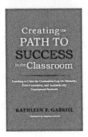

Creating the Path to Success in the Classroom
Teaching to Close the Graduation Gap for Minority, First-Generation, and Academically Unprepared Students
Kathleen F. Gabriel
Foreword by Stephen Carroll

Race & Diversity books from Stylus Publishing

Advancing Black Male Student Success From Preschool Through Ph.D.
Edited by Shaun R. Harper and J. Luke Wood

Contested Issues in Troubled Times
Student Affairs Dialogues on Equity, Civility, and Safety
Edited by Peter M. Magolda, Marcia B. Baxter Magolda and Rozana Carducci
Foreword by Lori Patton Davis

Critical Race Spatial Analysis
Mapping to Understand and Address Educational Inequity
Edited by Deb Morrison, Subini Ancy Annamma, and Darrell D. Jackson

Closing the Opportunity Gap
Identity-Conscious Strategies for Retention and Student Success
Edited by Vijay Pendakur
Foreword by Shaun R. Harper

Beyond Access
Indigenizing Programs for Native American Student Success
Edited by Stephanie J. Waterman, Shelly C. Lowe, and Heather J. Shotton
Foreword by George S. McClellan

Critical Mentoring
A Practical Guide
Torie Weiston-Serdan
Foreword by Bernadette Sánchez

Community Colleges as Incubators of Innovation
Unleashing Entrepreneurial Opportunities for Communities and Students
Edited by Rebecca A. Corbin and Ron Thomas
Foreword by Andy Stoll
Afterword by J. Noah Brown

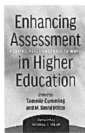

Enhancing Assessment in Higher Education
Putting Psychometrics to Work
Edited by Tammie Cumming and M. David Miller
Foreword by Michael J. Kolen

High-Impact Practices in Online Education
Research and Best Practices
Edited by Kathryn E. Linder and Chrysanthemum Mattison Hayes
Foreword by Kelvin Thompson

Facilitating Intergroup Dialogues
Bridging Differences, Catalyzing Change
Kelly E. Maxwell, Biren Ratnesh Nagda, and Monita C. Thompson
Foreword by Patricia Guirin

A Good Job
Campus Employment as a High-Impact Practice
George S. McClellan, Kristina L. Creager, and Marianna Savoca
Foreword by George D. Kuh

Building the Field of Higher Education Engagement
Foundational Ideas and Future Directions
Edited by Lorilee R. Sandmann and Diann O. Jones

(Continued)

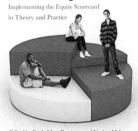

Confronting Equity Issues on Campus

Implementing the Equity Scorecard in Theory and Practice

Edited by Estela Mara Bensimon and Lindsey Malcom

Foreword by David Longanecker

"This volume examines how colleges and universities are using the Center for Urban Education's Equity Scorecard to create racial equity on campus. With in-depth examinations of the Equity Scorecard process as well as reflections from practitioner teams and researchers, the book is a testament to the role thoughtful data assessment can play in generating more racially equitable outcomes for students. The book calls educators and administrators to take personal responsibility for their roles in moving from a deficit model to an equity model and provides helpful context for anyone currently using or considering the scorecard as a tool for change." —**Diversity & Democracy**

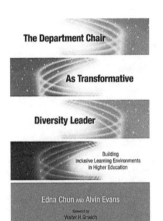

The Department Chair as Transformative Diversity Leader

Building Inclusive Learning Environments in Higher Education

Edna Chun and Alvin Evans

Foreword by Walter H. Gmelch

"Edna Chun and Alvin Evans recognize the pivotal role that department heads and departments play in the structure, culture, and climate of our colleges and universities. For diversity and inclusion efforts to really make progress, they must be nurtured and implemented at the grassroots level in each department where personnel decisions are made." —**Santa J. Ono**, *President, University of Cincinnati*

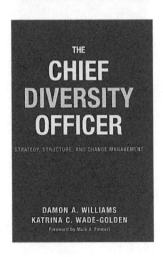

The Chief Diversity Officer

Strategy, Structure, and Change Management

Damon A. Williams and Katrina C. Wade-Golden

Foreword by Mark A. Emmert

"*The Chief Diversity Officer* provides an extremely thorough and thoughtful overview of the importance of the evolving role and responsibilities of this position in higher education. This timely volume includes a sophisticated discussion of the structural issues involved in diversity leadership, incorporating both educational theory and practical wisdom and advice. It will be a valuable resource for academic leaders across the country who care about the educational imperatives of diversity in higher education." —**Jonathan Alger**, *President, James Madison University*

22883 Quicksilver Drive
Sterling, VA 20166-2019

Subscribe to our e-mail alerts: www.Styluspub.com

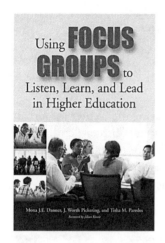

Using Focus Groups to Listen, Learn, and Lead in Higher Education

Mona J.E. Danner, J. Worth Pickering, and Tisha M. Paredes

Foreword by Jillian Kinzie

"A friendly, practical, and principled DIY guide, *Using Focus Groups* will help educators at any type of institution. Its process approach aims for the relevance of qualitative research combined with the rigor of quantitative methods. Guiding readers from first steps through data analysis and reporting, the book offers extended vignettes as well as templates and models. Engaging both faculty and staff in the process, the book identifies resources ready to hand on every campus."— **Susan Albertine**, *Senior Scholar, Association of American Colleges & Universities*

Search Committees

A Comprehensive Guide to Successful Faculty, Staff, and Administrative Searches

Second Edition

Christopher D. Lee

Foreword by Edna Chun

"Selecting the right person for an academic appointment has become increasing challenging in a competitive environment with dwindling resources. In his guide Christopher D. Lee provides a clear process for a search including helpful tools, hints, and warnings to improve the likelihood of success for the institution. Woven through the guide is an evidence-based rationale for the recommended approach, including vignettes that make the theoretical come to life. This reference is a must for both novice and seasoned search committee members." —*Patricia Maguire Meservey*, *President, Salem State University*

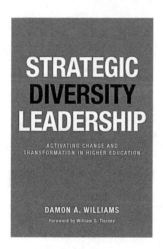

Strategic Diversity Leadership

Activating Change and Transformation in Higher Education

Damon A. Williams

Foreword by William A. Tierney

"Williams has done a masterful job of integrating organizational planning savvy with both practitioner wisdom and scholarly research from over four decades of campus diversity initiatives. He keeps his eye firmly on the human side of diversity change and provides a wealth of practical guidance for leaders who see the need to move beyond episodic diversity interventions toward comprehensive institutional engagement and change. I warmly recommend this exceptionally useful book for any educational institution that already sees diversity as an educational value and now wants to reach toward the next and more challenging level of making excellence inclusive." —*Carol Schneider*, *President, Association of American Colleges & Universities*

(Continues on preceding page)